Sir Richard Blackmore

Prince Arthur

An Heroick Poem in Ten Books

Sir Richard Blackmore

Prince Arthur

An Heroick Poem in Ten Books

ISBN/EAN: 9783742823632

Manufactured in Europe, USA, Canada, Australia, Japa

Cover: Foto ©Andreas Hilbeck / pixelio.de

Manufactured and distributed by brebook publishing software (www.brebook.com)

Sir Richard Blackmore

Prince Arthur

Prince ARTHUR.

An Heroick

POEM.

In Ten Books.

BY
RICHARD BLACKMORE, M.D.
AND
Fellow of the College of Physitians in *London*.

The Second Edition Corrected.

To which is added, An INDEX, Explaining the Names of *Countries, Cities,* and *Rivers,* &c.

LONDON:

Printed for *Awnsham* and *John Churchil* at the *black Swan* in *Pater-Noster-Row,* MDCXCV.

THE
PREFACE.

TO what ill purposes soever Poetry has been abus'd, its true and genuine End is by universal Confession, the Instruction of our Minds, and Regulation of our Manners; for which 'tis furnish'd with so many excellent Advantages. The Delicacy of its Strains, the Sweetness and Harmony of its Numbers, the lively and admirable manner of its Painting or Representation, and the wonderful Force of its Eloquence, cannot but open the Passages to our Breasts, triumph over our Passions, and leave behind them very deep Impressions. 'Tis in the power of Poetry to insinuate into the inmost Recesses of the Mind, to touch any Spring that moves the Heart, to agitate the Soul with any sort of Affection, and transform it into any Shape or Posture it thinks fit. 'Tis therefore no wonder that so wise a State, as that of Athens, should retain the Poets on the side of Religion and the Government. The Stage there was set up to teach the People the Scheme of their Religion, and those Modes of Worship the Government thought fit to encourage, to convey to them such Ideas of their Deities, and Divine Providence, as might engage their Minds to a Reverence of superiour, invisible Beings, and to observe and admire their Administration of humane Affairs. The Poets were look'd on as Divine, not only upon the account of that extraordinary Fury and Heat of Imagination, wherewith they were thought to be-inspir'd, but likewise upon the account of their Profession and Imployment, their Business being to re-

present

The PREFACE.

present Vice *as the most odious, and* Virtue *as the most desirable thing in the World.*

Tragedy *was at its first Institution a part of the Ancient Pagans Divine Service, when the* Chorus *which originally was so great a part, contain'd many excellent Lessons of* Piety *and* Morality, *and was wholly imploy'd in rectifying their mistakes about the* Gods, *and their Government of the World, in moderating their Passions, and purging their Minds from Vice and Corruption. This was the noble Design of the* Chorus. *And the Representation of great and illustrious Characters, gradually afterwards introduc'd, their Impious, or their Generous Actions, and the different Event that attended them, was to deter Men from Vice and Impiety, and encourage them to be Generous and Virtuous, by shewing them the Vengeance that at last overtook the one, and the Rewards and Praises that crown'd the other. The End of Comedy was the same, but pursu'd in another way. The business of Comedy being to render Vice ridiculous, to expose it to publick Derision and Contempt, and to make Men asham'd of Vile and Sordid Actions.*

Tragedy *design'd to Scare Men,* Comedy *to Laugh them out of their Vices. And 'tis very plain, that* Satyr *is intended for the same End, the Promotion of Virtue, and exposing of Vice; which it pursues by sharp Reproaches, vehement and bitter Invectives, or by a Courtly, but not less cutting Raillery. The Odes of the Lyric Poet were chiefly design'd for the Praises of their Gods, their Heroes and extraordinary Persons, to draw Men to an Admiration and Imitation of them.*

But above all other kinds, Epick Poetry, *as it is first in Dignity, so it mostly conduces to this End.*

In

The PREFACE.

In an *Epick Poem, where Characters of the first Rank and Dignity, Illustrious for their Birth or high Employment are introduc'd, the Fable, the Action, the particular Episodes are so contriv'd and conducted, or at least ought to be, that either Fortitude, Wisdom, Piety, Moderation, Generosity, some or other Noble and Princely Virtues shall be recommended with the highest Advantage, and their contrary Vices made as odious.* To give Men right and just Conceptions of Religion *and* Virtue, *to aid their Reason in restraining their Exorbitant Appetites and Impetuous Passions, and to bring their Lives under the Rules and Guidance of true Wisdom, and thereby to promote the publick Good of Mankind, is undoubtedly the End of all Poetry.*

'Tis true indeed, that one End of Poetry is to give Men Pleasure and Delight; but this is but a subordinate, subaltern End, which is it self a Means to the greater, and ultimate *one before mention'd. A Poet should imploy all his Judgment and Wit, exhaust all the Riches of his Fancy, and abound in Beautiful and Noble Expression, to divert and entertain others; but then it must be with this Prospect, that he may hereby engage their Attention, insinuate more easily into their Minds, and more effectually convey to them wise Instructions. 'Tis below the Dignity of a true Poet to take his Aim at any inferiour End. They are Men of little Genius, of mean and poor Design, that imploy their Wit for no higher Purpose, than to please the Imagination of vain and wanton People.*

I think these Poets, if they must be called so, whose Wit as they manage it, is altogether unuseful are justly reproach'd; but I am sure those others are highly to be condemned, who use all their Wit in Opposition *to*

A   Re-

The PREFACE.

Religion, and to the Destruction of Virtue and good Manners in the World. There have been in all Ages such ill Men that have perverted the right Use of Poetry, but never so many, or so bold or mischievous as in ours. Our Poets seem engag'd in a general Confederacy to ruin the End of their own Art, to expose Religion and Virtue, and bring Vice and Corruption of Manners into Esteem and Reputation. The Poets that write for the Stage (at least a great part of 'em) seem deeply concern'd in this Conspiracy. These are the Champions that charge Religion with such desperate Resolution, and have given it so many deep and ghastly Wounds. The Stage was an Outwork or Fort rais'd for the Protection and Security of the Temple, but the Poets that kept it, have revolted, and basely betray'd it, and what is worse, have turn'd all their Force and discharg'd all their Artillery against the Place their Duty was to defend. If any Man thinks this an unjust Charge, I desire him to read any of our modern Comedies, and I believe he will soon be convinc'd of the Truth of what I have said.

The Man of Sense and the Fine Gentleman in the Comedy, who as the chiefest Person propos'd to the Esteem and Imitation of the Audience, is enrich'd with all the Sense and Wit the Poet can bestow; this Extraordinary Person you will find to be a Derider of Religion, a great Admirer of Lucretius, not so much for his Learning, as his Irreligion, a Person wholly Idle, dissolv'd in Luxury, abandon'd to his Pleasures, a great Debaucher of Women, profuse and extravagant in his Expences, and in short, this Finish'd Gentleman will appear a Finish'd Libertine.

The Young Lady that must support the Character of a Vertuous, Well-manner'd Sensible Woman, the most

The PREFACE.

perfect Creature that can be, and the very Flower of her Sex, this Accomplish'd Person *entertains the Audience with confident Discourses, immodest Repartees, and prophane Raillery. She is throughly instructed in* Intreagues *and* Assignations, *a great* Scoffer *at the prudent Reservedness and Modesty of the best of her Sex, She despises the wise Instructions of her Parents or Guardians, is disobedient to their Authority, and at last, without their* Knowledge *or* Consent, *marries her self to the* Fine Gentleman *above mentioned. And can any one imagine, but that our Young Ladies and Gentlemen are admirably instructed by* such Patterns of Sense *and* Virtue? *If a Clergy-man be introduc'd, as he often is, 'tis seldome for any other purpose, but to abuse him, to expose his very* Character *and* Profession: He must be a Pimp, *a* Blockhead, *a* Hypocrite; *some wretched* Figure *he must make, and almost ever be so manag'd, as to bring his very* Order *into* Contempt. *This indeed is a very common, but yet so gross an Abuse of* Wit, *as was never endur'd on a* Pagan Theater, *at least in the ancient, primitive Times of* Poetry, *before its* Purity *and* Simplicity *became corrupted with the Inventions of after Ages.* Poets *then taught* Men *to reverence their* Gods, *and those who serv'd them. None had so little Regard for his* Religion, *as to expose it publickly, or if any had, their Governments were too wise to suffer the Worship of their Gods to be treated on the* Stage *with* Contempt.

In our Comedies *the* Wives *of* Citizens *are highly encourag'd to despise their Husbands, and to make great Friendship with some such* Vertuous Gentleman

The PREFACE.

tleman *and* Man of Senſe *as is above deſcrib'd. This is their Way of recommending* Chaſtity *and* Fidelity. *And that* Diligence *and* Frugality *may be ſufficiently expos'd, tho'* the two Virtues *that chiefly ſupport the* Being *of any State, to deter Men from being* Induſtrious *and* Wealthy, *the* Diligent, *Thriving Citizen is made the moſt Wretched, Contemptible Thing in the World: and as the Alderman that makes the beſt* Figure *in the* City, *makes the worſt on the* Stage, *ſo under the Character of a* Juſtice *of* Peace, *you have all the* Prudence *and* Virtues *of the* Country *moſt unmercifully inſulted over.*

And as theſe Characters are ſet up on purpoſe to ruin all Opinion and Eſteem of Virtue, ſo the Conduct throughout, the Language, *the* Fable *and* Contrivance *ſeem evidently deſign'd for the ſame* Noble *End. There are few Fine Conceipts, few Strains of Wit or extraordinary Pieces of Raillery, but are either* immodeſt *or* irreligious, *and very few* Scenes *but have ſome* ſpiteful *and* envious Stroke *at Sobriety and Good Manners, whence the Youth of the Nation have apparently receiv'd very bad Impreſſions. The* univerſal *Corruption of Manners and irreligious Diſpoſition of Mind that infects the Kingdom, ſeems to have been in a great Meaſure deriv'd from the Stage, or has at leaſt been highly promoted by it. And 'tis great Pitty that thoſe in whoſe Power it is, have not yet reſtrain'd the* Licentiouſneſs *of it, and oblig'd the Writers to obſerve more* Decorum. *It were to be wiſh'd that* Poets, *as Preachers are in ſome Countries, were paid and licens'd by the State, and that none were ſuffer'd to write in Prejudice of* Religion *and the* Government, *but that all ſuch Offenders,*

The PREFACE.

fenders, as publick Enemies of Mankind should be silenc'd and duly punish'd. Sure some Effectual Care should be taken that these Men might not be suffer'd by Debauching our Youth, to help on the Destruction of a brave Nation.

4. Some of these Poets, to excuse their Guilt, alledge for themselves, that the Degeneracy of the Age makes their leud way of Writing necessary; they pretend the Auditors will not be pleas'd, unless they are thus entertain'd from the Stage; and to please they say it the chief business of the Poet. But this is by no means a just Apology; 'tis not true, as was said before, that the Poet's chief business is to please. His chief business is to instruct, to make Mankind Wiser and Better; and in order to this, his Care should be to please and entertain the Audience with all the Wit and Art he is Master of. Aristotle and Horace, and all their Criticks and Commentators, all Men of Wit and Sense agree, that this is the End of Poetry. But they say 'tis their Profession to Write for the Stage; and that Poets must starve if they will not in this way humour the Audience. The Theater will be as unfrequented, as the Churches, and the Poet and the Parson equally neglected. Let the Poet then abandon his Profession, and take up some honest, lawful Calling, where joyning Industry to his great Wit, he may soon get above the Complaints of Poverty, so common among these ingenious Men, and lye under no necessity of prostituting his Wit to any such vile Purposes as are here censur'd. This will be a course of Life more Profitable and Honourable to himself, and more useful to others. And there are among these Writers some, who think they might have risen to the highest Dignities in other Professions, had they imploy'd their Wit in those Ways.

a   'Tis

The PREFACE.

'Tis a mighty Dishonour and Reproach to any Man, that is capable of being useful to the World in any Liberal and Virtuous Profession, to lavish out his Life and Wit *in propagating* Vice and Corruption of Manners, *and in battering from the Stage the strongest Entrenchments and best Works of* Religion *and* Virtue. *Whoever makes this his Choice, when the other was in his Power, may he go off the Stage <u>unpity'd, complaining of Neglect and Poverty</u>, the just Punishments of his* Irreligion *and* <u>Folly</u>.

'Tis *no dishonour to be a true* Poet, *if indeed a Man be one ; that is, a noble* Genius *well cultivated, and employ'd in Writing in such a way, as reaches the End of his Art, and by discouraging Vice, promotes the Good of Mankind.* But 'tis a mighty *Dishonour and Shame, to employ excellent Faculties and abundance of Wit, to humour and please Men in their Vices and Follies. Such a one is more hateful, as an* ill Man, *than valuable, as a* good Poet. *The great Enemy of Mankind, notwithstanding his* Wit *and* Angelick Faculties, *is the most odious Being of the whole Creation.*

Nor is *this Abuse confin'd to the Stage, the same Strain runs thro' the other kinds of Poetry. What monstrous leud and irreligious Books of Poems, as they are call'd, have been of late days publish'd, and what is the greater wonder, receiv'd in a Civiliz'd and Christian Kingdom, with* Applause *and* Reputation? *The sweetness of the* Wit, *makes the* Poison *go down with Pleasure, and the Contagion spreads without Opposition. Young Gentlemen and Ladies are generally pleas'd and diverted with* Poetry, *more than by any other way of Writing ; but there are few Poems they can fix on, but they are like to pay too dear for their Entertainment. Their Fancies are like to be fill'd with impure* Ideas,

and

The PREFACE.

and their Minds engag'd in hurtful *Paſſions, which are the more laſting, by being convey'd in lively Expreſſions, and all the Addreſs of an artful Poet.*

For this End among others, I undertook the writing of this Poem, hoping I might be able to pleaſe and entertain, not only without hurting the Reader, but to his advantage. I was willing to make one Effort *towards the reſcuing the* Muſes *out of the hands of theſe* Raviſhers, *to reſtore them to their ſweet and chaſt Manſions, and to engage them in an Employment ſuitable to their* Dignity. *If I ſucceed not my ſelf in this good Deſign, I hope at leaſt I ſhall awaken the Courage and Compaſſion of ſome other* brave Adventurers, *that may more happily attempt this honorable Work.*

To write an Epick Poem is a work of that Difficulty, that no one for near ſeventeen hundred years paſt has ſucceeded in it ; and only thoſe two great Wits Homer *and* Virgil *before. That the modern Poets have been ſo unſucceſsful, has not, I imagin, proceeded ſo much from want of* Genius, *as from their Ignorance of the Rules of writing ſuch a Poem; or at leaſt, from their want of attending to them. Tho'* Ariſtotle's *excellent Rules of Poetry were early publiſh'd, and ſoon after illuſtrated by the Comments of ſeveral* Criticks, *yet we do not find that our modern* Writers *were very careful to obſerve them. And indeed, as our modern* Poets *ſeem not to have attended to thoſe incomparable Rules, ſo neither have they carefully conſider'd the great* Models *that* Homer *and* Virgil *left them. Some Readers that are not vers'd in this matter, imagin every thing written in* Heroick Verſe, *is an* Heroick Poem; *but theſe have not conſider'd the* Nature of ſuch a Work, *nor look'd into the* Criticks, *who have written*

on

The PREFACE.

on this Subject. I shall therefore give the Definition *of an* Epick *or* Heroick Poem, *that those that have it not already, may now have a true Idea of its Nature.*

An Epick Poem *is a feign'd or devis'd Story of an* Illustrious Action, *related in* Verse, *in an* Allegorical, Probable, Delightful *and* Admirable *manner, to cultivate the* Mind *with* Instructions *of* Virtue. *'Tis a feign'd or devis'd Discourse; that is, a* Fable; *and so it agrees with* Tragedy *and* Comedy. *The word* Fable *at first signified indifferently a true or false Story, therefore* Cicero *for distinction, uses* Fictas Fabulas *in his Book* de Finibus. *But afterwards Custom obtain'd to use the word always for a feign'd Discourse. And in the first Ages, especially in the Eastern World, great use was made by Learned and Wise Men of these* feign'd Discourses, Fables *or* Apologues, *to teach the ruder and more unpolish'd Part of Mankind.* Theologians, Philosophers, *and great* Law-givers, *every where fell into this way of instructing and cultivating the People in the Knowledge of Religion, Natural Philosophy, and Moral and Political Virtues. So* Thales, Orpheus, Solon, Homer, *and the rest of the great Men in those Ages have done, and the famous Philosopher* Socrates *is by some affirm'd to be the Author of many of the Fables that pass under* Æsop's *name. Most of them made their Fables in Verse, that by the addition of* Harmony *and* Numbers *they might the better attain their End.* Strabo *and* Plutarch *greatly commend this way of teaching the People; and these Reasons may be given for the usefulness of it. Naked Philosophical Precepts and Doctrines are of themselves* harsh *and* dry, *hardly attended to, and ungratefully entertain'd. If the Hearers are* rude *and* course, *or very vicious, there is no hope of gaining them by a*

grave

The PREFACE.

grave *and* solemn *Discourse of Virtue, and even the better and more civiliz'd Auditors are hardly kept attentive to it.* Man *is naturally a lover of* Pleasure, *and if you would do him* Good, *it must be, by pleasing him; you must give him* Delight, *and keep his Mind in a constant agreeable Agitation, else he will not attend to the most useful* Counsel *and* Instruction. *He is pleas'd already with the* Notions *and* Habitudes, *howsoever* false *or* vicious, *that have the* present *Possession of him, and you must give him a great deal of* Pleasure *and* Entertainment *to engage him to hear you, when you would perswade him to the trouble, of becoming* Wiser *and* Better. *Now the first Wise Men that undertook to civilize and polish the barbarous World, found this way of* Fables *especially in Verse, to be mighty* Acceptable *to the People : The Contrivance gave them* Delight, *and the Novelty rais'd their Admiration. They could learn them perfectly, and repeat them often, by which means the Instructions of Virtue covertly contain'd in them, were inculcated on their Minds.*

And we find, that many Ages after Orpheus, Solon, Homer, &c. *the Divine Law-giver of the Christians thought fit to teach the People by* Apologues, Parables *or* Fables, *under which he cover'd and disguis'd his Heavenly Instructions.*

The Action must be Illustrious *and* Important ; *Illustrious in respect of the Person, who is the Author of it, who is always some* Valiant, *or* Wise, *or* Pious *Prince or great Commander : But let his Character be what it will in other respects (for there is no Necessity the* Hero *should be a good or a wise Person)* 'tis *always necessary he should have* Courage ; *which single Quality is sufficient to make the* Hero. *And the*

b *Action*

The PREFACE.

Action must be important, *both in respect of its* Object *and its* End. *'Tis the Action of some great Person, about some* noble *and* weighty *Affair. 'Tis true, there are many other Persons concern'd, but 'tis the Action of the* chief *Person that gives the* Being *and* Denomination *to the Poem. This Action must be but one ; when it ceases, the Poem is ended ; and if it be reviv'd, and taken up again, 'tis a new Poem begins. Action is Motion ; and if it ceases cannot be reviv'd, so as to be numerically the same. There are indeed many other Actions besides the* Principal *one, but they all depend on, and have relation to that which is* Principal, *with the* Unity *of which, the* Unity *of the Poem stands or falls. If this principal Action be* broken, *the Poem is* broken *too, if there be any other Action* coordinate *and* independent *on this, the Poem is* monstrous, *and has as many* Heads, *as there are found* independent *Actions. The Narration therefore of many Actions successively of one great Person, or the History of his Life related in Verse, is by no means an* Heroick *Poem, any one great Action being sufficient for that. That which makes the* Unity *of the Action, is the regular Succession of one* Part *or* Episode *to another, not only as* Antecedents *and* Consequents, *but as it were* Causes *and* Effects, *wherein the Reader may discern that the former Episode makes the following necessary, and the* Connection *between them is such, that they* assist *and* support *each other, as the* Members *of the Body do, no Episode being out of its place, of a* disproportion'd *size to the* Rest, *or that could be spar'd from its place, without* maiming, *or at least* deforming *the Whole. If this order of the Episodes be preserv'd, and there appears none but what* naturally *and* probably *results from the* principal *Action, then the Action may be look'd on as one.*

The

The PREFACE.

The Action must be related in an Allegorical *manner; and this Rule is best observ'd, when as* Divines *speak; there is both a* Literal *Sense obvious to every Reader, and that gives him satisfaction enough if he sees no farther; and besides another* Mystical *or* Typical *Sense, not hard to be discover'd by those Readers that penetrate the matter deeper.* Virgil *seems most happy in this Conduct, whose Poem all along contains this double Sense,* Homer *has often only an* Allegorical *Sense without the* Literal, *and therefore is not so well accommodated to this Age, as he was not to that of* Augustus. *But* Ariosto *and* Spencer, *however great* Wits, *not observing this judicious Conduct of* Virgil, *nor attending to any sober Rules, are hurried on with a* boundless, impetuous *Fancy over Hill and Dale, till they are both lost in a Wood of Allegories. Allegories so* wild, unnatural, *and* extravagant, *as greatly displease the Reader. This way of writing mightily offends in this Age; and 'tis a wonder how it came to please in any. There is indeed a way of writing purely Allegorical, as when* Vices *and* Virtues *are introduc'd as* Persons; *the first as* Furies, *the other as* Divine Persons *or* Goddesses, *which still obtains, and is well enough accommodated to the present Age. For the* Allegory *is presently discern'd, and the Reader is by no means impos'd on, but sees it immediately to be an* Allegory, *and is both delighted and instructed with it. The devis'd Story must be related in a* probable *manner; without this all things will be* harsh, unnatural, *and* monstrous; *and consequently most* odious *and* offensive *to the Judicious.* Probability *must be in the* Action, *the* Conduct, *the* Manners; *and where humane means cannot,* Machines *are introduc'd to support it. Nothing is more necessary*
then

The PREFACE.

then Probability; *no Rule more chastly to be observ'd.*

An Epick Poem must likewise be delightful *and* admirable; *and to make it so, must concur sublime Thoughts, clear and noble Expression, Purity of Language, a just and due Proportion, Relation, and Dependance between the Parts, and a beautiful and regular Structure and Connection discernable in the* Whole. *Without these it will not be capable of giving* Delight, *or raising* Admiration. Admiration *is the* Formal Object *of an Epick Poem, nothing is to be admitted there, but as it is* admirable; *and by this it is discriminated from all other sorts of Poetry. Every kind endeavours to* please *and* delight, *but this only attempts to please by* astonishing *and* amazing *the Reader. In an Epick Poem every thing should appear great and* wonderful, *the Thoughts cannot be too much* Elevated, *the Episodes too* Noble, *the Expression too* Magnificent, *nor the Action too* Wonderful *and* Surprising, *if Probability be preserv'd. No Riches of* Fancy, *no* Pomp *of* Eloquence *can be laid out too much on such a Work where the* Design *is throughout to raise our* Admiration. *To render the Action the more* Admirable, Homer *and* Virgil *have introduc'd the* Gods, *and engag'd them every where as* Parties; *and tho' I cannot say this is* Essential *and* Necessary *to an Epick Poem, yet 'tis evident, that interesting* Heaven *and* Hell *in the matter, does mightily raise the Subject, and makes the Action appear more wonderful. The Pagan Poets had in this a great advantage, their* Theology *was such, as would easily mix it self with their Poems, from whence they receiv'd their greatest Beauties.* Homer *indeed to raise his Subject by his frequent* Machines, *seems to have debas'd his* Religion. Virgil's *Conduct, in my Opinion, is more care-*
ful

The PREFACE.

ful and chast. But some of our modern Criticks *have believ'd 'tis scarce possible for a* Christian Poet *to make use of this advantage, of introducing* Superiour, Invisible *Powers into the Action, and therefore seem to despair of seeing an* Heroick Poem *written now, that shall reach to the* Dignity *of those of the Pagans. They think the* Christian Religion *is not so well accommodated to this matter, as the* Pagan *was; and that if any Attempt be made this way,* Religion *will suffer more, than the* Poem *will gain by it.* My Opinion *has always differ'd from these Gentlemen's, I believe a* Christian Poet *has as great advantages as the* Pagan *had; and that our* Theology *may enter into an Epick Poem, and raise the Subject without being it self debas'd. And this indeed was a second Reason why I undertook this Work, so full of* Difficulty *and* Hazard. *I was willing to give an Instance wherein it might appear, that the Assertion I have advanc'd, is* actually true.

In the Definition which I have given of an Heroick Poem, according to the Sense and Judgment of the best Criticks, I have said, its End is to convey some Instruction of Virtue. But of this, I have discours'd at large at the beginning of this Preface, *and there is no need of repeating it.*

'*Tis not for me to proceed to Censure other Mens Performances of this Kind; whoever will be at the Pains to read the Commentators on* Aristotle, *and* Horace's Rules of Poetry; *or that will but carefully consider* Rapin, Dacier, *and* Bossu, *those great Masters among the* French, *and the Judicious Remarks of our own excellent Critick Mr.* Rymer, *who seems to have better consider'd these matters, and to have seen farther into them, than any of the* English Nation; *will be soon able to see wherein the Heroick Poems that*

c   have

The PREFACE.

have been publish'd since Virgil *by the* Italian, French, *and* English Wits *have been defective, by comparing them with the* Rules *of Writing set down by those great Masters. Whether I have succeeded better, must be left to the determination of the Judicious Reader.*

In this Work I have endeavour'd mostly to form my self on Virgil's *Model, which I look on, as the most just and perfect, and which is most easily accommodated to the present Age, supposing the* Christian Religion *in the place of the* Pagan. *I do not make any Apology for my* Imitation *of* Virgil *in so many places of this Poem; for the same great* Master *has imitated* Homer *as frequently and closely; and I do not find that any of his* Criticks *have condemn'd him for his doing so. Nor is it at all* improbable, *but that the* Greek Poet *himself imitated his Predecessors of the same Nation, tho' no doubt he wonderfully improv'd their Model.* Homer, *I believe, was not the first Writer of an* Epick Poem. *We find* Aristotle *in his Book of the Art of Poetry makes mention of several, I suppose, before him: He tells us of an* Epick Poem, *intituled,* The Little Ilias, *and another the* Cyprica *; and censures them both, as containing many* perfect, distinct, *and* independent Actions. *The last of these Poems is likewise mention'd by* Herodotus *in* Euterpe, *by* Athenæus *and* Pausanias. *And 'tis likely many more such Poems were written before* Homer's *time, who might be well suppos'd to have imitated them in what they had done well, as well as to have improv'd them in avoiding many of their Errors.*

What Homer *and* Virgil *have* perform'd *with Honour and universal Applause, I have* attempted: *What they have been* able, *I have been willing to do. If I have not succeeded, my disappointment will be the less,*

in

The PREFACE.

in that Poetry has been so far from being my Busineſs *and* Profeſſion, *that it has imploy'd but a small part of my Time ; and then, but as my* Recreation, *and the Entertainment of my idle hours. If this Attempt ſucceeds so far, as to excite some other Perſon that has a noble* Genius, Leisure, *and* Application, *to Honour his Country with a juſt* Epick Poem, *I shall think the* Vacancies *and* Intervals *that for about two years paſt, I have had from the* Busineſs *of my* Profeſſion; *which notwithſtanding was then greater then at any time before, have been very well imploy'd.*

Books lately Printed for, and Sold by A. & J. Churchil, *at the* Black Swan *in* Pater-Noſter-Row.

A View of Univerſal Hiſtory, from the Creation to the Year of Chriſt 1695. wherein the moſt memorable Perſons and Things in the known Kingdoms and Countries of the World, are ſet down in ſeveral Columns by way of Synchroniſm, according to their proper Centuries and Years: By *Francis Tallents*, ſometime Fellow of *Magdalen* College, *Cambridge*. The whole graven in 16 Copper-plates, each 15 Inches deep, and 22 broad ; bound up into Books, the Sheets lined. A Work of great Exactneſs and Curioſity. Price 16 s.

Camden's Britannia, newly Tranſlated into Engliſh, with large Additions and Improvements. By *Edmund Gibſon* of Queens College in *Oxford*.

The General Hiſtory of the Air. By *Robert Boyle*, Eſq; 4°.

A Compleat Journal of the Votes, Speeches and Debates, both of the Houſe of Lords and Houſe of Commons, throughout the whole Reign of Queen *Elizabeth*. Collected by Sir *Simonds Dewes* Baronet, and Publiſhed by *Paul Bowes* of the Middle-Temple, Eſq; The Second Edition. Fol.

The Works of the famous *Nicholas Machiavel*, Citizen and Secretary of *Florence*. Written Originally in Italian, and from thence faithfully Tranſlated into Engliſh.

Mr. *Lock's* Eſſay concerning Humane Underſtanding. The Second Edition, with large Additions. Fol.

------ his Thoughts of Education, 8°.

The Fables of *Æsop* and other Mithologiſts ; made Engliſh by Sir *Roger L'Eſtrange*, Kt. Fol.

Two Treatiſes of Government : The firſt an Anſwer to *Filmer's Patriarcha*. The latter an Eſſay concerning the true Original, Extent, and End of Civil Government. 8°.

Notitia Monaſtica, or a ſhort Hiſtory of the Religious Houſes in *England* and *Wales*, &c. By *Thomas Tanner*, A. B. 8°. The

The Refurrection of the (fame) Body afferted from the Traditions of the Heathens, the Ancient Jews, and the Primitive Church: With an Anfwer to the Objections brought againſt it. By *Humphry Hody*, D.D.

Biſhop *Wilkins* of Prayer and Preaching; Enlarged by the Biſhop of *Norwich*, and Dr. *Williams*, &c.

Conſiderations about lowering the Intereſt, and raiſing the Value of Money, 8o.

Short Obſervations on a Printed Paper, intituled, *For encouraging the Coining Silver Money in* England, *and after for keeping it here*. 8°.

Sir *William Temple*'s Hiſtory of the *Netherlands*, 8°.

------ *Miſcellanea*, 8°.

Dr. *Gibſon*'s Anatomy of Humane Bodies, with Figures, 8°.

Dr. *Patrick*'s new Verſion of all the Pſalms of *David* in Metre, 12°.

Two Treatiſes of Rational Religion, 8°.

Gentleman's Religion, with the Grounds and Reaſons of it. In which the Truth of Chriſtianity in general is vindicated; its Simplicity aſſerted; and ſome Introductory Rules for the diſcovering of its particular Doctrines and Precepts, are propoſed. By a private Gentleman.

The Novels and Tales of the renowned *John Boccacio*, the firſt Refiner of *Italian* Proſe; containing an hundred Curious Novels: By ſeven honorable Ladies, and three Noble Gentlemen, Framed in ten Days. The Fifth Edition much Corrected and Amended.

Logica: five, Ars Ratiocinandi. Ontologia; five de Ente in Genere. Pneumatologia, ſeu Deſpiritibus. Auctore Joanne Clerico. 12°.

The Hiſtory of *Scotland*. Written in Latin by *George Buchanan.* Faithfully rendered into Engliſh. Fol.

The Lives of the Popes, from the time of our Saviour Jeſus Chriſt, to the Reign of *Sixtus* IV. Written Originally in Latin by *Baptiſta Platina*, Native of *Cremona*, and Tranſlated into *Engliſh*. And the ſame Hiſtory continued from the year 1471. to this preſent time; wherein the moſt remarkable Paſſages of Chriſtendom, both in Church and State, are treated of and deſcribed. By Sir *Paul Rycaut*, Kt. The Second Edition Corrected.

The Meditations of *Marcus Aurelius Antoninus*, the *Roman* Emperor, concerning himſelf. Treating of a Natural Man's Happineſs; wherein it conſiſteth, and of the means to attain unto it. Tranſlated out of the Original Greek, with Notes; by *Meric Caſaubon*, D.D. The Fifth Edition. To which is added, The Life of *Antoninus*, with ſome Remarks upon the whole. By Monſieur and Madam *Dacier.* Never before in Engliſh. 8°.

Sermons Preached by Dr *Robert Leighton*, late Archbiſhop of *Glaſgow*. Publiſhed at the deſire of his Friends after his Death, from his Papers written with his own hand. The Second Edition. 8°.

The *Roman* Hiſtory written in Latin by *Titus Livius*, with the Supplements of the Learned *John Freinſhemius*, and *John Dujatius.* From the Foundation of *Rome* to the middle of the Reign of *Auguſtus.* Faithfully done into Engliſh. Fol.

Anicius Manlius Severinus Boetius, of the Conſolation of Philoſophy. In five Books. Made Engliſh by the Right Honorable *Richard* Lord Viſcount *Preſton*. 8°.

In the Preſs.

Leland de Viris illuſtribus, from the MSS. with large Improvements; and *Boſton* of *Bury*, and a Continuation. By Mr. *Tanner.*

Sir *Richard Baker*'s Chronicle of the Kings of *England*, continued down to this time. *Cambridge* Concordance, Fol.

Prince Arthur.

BOOK I.

I Sing the *Briton*, and his Righteous Arms,
Who bred to Suff'rings, and the rude Alarms
Of bloody War, forsook his Native Soil,
And long sustain'd a vast Heroick Toil,
Till kinder Fate invited his Return,
To bless the Isle, that did his Absence mourn:
To re-enthrone fair Liberty, and break
The Saxon Yoke, that gall'd *Britannia*'s Neck.

Tell, sacred Muse, what made th' Infernal King
Use all his Arts, and all his Forces bring
The gen'rous *Briton*'s Triumphs to oppose,
Afflict his Friends, and aid his cruel Foes.
Tell, why the angry Pow'rs below, combine
T' oppress a valiant Prince, and thwart his brave Design.

Ambitious *Lucifer*, depos'd of late
From Bliss Divine, and high Angelick State,
Sinks to the dark, unbottom'd Deep of Hell,
Where Sin, and Death, and endless Sorrow dwell:
Here plung'd in Flame, and tortur'd with Despair
He plots Revenge, and meditates new War.
His Thoughts on deep Designs th' Apostate spent,
When this Conjuncture favour'd his Intent.
A spacious, dusky Plain lay waste and void,
Where yet Creating Power was ne'er imploy'd

To fashion Elements, or strike out Light;
The silent, lonesome Walks of ancient Night.
In th' Archives kept in Heav'n's bright Towers, was found,
A sacred old Decree, wherein the Ground
Was set distinctly out, from Ages past,
For a new World, on this unbounded Waste.
Here did th' Artificer Divine of late,
The World so long before markt out, create.
And gave it to the Man he newly made,
Where all things him, as he did Heav'n, obey'd.
In *Eden's* Walks he made his blest Abode,
All full of Joy, of Glory, full of *God*.
Nature with vast Profusion on him pours,
Unmeasur'd Bliss, from unexhausted Stores.

Th' Apostate raging at his own Defeat,
And envying this new Prince his happy Seat;
Labours to win him to his Side, to bear
Arms against Heav'n, and wage Confed'rate War.
Nor did his Arts in vain weak Man assail,
His false Seraphick Tongue, and Charms prevail.
Deluded Man from his high Station fell
Deserting Heav'n, to serve the Cause of Hell.
This fatal Conquest o'er fall'n *Adam* gain'd,
A mighty Empire *Lucifer* maintain'd;
Till the blest Prince of Peace, Heav'n's Lord and Heir,
By Pity's Tears, and charming Mercy's Prayer
Drawn down from Heav'n, freed lost Mankind, and broke
The Pow'r of Hell, and Sin's Tyrannick Yoke.
He makes Proud *Lucifer* his Host disband,
And wrests the Scepter from th' Usurper's Hand.
The Prince of Darkness owns the Conquerour,
And yields his Empire to a mightier Pow'r.

From

From Idols and their Priests the Nations freed,
Celestial Light, and Truth divine succeed.
Religion large Dominions soon obtain'd,
And daily Conquests, and fresh Laurels gain'd.
To *Albion*'s Shore she early pass'd the Main,
And brought along her bright Etherial Train:
From thence she chas'd Infernal Shades away,
And o'er the Isle, diffus'd a Heav'nly Day.
The Prince of Hell at her Appearance flies,
Spoil'd of his Altars, and his Votaries.
Confin'd to Barb'rous Northern Lands he staid,
Till the fierce Saxon, *Albion* did invade.
Victorious *Octa* who his Shrines ador'd,
Rebuilt his Altars, and his Groves restor'd.
Long abdicated Gods make *Albion* mourn,
At theirs, and their devouring Priests Return.
Th' Arch-Traytor's Rage hence against *Arthur* rose,
And all th' infernal Pow'rs his Arms oppose:
Conscious should he his glorious End acquire,
And force th' intruding Pagan to retire,
Theirs, with the Saxon Empire must expire.
They must again forsake fair *Albion*'s Land,
And leave Divine Religion to Command.

 Scarce had they left the happy Neustrian Coast,
Born with a Prosperous Gale, scarce had they lost
The Tops of Spires, and rising Points of Land,
When *Lucifer*, that did observing stand
On the high Southern Promontory's Head,
Of *Vecta's* Isle, the Seas beneath him spread;
With sharp Angelick Ken, views far and wide,
And soon Prince *Arthur*'s hateful Fleet descry'd.
The Heav'ns serenely smil'd, and every Sail
Fill'd its wide Bosom, with th' indulgent Gale.

Mercy, Deliverance, Pity, Hope difplaid
Their Silver Wings, and glad attendance paid,
Sung on the Shrowds, or with the Streamers plaid.
Rage flaſh'd, like Lightning, from th' Apoſtate's Eyes,
And Envy fwell'd him to the vafteſt Size.
Then thus he to himſelf.
Was not to me in the fam'd Wars of Heav'n,
The chief Command of all the Forces giv'n,
Sent by Confederate Potentates to wage
Unheard of War, and all Heav'n's Pow'r engage ?
When I, to end with Honour the Campaign,
Drew my bright Troops out on the Etherial Plain;
And puſh'd on that great, laſt deciſive Day,
With God-like Vigour, for th' Imperial Sway.
In Luſture chief, in Danger and Command,
Did I proud *Michael's* Veteran Troops withſtand.
Michael, than whom a Braver Combitant,
For Skill and Strength the Foe could never vaunt.
'Gainſt freſh Battalions ſtill pour'd on I ſtood,
Smeer'd with Celeſtial Duſt, and Seraphs Blood.
Had not our Mould been Æther, Pure and Fine,
Labour'd with Care, anneel'd with Skill divine;
The Blows of mighty Cherubs Death had cloy'd,
Unpeopl'd Heav'n, and the bright Race deſtroy'd.
With *Michael* pain'd with ghaſtly Wounds, at length
I clos'd, and grafp'd him with Immortal Strength;
And down Heav'n's Precipice, had headlong hurl'd
The great Arch-Angel, to th' Infernal World,
Had not ſwift *Uriel* trembling at the Sight,
That fill'd all Heav'n, with Horrour and dire Fright,
Ruſh'd in, to ſave him from unequal Fight.
Their ſtagg'ring Army ſhrunk, and we had won
The Throne we fought for, But th' Almighty's Son

Brought

Brought strong Recruits, to reinforce their Host,
And win back what their general *Michael* lost.
Tho' overmatcht, did I not firmly stand,
The chiefest Mark of his Revenging Hand?
Did I from Posts of greatest Danger run,
Or once his bright Triumphal Chariot shun?
Did I once shrink, when showers of poison'd Darts,
Dipt in Eternal Wrath, shot thro' our Hearts?
When massy Rocks of Heav'nly Crystal flew,
Which the strong Arms of mighty Seraphs threw?
Did I not run and timely Help afford,
Where Storms of Fire, and loudest Thunder roar'd?
'Tis true, o'er-born with Force, at last I fell,
But got immortal Fame, tho' with it Hell.
Scarce was I vanquish'd and o'erthrown but late
By Power Almighty, and Eternal Fate.
Since that chief Lord, and Prince of Hell I've reign'd
And from the Foe, his new-made World have gain'd'
And long maintain'd the Conquests I had won;
Now much lost back to his Almighty Son.
But faithful *Octa* has once more restor'd
This happy Isle to me its ancient Lord.
Have I been thus for great Atchievements fam'd,
My Deeds throughout all Heav'n and Hell proclaim'd;
And shall this British, despicable Wight,
Me and my Priests, force to a second Flight?
Rifle my Temples, and in Triumph bear,
Thro' shouting Throngs, the Spoils high in the Air?
Who then to me will Hymns of Praise return,
Who on my Altars Odorous Incense burn?
If I chastise not this vain *Briton*'s Pride,
That does insulting on the Ocean ride.
If I secure not my new conquer'd Seat,
And all his wild, ambitious Arms defeat.

This

This having said, to Heav'n he mounts upright,
And to the Northern Pole directs his Flight.
All fir'd with Rage, and full of anxious Care,
With his swift Wings, he cuts the yielding Air.
As when the Sun pours from his Orb of Light,
A glorious Deluge, on the Face of Night.
His golden Rays shot from the Rosy East,
Reach in a Moment, the remotest West,
And smiling on the Mountains Heads are seen,
Th' immense Expansion past, that lies between.
The Prince of Darkness now, once Prince of Light,
With equall Swiftness takes his Airy Flight,
And the vast interval of Seas, and Isles,
Wild Desarts, spacious Forrests, snowy Hills,
Past in a Moment, does on *Fiœl* Light;
Of *Lapland Alpes*, chief for amazing Height.
Where *Thor* resides, who heretofore by Lot
The Sovereign Rule o'er Winds and Tempests got.
Here in strong Prisons bound with heavy Chains,
His howling, savage Subjects he restrains,
And in Eternal Din, and Uproar reigns.
In close Apartments round his Desart Court,
Fierce Pris'ners are confin'd of different sort.
Here boundless Stores, and Treasures Infinite
Of Vapours, Steams, and Exhalations, fit
T' engender Winds, or Snow, or Hail, or Rain,
In Subterranean Magazins remain.
Here new fledg'd Winds, young yelping Monsters try
Their Wings, and sporting round their Prisons fly.
Here whistling East-winds prove their shriller Notes:
Here the hoarse South-winds, strain their hollow Throats.
Boreas the fiercest and most turbulent,
Of the mad Race, raves in his Dungeon pent.

At

At th' Adamantine Door vaſt Hills are thrown,
And abrupt Rocks of Ice, pil'd ſevenfold on.
Capricious Whirlwinds, of more Force than Sound,
In everlaſting Eddys turning round,
Grow Giddy, Furious and Extravagant,
And ſtrive to break from their cloſe Den's reſtraint.
When *Thor* unlocks their Priſons, out they fly,
A lawleſs Rout, and with their Helliſh Cry
Out-howl the hideous Monſters of the Seas,
Or ſavage Roarings of the Wilderneſs.
Some range the Flats, and ſcour the Champain Land,
Or roll in tott'ring heaps the Deſart Sand.
Some to the lofty Woods direct their Courſe,
And with an uncontroul'd, impetuous Force
O'erturn oppoſing Structures in their haſt,
Tear up tall Pines, and lay the Foreſt waſt.
Some to the Ocean with like Speed reſort,
And in loud Tempeſts on the Billows ſport.
Embroil the Coaſts, and in wild Outrages
Turn up to Heav'n, the Bottom of the Seas.
But huſht at *Thor*'s Command they all obey,
And to their ancient Priſons haſte away.

To him, thus *Lucifer:* Great Prince, on thee
Fate has beſtow'd the Empire of the Sea,
All there concern'd, invoke thy Deity.
The Merchants pray to thee to fill their Sails,
Enrich thy Prieſts, and purchaſe proſperous Gales.
I too thy Suppliant, ask thy powerful Aid,
A haughty Prince, deſigning to invade
My faithful Subject *Octa*, and beguile
Me of my Hopes of fair *Britannia*'s Iſle;
Sails with a numerous Fleet, with Men and Arms,
And *Octa* trembles at his proud Alarms.

Let him in furious Hurricanes be tost,
Be sunk, or wreckt, or on the Ocean lost,
Beat him at least, from his intended Coast.
Make him thy Vengeance feel, thy Power regard,
And be what e'er thou askest, thy Reward.

Great Prince, then *Thor* reply'd,
Who rul'st the Realms of Hell with Soveraign Sway,
Whom all th' Infernal Thrones, and Pow'rs obey,
I own Obedience to thy high Command,
Who putt'st this Scepter first into my Hand.
Thou led'st in Heav'n our bright Battalions on,
And bravely didst attempt th' Almighty's Throne;
I saw thy mighty Deeds, and kept my Post
Close by thee, till that Glorious Day was lost.
Thy faded Splendor, and illustrious Scars,
From ghastly Wounds, receiv'd in those just Wars,
I view with Reverence, 'tis true subdu'd
Headlong we fell from Heav'n's high Tow'rs, pursu'd
With Whirlwinds, and loud Thunder, down to Hell,
And Storms of Fire beat on us as we fell.
Yet after that, thou ledst us to invade
This Globous World, which we our Conquest made.
And my Election Patroniz'd by thee,
This great Command and Province fell to me.

That said, by him their heavy Gates unbarr'd,
Which loud on mighty Iron Hinges jarr'd,
Out-ratling *Eurus*, and loud *Boreas* fly,
And with Outrageous Tempests fill the Sky.
They bend their Course strait to the British Coast,
And on those Seas lay out their Anger most.
Their furious Wings the swelling Surges beat,
And rouze old Ocean from his peaceful Seat.

The

The raging Seas in high ridg'd Mountains rise,
And cast their angry Foam against the Skies.
Then gape so deep, that Day Light Hell invades,
And shoots grey Dawning thro' th' affrighted Shades.
Low bellying Clouds soon intercept the Light,
And o'er the *Britons* spread a Noon Day Night.
Exploded Thunder tears th' Embowel'd Sky,
And Sulphurous Flames a dismal Day supply.
The Dire Convulsions, for a certain Space
Distorted *Nature*, wresting from it's Place
This *Globe*, set to the Sun's more oblique View,
And wrench'd the *Poles* some Leagues yet more askew.
Horrour, Confusion, Uproar, Strife and Fear
In all their wild amazing Shapes appear.
Mean time old *Chaos* joyful at the Sight,
Look'd and smil'd horrible on older *Night*,
Hoping that *Nature*, their grand Foe would crack
With universal Ruin, and her Wreck
Would give them all their lost Dominions back.
The Sailor's Clamour, and enormous Cries,
The Crack of Masts, mixt with th' outrageous Noise
Of Storms and Thunder, rending all the Air,
Form the last Scene of Horror and Despair.

When the Just *Arthur* fill'd with Grief and Dread,
And Pale Confusion deeply sigh'd, and said,
O righteous Heav'n, why hast thou rang'd this Day
Against me all thy Terrors in Array!
Arm'd in thy Cause thy Temples to restore,
And give that Aid thy sacred Priests implore.
If thou such fierce Destruction dost dispence,
To punish some unpardon'd old Offence,
On me let all thy fiery Darts be spent,
Let not my Crime involve the innocent.

C   Whelm

Whelm o'er my guilty Head thefe raging Seas,
And let this Sacrifice thy Wrath appeafe,
But let the *Britifh* Youth return in Peace.
That faid, his Ship unmafted, without Guide,
Driv'n by the Winds and Seas impetuous Tyde,
The Sight of all the fcatter'd Navy loft,
Strikes on the Quickfand of an unknown Coaft.

Mean time bright *Uriel*, Heav'n's high Favourite,
Left the celeftial Palaces of Light,
Sent by fupream Command, and down he flies,
Let by a Golden Sun-beam thro' the Skies.
Meeknefs divine, ferene and Heav'nly Grace,
And frefh immortal Youth fhone on his Face.
God-like his Form, his Looks fo charming mild
That where fhe came all ravifh'd Nature fmil'd.
He ftrait alights on lofty *Gobeum's* Head,
Which wonder'd at the Heav'n about it fhed,
From the bright *Cherubim*, who touch'd his Lyre,
Fam'd for its Sweetnefs in the Heav'nly Quire.
Th' enchanted Winds ftraightway their Fury laid,
Grew wondrous ftill, and ftrict Attention paid.
Aerial Demons that by Twilight ftray,
Sport in loud Thunder, and in Tempefts play,
Spread their brown Wings, and fly in Clouds away.
The Day returns, the Heav'ns no longer fcowl,
And fierce Sea-Monfters charm'd forget to howl.
The Winds retreat, and leave the peaceful Waves;
To reft their Wings, and fleep in *Lapland* Caves.
Soft *Zephirs* only ftay to fan the Woods,
And play in gentle Gales along the Floods.
The Ocean fmiles to fee the Tempeft fled,
New lays his Waves, and fmooths his ruffled Bed.

All

All things thus hufht, great *Arthur* gave Command,
To quit their Ship, ftuck in the barren Sand,
And in their Boats to make the neighb'ring Land.
They fpy a Creek not far a peaceful Seat,
Where flying Waves by furious Tempefts beat,
Find from the fierce Purfuit a fafe Retreat.
Free from th' outrageous Clamours of the Deep,
They reft fecure, and unmolefted fleep.
Stretcht fmooth beneath the fhady Trees and Rocks
That guard them from the Winds impetuous Shocks.
Here fmaller Veffels may fecurely ride
And all th' Affaults of angry Storms deride.
Here they arriv'd, and Heav'n they firft ador'd,
Which gave the Aid, their earneft Cries implor'd.
Which fav'd them from the Winds, Waves, Rocks, and Storms,
Deaths of fo many, and fuch hideous Forms.
Then for their parted Friends, with humble Prayer,
They ask Heav'n's Pity, and indulgent Care.
Now *Arthur* from the Rock, views far and wide
The Seas beneath, if thence might be defcry'd
The Friends he lately loft, but views in vain,
No Friend appears on all the Defart Main.

Return'd he thus began:
Too dark th' Eternal's ways are, too profound,
For the moft fharp created Wit to found.
Clouds black, as thofe that rife the facred Fence
Of his high Throne, furround his Providence.
Whofe walks are tracklefs, and on ev'ry Hand
About her Paths, fhades and thick Darknefs ftand.
Her ways are fo perplext, fo wide her fteps,
Such turns and windings, and fuch frightful leaps;

Such Gulphs, and interpofing Rocks appear,
There fuch Afcents, fuch dreadful Downfalls here,
That Reafon ftrait affrighted ftops her Pace,
Is foon thrown off, and quits th' unequal Chafe.
Th' Almighty's Councils are fo high and fteep,
Immenfe, unbounded, without Bottom deep;
Angels amaz'd from their high Thrones of Blifs,
Trembling look down on this profound Abyfs.
Sometimes he feems to thwart his own Intent,
Stop and defeat his long defign'd event;
Yet which way e're he fteers, his end's attain'd,
By uncouth means, with greater Wonder gain'd.
Sometimes his high Permiffion, leaves oppreft
The Men moft like him, and that ferve him beft:
But ftill their Sufferings and feverer Fate,
Prepare them for fome glorious, future ftate.
Invited by fad *Britain*'s Prayers, and Tears,
To fave her State; and eafe her deadly Fears,
We arm'd, depos'd Religion to enthrone,
T' enlarge the Chriftian Empire, not our own.
We arm'd thus, to reftore in Hell's Defpight,
To Heav'n it's Worfhip, and to Men their Right.
Refume your Courage then, it can't be true,
That Heav'n's Revenge, fhould Heav'n's own Caufe purfue.
Thefe Evils are not in Difpleafure meant,
Heav'n is too Juft, and you too Innocent.
Succefs and Triumph will our Arms attend,
And thefe rough Ways lead to a glorious End.
With Pleafure we hereafter fhall relate
Thefe fufferings, that will greater Joys create.

   He faid, and all his anxious Cares fuppreft,
And kept conceal'd his trouble in his Breaft.

With looks compos'd, 'twixt Pleasure and Despair,
Grave but serene, he bids them all repair
Their strength, exhausted with much toil and care.
Of Meats and Fruits part of their Naval Store,
Which with them from their Ship they brought ashore:
Their weary Limbs repos'd, beneath the shade
Of well spread Trees, a grateful Meal they made.
Rich Wine of *Burgundy*, and choice Champaign,
Relieve the Toil, they suffer'd on the Main.

But what more chear'd them than their Meats and Wine,
Was wise Instruction, and Discourse Divine,
From God-like *Arthur*'s Mouth, by Heav'n inspir'd;
Which all their Breasts with sacred Passions fir'd.
Great were his Thoughts, strong and sublime his Sense
Of Heav'n's Decrees, Foreknowledge, Providence.
He reason'd deep of Heav'n's mysterious Ends,
And made stern Justice, and fair Mercy Friends.
How high he soar'd, how noble was his Flight,
Speaking of Truth divine, and Wisdom infinite!
He opens all the Magazins above,
Of boundless Goodness and Eternal Love,
From these rich Stores of Heav'n, these sacred Springs
Of everlasting Joy and Peace, he brings
Ambrosial Food, and rich Nectarean Wine,
Which chear pure Souls, and nourish Life Divine.
He then compar'd this transient, mortal state,
To the fierce Tempest they escap'd so late,
Which here is every great and good Man's Fate.
If God-like Men for Heav'n embark, and stand
Their Course direct, to make the blisful Land;
Strait Hell the bloody signal gives to Arm;
Cain's cruel Offspring takes the dire Alarm;

And

And potent Fiends by Sea their Forces joyn,
T'' obstruct their way, and break their brave design.
All with consummate Malice, furious Rage,
Against th' adventurous Voyagers engage.
Through all the Sky they raise outrageous Storms,
And Death stands threat'ning in a thousand Forms.
Clouds charg'd with loud Destruction drown the day,
And airy Dæmons in wild Whirlwinds play.
Thick Thunderclaps, and Lightning's livid glare
Disturb the Sky, and trouble all the Air.
Outrage, Distraction, Clamour, Tumult Reign
Through the Dominions of th' unquiet Main.
The labouring Bark with Heav'nly Treasure fraught
Now almost sunk, now up in Tempests caught,
Near Sands and Rocks, rides on the dark Abyss,
Long beaten off from the bright Coasts of Bliss.
At last Calm Day succeeds this stormy Night,
And the glad Voyagers find in their sight,
The Realms of Peace, and the bleft Shores of Light.
Here they arrive, and find a safe Retreat,
And all their Pain, and Labours past forget.

There was a Cave hard by, which Nature made
In the hard Rock, and cover'd with the shade,
Of spreading Trees, that Day could not invade.
Hither the pious British Prince retires,
To offer Praises up, and pure Desires.
Here rapt'rous Converse he with Heav'n maintains,
And aided by *Devotion's* purest strains,
Combates Almighty Power, and Conquest gains.
Devotion, that oft binds th' Almighty's Arms,
And with her Prayers and Tears, her powerful charms,
Of all its Thunder, his right hand disarms.

She

She passes quick Heav'ns lofty Crystal Walls,
And the high Gates fly open, when she calls.
The lovely Goddess of Divine Address,
Has to th' Almighty's Presence free Access.
Her Pow'r can sentenc'd Criminals reprieve,
Judgment Arrest, and bid the Rebel live.
Her Voice did once the Sun's swift Chariot stay,
And on the Verge of Heav'n, held back the falling Day.
She makes contentious Winds forget their Strife,
And calls back to the Dead, departed Life,
Charm'd by her Voice, Rivers have stop'd their Course,
And the chill'd Fire laid down its burning Force.
Such is *Devotion*'s Power, which *Arthur* knew,
And when distress'd still to this Refuge flew.
Much to his Conduct he, much to his Arms,
But more he trusted to *Devotion's* Charms.
Of Triumph and Success he rarely fail'd,
For those on Earth, and these in Heav'n prevail'd.

Now in the silent, shady Cave retir'd,
He with her sacred Fury lay inspir'd.
The Prince being thus entranc'd, a Heav'nly Light
Shoots smiling through the Wood with silent flight.
The Trees admire the Glory on them shed,
And seem'd to start, and humbly bow their Head;
When fresh arriv'd on Earth, with Heav'n's Commands,
Great *Raphael's* glorious Form by *Arthur* stands.
Celestial Sweetness, Mild and Godlike Grace
Ineffable, sate on his blooming Face.
His Cheeks such Beauty shew'd, such Light and Joy his Eyes,
As from full Bliss, fresh Youth, and Strength immortal rise.
The purest piece of Heav'n's Etherial Blue,
In a rich Mantle, from his Shoulders flew.

Celestial

Celestial Linnen, finely Spun and Wove
On Looms divine, by all the Skill above,
Bleach'd on th' Empyreal Plains till white as Snow,
Made the long Robe which to his Feet did flow.
Immortal Gold, Illustrious as the Morn,
And dazling Gemms by high Arch Angels worn,
With pond'rous Pearl from Heav'n's bright Eastern Shore,
Adorn the shining Garments that he wore.
A Purple Girdle, from the Morning Sky
New rent, does round his starry Vesture tye.
Thus he appear'd, and with the Light he gave,
And unknown fragrancy, fill'd all the Cave.

 Then thus he spake, Hail mine and Heav'n's kind Care,
Hither I come, drawn by thy powerful Prayer.
Know Righteous Prince, th' Almighty does approve,
Your firm Adhesion, and unshaken Love.
Ends Great and Wise lodg'd in his secret Breast,
Obstruct your Wishes, and your Course molest.
Yet still pursue your great and just intent,
No Force or Arts shall your Design prevent,
Propitious Heav'n Decrees your wish'd Event.
You on these Coasts for happy Ends are thrown,
And after this, expect the British Crown.
Your Friends and Navy on the Ocean lost,
Are All arriv'd safe on th' *Armoric* Coast:
By the impetuous Tempest beaten back,
But Men and Ships sav'd from the threatn'd Wreck.
You're cast on *Hoel's* Lands amidst your Foes,
Who hate your Cause, and your just Arms Oppose.
But fear not *Hoel's* Power, though now your Foe,
By Hell incens'd, he will not long be so.
Go then directly to his Court, for there,
A Glorious Work demands your pious Care.

That said, with outſtrecht Wings he ſoars upright,
And through the Winds vaſt Empire takes his flight.
He cuts the Clouds, and by the Planets flies
Up the ſteep Cryſtal Mountains of the Skies.

And ſwiftly paſſing through the Starry Sphears,
Before the Throne he in his Place appears:
The Cherub's gone, and with him *Arthur*'s fears.
Who to his Lords returns, and to their Heart,
Courage and Joy, his Words and Looks impart.
His God-like Language does their Fears abate,
And with freſh hopes their troubled Breaſts dilate.

Mean time th' Infernal Thrones and Powers reſort,
At their great Monarch's Summons to his Court.
There they in Council meet, and there debate
Important matters, high Deſigns of State.
Their Prince with Pride extended, mounts his Throne,
Of poliſh'd Gold, whence horrid ſplendor ſhone:
And mingled with the Shades tremendous Light,
More dreadfull thus, as Fires which flame by Night.
In ſad Magnificence, and diſmal State,
He ſits, and round th' Infernal Orders ſate.

Then *Lucifer* began:
Immortal Potentates, Illuſtrious Lords,
The *Britiſh* Youth's ambitious Aim affords,
A weighty Subject for your high debate;
Who ſeeks the Ruin of your Pow'r and State.
You all have heard how with a mighty Force
Embark'd, he ſtraight for *Albion* ſteer'd his Courſe,
King *Octa* to attack, our Votary,
And make our Prieſts from our new Altars fly.
I watch'd, and aided by the Power of *Thor*,
I ſhew'd the Miſcreant another Shore.

His Fleet beat back, and haughty purpose crost,
He wanders, Shipwreckt on th' *Armorick* Coast,
Where faithful *Hoel* does the Scepter hold,
Mighty in Arms, and in our Service bold.
Spirits *Divine*, high Peers of Hell suggest;
By what sure Plagues he may be more distrest,
His Ruin finish'd, and his Sect opprest.

That said, a *Fury* crawl'd from out her Cell,
The bloodiest Minister of Death and Hell.
A monstrous Shape, a foul and hideous sight,
Which did all Hell with her dire Looks affright.
Huge, full gorg'd Snakes on her lean Shoulders hung,
And Death's dark Courts with their loud hissing rung.
Her Teeth and Claws were Iron and her Breath,
Like Subterranean Damps, gave present Death.
Flames worse than Hells, shot from her bloody Eyes.
And Fire and Sword Eternally she cries.
No certain Shape, no Feature regular,
No Limbs distinct in th' odious Fiend appear.
Her squallid, bloated Belly did arise,
Swoln with black Gore to a prodigious Size:
Distended vastly, by a mighty Flood
Of slaughter'd Saints, and constant *Martyr*'s Blood.
Part stood out prominent, but part fell down,
And in a swagging heap, lay wallowing on the Ground.
A Monster so deform'd, so fierce as this,
It Self a Hell, ne'er saw the dark Abyss.
Horrour till now the ugliest Shape esteem'd,
So much out-done, a harmless Figure seem'd.
Envy and *Hate*, and *Malice* blush'd too see,
Themselves Eclips'd by such Deformity.
Her Feav'rish Thirst drinks down a Sea of Blood,
Not of the impious, but the *Just* and *Good*.

'Ginst

'Gainſt whom ſhe burns with unextinguiſh'd Rage,
Nor can th' exhauſted World her Wrath aſſwage.

Then thus the Fury *Perſecution* ſpake:
I mighty Prince of Hell, will undertake
This glorious Work, I quickly will inſpire
Hoel, with my ungovernable Fire.
Without remorſe he ſhall my Will Obey,
And cruſh this *Briton*, now his eaſy Prey.
Nero by me rais'd his illuſtrious Name,
And *Dioclesian* got Immortal Fame.
I their rude, inbred Cruelty refin'd,
And ſtampt my perfect Image on their Mind.
My flames all Love's courſe mixture did deſtroy,
And purg'd off ſoft Compaſſion's baſe alloy;
I form'd and diſſiplin'd their untaught Hate,
And rais'd their fierceneſs to a perfect State:
Where ſhame, and all reflecting Senſe is loſt,
And Hell can't purer ſtrains of Malice boaſt.
Inexorable they all Cries withſtood,
Raviſh'd with Slaughter, and regal'd with Blood.
Hard marble Rocks might with more eaſe relent,
And Fire and Plague learn ſooner to repent.
Then *Chriſtian Kings* my Fury entertain'd,
And taught by me, in Blood and Slaughter reign'd.
With pious Rage and fierce deſtructive Zeal,
I firſt inſpir'd their Minds, and did reveal
The myſtery, how deep Revenge to take,
And ſlay the Servants for the Maſters ſake.
How bloody Wrath might with Devotion joyn,
And ſacred Zeal with Cruelty combine.
By me the unknown way they underſtood,
T' attone the *Chriſtian's God* with *Chriſtian Blood*.

By me they shook off Fear's and Love's Restraints;
And on God's Altars burnt his slaughter'd Saints.
I made them call, that all Remorse might cease,
Murder Compassion, Desolation Peace.
Whilst my infernal Heats their Breasts inspir'd,
To the vile Sect their own mad Zeal acquir'd,
Wider Destruction, and more fatal Harms,
Then all your *Scythian*, or your *Gothick* Arms:
And *Rome*, proud *Rome* her self must owe to me
Her present State, and future Dignity.
The greatest *Genius* this, I e'er could find,
And to receive my Image best inclin'd.
I will her Mind inspire, and to her Heart
Immortal hate, to *Abel's* Race impart.
These Breasts she empties with her Infant Jaws,
I file her Teeth, and shape her tender Claws.
I Nurse her on the horrid *Alps* high Tops,
And feed her hunger with *Cerberean* Sops
Dipt in *Tartarean* Gall, and Hemlock Juice,
That in her Veins will noble Blood produce.
Fierce Tygers, Dragons, Wolves about her stay,
They grin, and snap, and bite, and snarling play.
I to her Jaws, throw Infants newly Born;
She sucks their Blood, and by her Teeth are torn
Their tender Limbs, while I rejoyce to see
Such noble Proofs of growing Cruelty.
To her wide Breast, and vast capacious Soul,
I often Torrents of black Poison rowl:
She drinks the livid Flood, and thro her Veins
Mad Fury runs, and wild Distraction reigns.
I'll lead her from the Rocks, her Strength full grown,
Fix her high Seat in the imperial Town,
And give her Scarlet, and a threefold Crown.

No Blood will then her mighty Thirst asswage,
No Ravage cloy her *Antichristian* Rage.
Her mitred Sons that never can relent,
From the great *Cain* shall prove their high Descent.
Their Deeds of strange infernal Cruelty,
Shall shew their Race worthy of Him and me.
Lay-Bigots, I with Time and Labour wrought,
Some inward Grudgings still against me fought:
'Twas hard to raise their hate to a degree,
From struggling Nature, and all Pity free.
But these Church-Zealots, of a truer Breed,
Are form'd with Ease, and scarce my Labour need.
Their forward Genius without teaching grows,
And all my hopes, and ev'n my Wish out-does.
How often shall thy Glorious Sons, O *Rome*,
With *Martyrs* Flames inlighten *Christendom* ?
How often shall they, to deride their God,
Lift up in Prayer, their Hands all full of Blood ?
The wasted World shall feel their loud Alarms,
Their blest Massacres, and their hallowed Arms.
As if their high intent were to Efface,
All Foot-steps left of *Abel*'s hateful Race.
Bloody Tribunals, Rapine, Fire and Sword,
And Desolation, daily Sport afford.
Mankind they shall with such dire Plagues attack,
As will their Church a holy Desart make.
Such is my Zeal to serve th' Infernal State,
And shall this *British* Prince escape my Hate ?
Forbid it *Hell*, and here she made a pause ;
The Lords in Council gave a loud Applause.
The Prince of Darkness leaping from his Place,
Did in his Arms, his darling Fiend embrace :
Her Anger then rose higher, and all Hell
Uneasie seem'd, she grew so terrible.

She

She strait contracts her vast dilated Size,
And thro' Hell's dusky Void, she upward flies.
As when rich Towns, great Cost and Art employ
In Fire-works, to express their publick Joy,
For some great Vict'ry won by Land or Sea,
Or on some Prince's Coronation Day.
The flaming *Rockets* hizzing fly by Night,
And fill the Sky with unknown Noise and Light.
The *Sphears* amaz'd stand, or move slowly on,
And wonder how the day returns so soon,
And what new Stars rise brighter than their own.
So does the *Fiend*, her Snakes all hissing rise,
Through the thick haggair'd Air, and as she flies,
Leaves tracks of Light, cast from her fiery Eyes.
And now arriv'd on the grey Coasts of Day,
Direct to *Hoel's* Court she takes her way:
Where she alighted when the *Sun* had hurl'd
His glorious *Orb* hence, to th' other World.
'Twas then when all thing's look'd, as if old *Night*
Had *Nature* crush'd, and seiz'd her ancient Right.
Whilst Silence, Shades, and Lights around create,
Sad solemn Pomps t' express her Death-like state.
Winds, and wild *Beasts,* lye in their Dens at rest,
Nor these the Woods, nor those the Seas molest.
The sleeping *Vultures* drop their Prey, the *Dove*
Ceases her Cooing, and forgets to love.
The Jocond *Fairies* dance their silent round,
And with dark Circles mark the trampled ground.
Tartarean Forms Skim o'er the Mountains Heads,
Or lightly sweep along the dewy Meads.
Ghosts leave their Tombs hid Murders to reveal,
Or Treasures which themselves did once conceal.

Visions thro' th' Air, and careless *Phantoms* stray,
Or round Mens troubled Heads while sleeping play.

The Fury *Alman*'s Reverend Shape assumes,
Odin's High Priest, and so to *Hoel* comes.
For the Priests Form is fittest to engage
Princes in Blood, and move destructive Rage.
Thus chang'd the *Fiend*, such is her Craft, appears,
And thus began, just *Hoel*, all those years
I liv'd, I did with studious Care employ,
How best I might the *Christian* Crew destroy.
I thy great Soul in this blest Cause engag'd,
Inspir'd with Heats Divine, not yet asswag'd.
I quit *Elysian* Pleasures to impart,
What does with greater Joy extend my Heart;
And will do thine, *Arthur*, curst be that Name,
Designing Empire, and Illustrious Fame
Embark'd with Arms, fair *Albion* to invade
But by just Heav'n, is thy cheap Captive made.
Pursu'd in Thunder, and in Tempests tost,
At last he's Shipwreckt on this happy Coast.
With his sad *Friends* he wanders up and down,
Naked, perplext, deserted, and undone.
But yet just Heav'n decrees him greater Harm,
But saves that Glory for your Zealous Arm.
To take his Life must be your pious Care,
And with the Gods divided Honour share.
Thus you their En'my, and your own remove,
Secure your Peace, and please the Pow'rs above.
To *Christians* this can be no Injury,
That call for *Torments*, and are pleas'd to *Dye*.
They all seem fond, to wear the *Martyr's* Crown,
And meet the Flames, with greater of their own.

No *Rights*, no Rules of *Juſtice* you invade,
For *Ruin*'s their Profeſſion, *Death* their Trade.
Go then, and grace the *Briton*, that comes on
To meet you, and receive the *Martyrs* Crown.
Remove this Pillar of the Church, and all
The unſupported Roof, will crack and fall.
Take this *Defender* of their Faith away,
The paſſive Rabble, tamely will Obey.
Their Lives in Sport you may at leiſure take,
They quickly fall, that no Reſiſtance make.
The Gods into your Hands have caſt your Foe,
To take his Life will pleaſe Heav'n, him, and you,

That ſaid, ſhe breath'd her Soul into his Breaſt,
And her wild Fury all his Veins poſſeſt.
Infernal Flames Rage in his poiſon'd Blood,
And his ſwoln Heart Boils with th' impetuous Flood.
The *Fiend* her Shape of thickned Air diſſolves,
And diſappears, *Hoel* ſurpriz'd revolves
The welcome meſſage in his Mind, and ſtrait
Commands his Lords and Guards ſhould on him wait,
On the firſt Shooting of the tender Day,
So eager did he ſeem to ſeize the Prey.

Now was the Eaſtern Sky-dy'd Purple ſpread,
For fair *Aurora*'s radiant Feet to tread;
She mounts ſerene, and with mild dawning Light,
Smiles on the lowring, duſky Face of Night;
That to victorious Day yields up her Seat,
Whilſt her black Forces ſilently Retreat.
As when a *Lyon* at the Fall of Day,
Rouz'd with fierce Hunger up to Hunt his Prey,
Stretches his Limbs out, Yawns, and tries his Paws,
And for ſure Death prepares his cruel Jaws.

He stands, and rolls about his angry Eyes,
Lashing his Sides to make his Fury rise.
Then scowrs the Hills, ranges the Forrests o'er,
And thunders thro the Desart with his hideous Roar.
The *Winds* all husht sit trembling on the Trees,
And scacely whisper out a gentle Breeze.
Wolves dare not Howl, but grinning softly creep,
And *Leopards* stretcht out, feign themselves asleep.
Th' affrighted *Herds* close in their Covert ly,
And to escape his Rage, with Terrour dy.
Thus *Hoel*, with infernal Rage possest,
With fierce desire speeds to the bloody Feast.
A deadly Storm does on his Forehead lowr,
Himself his Rage, *Arthur* his Hopes devour.
Breathing out *Death* he march'd, but at mid-day,
He stands by Heav'n arrested in his way.

The Air serene, a black thick Cloud appear'd,
And as it hover'd o'er their Heads, were heard
Celestial *Flutes*, and *Harps* divinely Strung,
With *Hymns* and *Hallelujahs*, Set and Sung
By the best Masters of the Quire above,
With Bliss transported, and inspir'd with Love.
Whilst *Hoel* and his Friends pleas'd, and amaz'd,
Listen'd, and on the Scene descending gaz'd:
The broken Cloud, pours out pure Floods of Light,
Show'rs of Celestial Rays transcendent bright,
And Storms of Splendor, dazling Mortal Sight.
Th' illustrious *Tempest* does on *Hoel* beat,
Who falls astonish'd, headlong from his Seat:
Confounded with unsufferable Day,
Groveling in *Glory* on the shining Way,
And with bright Ruin overwhelm'd, he lay.

E

'Twas then, a soft, still Heav'nly *Voice*, that broke
From out the Cloud, to trembling *Hoel* spoke.
'Gainst me, what Fury did thy Arms engage ?
What mov'd thee with inexorable Rage,
Vain Man, to persecute my Saints and Me ?
In vain thou seek'st to baffle Heav'n's Decree.
Vain is thy Force, and impotent thy Hate,
Too weak thy Arms, to stem the Tyde of Fate.
The Torrent bears thy faint Resistance down,
Retire, or in Eternal Ruin Drown.

Then *Hoel* thus, O tell me, who thou art,
Great *Spirit*, and thy Will to me impart.
Tell me if Error has my Feet misled,
What safer Paths I may hereafter tread.

The Voice reply'd :
I am the *Christians God*, whom you pursue;
Go meet my Servant *Arthur*, he shall shew
At large, what thou hast to *believe*, what *do*.
The Scene here disappear'd, his Lords came round,
And rais'd reviving *Hoel* from the Ground.
Who marches on, the *British* Prince to find,
And Act not what himself, but Heav'n design'd.
With anxious Thoughts the Vision he revolves,
And to Obey Heav'n's high Command resolves.
Whilst to his Lords the Vision he relates,
They find themselves advanc'd to *Conda*'s Gates.

Arthur mean time, to whom great *Raphael*'s word,
Unshaken Hopes, and Courage did afford ;
Proceeded on his Way, but sent before
Embassadors to *Hoel*, to explore

His

His temper, and the Genius of his Court,
That he juſt ſteps might take by their Report.
He choſe out to diſcharge this weighty Truſt,
Valiant *Pollandor*, *Roderick* the Juſt ;
And Faithful *Galbut*, Friends that in diſtreſs,
(A thing unknown to Courts) their Love expreſs.
Soon after *Hoel* had his Entrance made,
At the ſame City they arriv'd, and ſtaid
But little, for th' admiſſion which they pray'd.
Then *Hoel* firſt the *Britons* thus addreſt,
Let no ſad Thought your pious Prince moleſt :
A Meſſage ſent from Heav'n preventing yours,
To me great Joy, Safety to him procures.
Friendſhip and Love, fill my enlighten'd Mind,
From Hatred purg'd, from Treachery refin'd.
Return, and let your Valiant Leader know,
His *God* has to a *Friend*, transform'd his *Foe*.
Tell him he's ſafe from all intended Harms,
And that I haſt, t' Embrace him in my Arms.

With Regal Bounty, he to all preſents
Rich Swords, and various ſplendid Ornaments.
To *Arthur* ſends a *Chariot*, dazling Bright,
Which to the Sun return'd redoubled Light.
And *Horſes* of th' *Iberian* Noble Race,
That right Deſcent from the ſwift *Burus* trace.
Bold, Gen'rous, Sprightly, as th' Illuſtrious Breed,
Which in th' Etherial, blue Encloſures Feed.
That thro' Heav'n's Waſt, with the *Sun's* Chariot play,
And govern *Time*, by carrying round the Day.
Their Furniture of Gold, their Bridles Gold,
And golden Bits, their champing Mouths did hold.
They haſt, and all their Diligence employ,
To fill Juſt *Arthur*'s Mind, with Peace and Joy.

To him returning they impart at large,
The kind, endearing Things they had in Charge.
As when his Sons to *Jacob* did relate,
That *Joseph* liv'd, and liv'd in Regal State;
Telling of all his Riches, Power, Renown,
Egypt's Support, and Prop to *Pharoah*'s Crown.
Refiftlefs Floods of fudden Pleafure Roll
Along his Veins, and break in on his Soul.
He finks beneath the preffure of his Joy,
And *Joseph*'s Life, does almoft his deftroy.
Then Doubts and Fears, his Joys high Tyde oppofe,
From which Contention fiercer Tempefts rofe.
While his crofs Paffions fought with equal Power,
Each Triumphs in his turn, as Conquerour.
The *Patriarch* in this Diftraction loft,
Is in each Storm with equal Danger toft.
But when the Chariots and rich Train he faw,
He did from thence frefh Life and Vigour draw.
His Breaft from all contending Paffions freed,
Calm Joy, and unmolefted Peace fucceed.
Enough the *Patriarch* was heard to Cry,
I'll haft to *Joseph*'s Arms, and in them Dye.
So when Juft *Arthur* heard the Meffage firft,
His wavering Mind with Fears and wife Diftruft,
And rifing Tydes of fuddain Joy was toft,
Uncertain which ftrong Paffion prefs'd him moft.
But when he faw the Prefents *Hoel* fent,
His Doubts fupprefs'd, he grew more Confident:
And his calm Mind eas'd of his anxious Cares,
T' embrace his new, and generous Friend prepares.

And now advancing *Night* the Sky invades,
While clofe purfu'd by the Victorious Shades,

The Rayes that faintly from the Ground recoil,
On the green Fields, let fall their pearly spoil.
When *Arthur* to his secret Joys retires,
Where his exhaling Soul to Heav'n aspires,
In sacred *Anhelations*, and inflam'd *Desires*.
Fixt *Contemplation* feeds his Hope and Love,
With rapt'rous Preludes to the Joys above.
His ravish'd Eyes view the unmeasur'd Bliss,
In the next Life enjoy'd, believ'd in this.
So *David* often pass'd the silent Night,
And in his Transports felt sublime Delight.
Surpassing all that mighty Monarchs have,
Which his own Crown, and all his Triumphs gave.
While baser Birds the humble Valley love,
And sing contented with their little Grove;
The *Eagle*'s generous Pride does nobly rise
To Heav'n, and thence does this low World despise.
Scorning a Vulgar Bough, he thinks he sees
Woods in the Clouds, and hanging Groves of Trees.
Thither he hasts, and leaves th' ignoble Brood,
That aim no higher, to their Shrubs and Wood.
If to his Prey he stoops, ashamed he flies
Back to his airy Dwelling in the Skies.
Where in the Clouds he hides his Royal Head,
Safe from the Snares, which watchful Fowlers spread:
So Men of courser Mould, and baser Birth,
Pleas'd with the Dust lye grov'ling on the Earth.
For Food their Souls all foul and bloated, seek
The Damps and Steams, that from its Bowels reek.
While Men *divinely* Born, still upwards move,
And scorn this *World*, that courts in vain their Love.
In Flames of Zeal, and Pangs of pure Desire,
These to the Seats of *Light* and *Peace* aspire.

Where

Where they converſe with the bleſt *Minds* above,
And wonder what on Earth invites Mens Love.
This Molehill Earth has loſt its former Charms,
Molehill for Bulk, and Stings wherewith it ſwarms.
With Wonder they obſerve how Mortals Pride,
Can into Kingdoms this ſmall Heap divide.
How one t' enlarge the Empire he has got,
Invades the Borders of his Neighbour's Spot.
How this proud Monarch of a Turf, is vext
With reſtleſs cares, to diſpoſſeſs the next.
As Heav'ns vaſt *Globes* that fill the World with Light,
Seem little *Balls* to diſtant Mortals ſight,
That in the moſt capacious *Planets*, we
No room for States and large Dominions ſee.
So theſe more noble Minds advanc'd ſo high,
Believe the ſame of us, who from the Sky,
The low-hung *Earth*'s contracted Body Spy.
They keep above free from the fatal Nets,
Which for unwary Feet the Tempter ſets.
Free from the Earth's dark ſmoke, and endleſs Noiſe,
They dwell in Peace, and feed on Heav'nly Joys.
Such Pleaſures *Arthur* while retir'd, enjoy'd,
And wiſh'd he ever might be thus imploy'd.

And now the radiant Gates of th' Eaſtern Sky,
Unbar'd by bright *Aurora*, open fly;
Strait iſſues out the *Sun* with mighty Force,
As Giants do, prepar'd to run his Courſe.
The joyful *Britons* all things ready make,
And their new Friend to meet, their Journy take.
Scarce had the Sun his glitt'ring Chariot driv'n,
Up the ſteep Brow, and ſharp Aſcent of Heav'n,
When the glad Princes did each other meet,
And *Hoel* thus did firſt the Stranger greet.

As a faint Traveller in *Arabian* Sands,
Scorcht with the Burning Sun-beams, panting ſtands,
Views the dry Deſart with deſpairing Eyes,
And for the Springs, and diſtant Rivers ſighs.
As *Sailers* long for Land, Heav'n's Aid implore,
And with their greedy Wiſhes graſp the Shore;
When beaten from the hoſpitable Coaſt,
And in loud Storms upon the Ocean toſt;
Where Ruin in ſo many Shapes appears,
They ſcarcely can attend to all their Fears.
I've wiſh'd to ſee you with the like Deſire,
The *Oracle* of whom I muſt enquire,
The way to *Peace* and Everlaſting *Bliſs*,
Which loſt in Night, and unknown Paths, I miſs.
When firſt I ſet out with a hoſtile Mind,
And Evils which I dread to name, deſign'd;
The Powers that guard your ſacred Life alarm'd,
Soon interpos'd, and my wild Hand diſarm'd.
Kind Heav'n that both our Safeties did deſign,
Turn'd from your Head the Blow, the Guilt from mine.
For on the way a Glory dreadful Bright,
Around me ſhone, and with exceſſive Light,
As they do Stars, the weaker Sun-beams drown'd:
I, as tranſfixt, fell Headlong to the Ground.
'Twas then a wondrous Heav'nly *Voice* I heard,
The words were theſe, but no bleſt Face appear'd.
'Gainſt me what Fury does thy Arms engage?
What moves thee with inexorable Rage,
Vain Man, to perſecute my Saints and me?
In vain thou ſtriv'ſt to baffle Heav'n's Decree.
Vain is thy Force, and Impotent thy Hate,
Too weak thy Arms to ſtem the Tide of Fate.

The

The Torrent bears thy faint Refiftance down,
Retire, or in eternal Ruin drown.
I ftraight cry'd out, O tell me who thou art,
Great *Spirit*, and thy Will to me impart.
Tell me if Error has my Feet mifled,
What fafer Paths I may hereafter tread.
   The *Voice* reply'd:
I am the *Chriftian's God*, whom you purfue,
Go find my Servant *Arthur*, he fhall fhew
At large, what thou haft to believe, what do.

   Prince *Arthur* paus'd a while, then filence broke,
And friendly thus th' *Armoric* King befpoke.
Th' Eternal's Providence I muft adore,
That has compell'd me to th' *Armoric* Shore.
That I might here, ferve fuch a glorious End,
And to the Chriftian Caufe gain fuch a Friend.
Goodnefs Divine, King *Hoel* does invite
By Miracles, t' enjoy Celeftial Light.
Caft on your Coafts, with Pleafure I will ftay,
To aid and guide you in your Heav'nly way.
To whom th' *Armoric* Monarch thus Reply'd;
While we to *Nannetum* together ride,
Inftruct, O Pious Prince, my willing Mind:
It is a task your God has you defign'd.
Unfold his Heav'nly Will, and let me know,
What *Worſhip* to him, what *Belief*, I owe.
To whom the Prince, this favour firft I ask,
Before I undertake the pious Task:
That you'll difpatch your Servants to the Coaft,
To feek my Friends out, in the Tempeft loft.
And if by chance caft on th' *Armoric* Shore,
They wander up and down, diftrefs'd and poor,

Your angry Subjects, may not them annoy,
Nor with devouring Flames, their Ships deſtroy.
This Friendſhip ſhewn, I'll with a chearful Mind,
Attempt the Task by you, and Heav'n enjoyn'd.
When the paſt Night did with her dusky Train
Advance, o'er-ſhadowing all th' *Aerial* Plain;
A ſudden Tranſport did my Soul engage,
And all my Limbs ſhook with the ſacred Rage.
Straight caught up from the Body, through the Skies
To the third Heav'n, my raviſh'd Soul did riſe:
Where Things ineffable I ſaw, and heard
Divine *Inſtruction*, which my Mind prepar'd
To aid you in your Heav'nly Way, and ſhew
What *Worſhip* to th' *Eternal Mind* is due.
Straight *Hoel* to the Shores his Servants ſent,
Who might the Harms, that *Arthur* fear'd, prevent.
Who might the hapleſs *Britons* kindly treat,
And ſafe conduct them to his Royal Seat.
Such Love the King to *Arthur*'s Friends expreſt,
Who now prepar'd t' obey the King's Requeſt.

Prince Arthur.

BOOK II.

Attentive *Hoel's* Eyes on *Arthur's* Face
Were fixt, who thus began with God-like grace.
Before th' unshaken Pillars of the Earth
Were Reer'd, before prolifick *Nature's* Birth,
Before the Register of *Time* begun,
Or Heav'n's bright Forces throng'd about the Sun,
Was a wild *Void*, that no set Bounds restrain'd,
Where Silence, Night, and Desolation reign'd.
Where yet no glimmering track of Light appear'd,
No Discord yet, or Harmony was heard.
From Ages past lay in th' *Eternal's* Mind,
A finish'd Model of a *World*, design'd
To be Erected by Almighty Hands,
Where now this Round, Capacious Fabrick stands.
The deep Foundations laid, in Heav'n they said
A strange new *World* was making, Fame soon spread
The tydings through the Palaces of Bliss,
To see a work so wonderful as this;
Millions of *Angels* to Heav'n's Turrets fly,
And on the Crystal Terras of the Sky,
Stood in bright Throngs, and on *Creation* gaz'd,
And at the Sight were ravish'd, and amaz'd.

Almighty Vigour strove through all the Void,
And such prolifick Influence employ'd,

That ancient, barren *Night* did pregnant grow,
And quicken'd with the *World* in Embrio.
The struggling Seeds of unshap'd Matter ly,
Contending in her Womb for Victory.
No Order, Form, or Parts distinct and clear,
Did in the Crude Conception, yet appear.
Thick *Darkness* did the unripe *Light* Embrace,
Which faintly glanc'd on *Chaos* shady Face.
The unfledg'd *Fire* has no bright Wings to rise,
But scarce distinguish'd, with the *Water* lies.
It's sprightly, ruddy Youth not yet attain'd,
The glitt'ring Seeds, Mother of *Fire*, remain'd
Like golden Sands, thick scatter'd on the Shore,
Of the wild Deep, and shone in burning Oar.
In glowing Heaps the *Stars* lay dusky bright,
Rude and unpolish'd Balls of unwrought Light.
The *Sphears* pil'd up about their *Poles* were Furl'd,
Design'd the Swadling Bands of th' Infant World.
The Sky dispers'd, lay in Etherial Oar,
And azure Veins, betray'd th' Empyreal Store.
The watry Treasures in th' unfashion'd Birth,
Lay in the rough Embraces of the Earth.
But at the great Command will Thaw, and throw
The Dross off, and like melted Metals flow.
Besides vast numbers of loose Atoms stray,
And in the restless Deep of *Chaos* play.
In dark Encounters they for Empire strive,
And gain what *Chance*, and wild *Confusion* give.
Which joyntly here possess the Sov'raign Sway,
Pleas'd with those Subjects most, that least Obey.
Order, a banish'd Rebel, flies the Place,
And Strife and Uproar fill the noisy Space.
Tumult and Mis-rule please at *Chaos* Court,
And everlasting Wars his Throne Support.

Troops arm'd with *Heat* have here a Battel won,
But *Moist* and *Cold* the Victor soon dethrone.
Here heavier Seeds rush on in numerous Swarms,
And crush their Lighter Foes, with pond'rous Arms.
The lighter strait Command with equal Pride,
And on wild Whirlwinds in mad Triumph ride.
None long submits to a Superiour Power,
Each yields, and in his turn is Conquerour.
If some grown mild from fierce Contention cease,
And with calm Neighbours court a seperate Peace;
If Truce they make, and in kind Leagues combine,
Their short Embraces some rude Shocks disjoyn.
Th' *Eternal*'s Voice compos'd these *Atoms* jars,
And justling Elements intestine Wars.
He sets imprison'd *Heat* and *Vigour* free,
And suits and ranges Natures that agree.
He through the *Mass* a mighty Ferment spread,
And where it came mis-shap'd Confusion fled.
Dark *Chaos* now throws off his gloomy Face,
Puts on fresh Beauty, and a Heav'nly Grace.
Th' *Almighty spake*, and strait the sprightly *Light*
With lovely Looks broke from th' Abyss of Night;
On Golden Wings it mounts, and in its way
Its Smiles diffuse new Morn, and unripe Day.
Aloft vast spreading Sheets of *Ether* rise,
Matter for *Sphears*, and pure transparent Skies.
The *Sky* which for its Compass scarce finds room,
Spun thin, and wove on Nature's finest Loom:
The new-born World in its soft Bosom wraps,
And all around its Starry Mantle laps.
The *Sun*'s vast *Globe* which till the Birth of Day,
All Rough and Cloudy in wild *Chaos* lay;
Well wrought and polish'd, is advanc'd on high;
The vagrant Beams which stray'd about the Sky,

Now

Now becken'd by *Creating* Power obey,
And the bright Forces hither haſt away.
Then hov'ring on the Spungy Globe they wait,
And round their new appointed Manſion ſate.
The thirſty *Orb* drinks in the liquid Beams,
And now but one vaſt Sea of Glory ſeems:
It ſelf a Heav'n with dazling Luſtre bright,
Pours out pure Floods of overflowing Light.
Here as in Furnaces of boiling Gold,
Stars dipt come back, full as their *Orbs* can hold
Of glitt'ring *Light*, here too the *Moon* all drown'd,
Does with the Golden Metal fill her Round.
Sometimes half dipt, it but in part adorns
Her Face, and ſhines with Blunt, refulgent Horns.
Th' Etherial Plain now cultivated bears,
A ſhining Harveſt of Illuſtrious *Stars*.
Which at a diſtance ſeem ſmall Lights, but near
Capacious *Realms*, and glorious *Worlds* appear.
The *Sphear*s ſpread forth their Boſoms, now refin'd,
And Belly out, like Sails ſwoln big with Wind.
The *Air* beat out, and purified does lye,
A Cryſtal deep between the Earth and Sky.
Through this thin Void the Sun's indulgent Beams,
Flow gently on the Earth in Golden Streams;
Which kindly ſteal away the Watry Store,
And rob the Earth, but to enrich it more.
The *Earth* with its own Burden tir'd, and preſt
Down with its weight, lies in the midſt at reſt.
A *Deep* broke up, *God* calls the Waters, they
Feel the Command, and with quick Flight Obey.
In mighty Heaps the foaming Deluge flows,
High Liquid Walls and curling Ridges ſhows.
Some waters with a ſmooth and gentle Tyde,
On the Earth's plain and level Surface Glide.

Others

Others that meet a Steep abrupt Descent;
Run down in Floods more loud and turbulent.
At last they flow from the high Precipice,
In noisy Falls into the dark Abyss.
Till the vast Deluge with its liquid Store,
Fills up the Deep, and crowns the Ambient Shore.
Now their tall Heads the rising *Mountains* show,
And wide mouth'd *Vallies* sink themselves as low.
The Earth as yet all bare and naked lay,
For Heav'n's Command th' imprison'd Spirits stay.
God spake, and straight a lovely *Spring* appears,
And every Field fresh, verdant Cloathing wears.
Green *Herbs* adorn the Hills aspiring Heads,
And smiling *Flowers* enrich th' enamell'd Meads.
Trees starting up, lifted their Heads so high,
They met the Clouds descending from the Sky.
Some rang'd in beauteous Order, Stately stood,
Others press'd close, and throng'd into a Wood.
Some where the Sun gives more indulgent Heat,
Transparent Gums, and Od'rous Juices Sweet.
The fragrant *Balsom-Tree*, distills around,
Her healing Riches, on the neighbouring Ground.
The humble *Jess'mine*, breaths Perfumes abroad,
And wanton *Zephyrs* bear the balmy Load.
Pure Crystal *Rivers* through the Meadows flow,
Their flowry Banks smile on them, as they go:
Their watry Train in Snaky Windings slides,
And in their Streams the *scaly* Nation glides.
Birds glad to try their Wings rise from the Earth,
And with their Songs they celebrate their Birth.
Beasts in their various Kinds all Mild, and Tame,
Stood gazing round, and wonder'd whence they came.
The Bleating *Flocks* wander on every Hill,
And lowing *Herds* the Ecchoing Vallies fill.

The

The sporting *Lyon* paws the wanton *Bear*,
Wolves seek the Woods, the Lawns the timorous *Deer*.
The Crested *Snake* draws thro' the flowry Plain,
The shining Volumes of his Spiral Train.
Leviathan in th' Ocean takes his place,
Prince of the Waters, and the Finny Race.
Rolling amidst the Waves, he takes his Sport,
As a great Sea-God in his watry Court.
Swimming to Land he drives high Seas before,
Like a great Island floating near the Shore.
In wanton Pastime he sucks in with Ease,
Then spouts against the Skies th' exhausted Seas:
Like some prodigious Water-Engine, made
To play on Heav'n, if Fires should Heav'n invade.
So fair, so rich a Paradise as this,
Almighty Power call'd from the dark Abyss:

 To keep the Birth-Day of the World, the *Spring*
Does all her Joys and fragrant Riches bring.
Nature appearing in her brightest Dress,
Does all her Sweets and Heav'nly Charms express.
The *Sphears* in tuneful Measures Roll above,
And Heav'n's bright *Orbs* in beauteous Order move.
The smiling *Earth* discovers perfect Joy,
Where nothing noxious can its Peace annoy.
The *Air's* so soft, such balmy Odours fly,
So sweet the *Fruits*, so pure and mild the *Sky*,
The Blissful States, too great to be exprest,
By all the Pleasures of the wanton East,
By th' *Arab's* Sweets, from *Zephirs* tender Wings
Gently shook off, or what the Merchant brings
Of Forreign Luxury with tedious Toil,
From *Asia's* Coast, or soft *Campania's* Soil.

Thus

Thus after five days Labour *Nature* stood,
God view'd his Creatures, and pronounc'd them *Good*.
But still there wanted one who might adore
Divine Perfections, and Heav'n's Gifts implore.
Who might *himself*, and his great *Author* know,
Obey his *God*, and Rule as God below.
Then *Man* was made, the Author fram'd and wrought
The nobler Mould, with more Concern and Thought.
His *Mind* made up of pure Etherial Air,
Came from the Hands Divine all Bright and Fair.
And lodg'd in Clay, did at its Entrance give
So quick a touch, as made that Clay to live:
And both united with such wondrous Art,
In part he's *Angel*, *Animal* in part.
In whom the Bounds of both the Worlds are seen,
Where *Earth* does terminate, and *Heav'n* begin.
One part, like sprightly Flames, will upward move,
Kin to the blest, unbody'd *Minds* above;
The other, only shap'd and quicken'd Earth,
From moulded Dust receives its humble Birth;
Yet *Life* Divine, and high Perfection gains,
Ennobled by the Guest it entertains.
His *Form* erect, and Cherub-like his Face,
Where Sweetness temper'd Stern and Manly Grace.
Mild to be lov'd, and awful to be fear'd,
He, like some new discover'd God, appear'd.
Then did *th' Almighty* to his Bosom give,
To bless him perfectly, his Consort *Eve*.
Of a more soft and nicely temper'd Mould,
Her strokes were tender, his more strong and bold.
Sweetness that ravish'd, milder than the Morn,
And perfect Beauty did her Looks adorn.
She like a *Goddess*, with the Heav'nly Charms
Of blushing Innocence, comes to his Arms.

What Joys Divine did on the Fav'rite wait,
These happy Hours that knew his Native State!
His *Work* thus finish'd, and *Creation* done,
Th' Almighty rests on his Eternal Throne.
Straight the loud Shouts and Acclamations giv'n,
Shook the high Towers and jarring Gates of Heav'n.
There stood an *Alabaster* Mount that shone,
In th' Air sublime, from the Imperial Throne
Remov'd at distance, and between them lay,
All pav'd with Stars, a broad, frequented way.
Hither for great Assemblies they repair,
From all the Regions of th' Etherial Air.
Here they in perfect Love and Peace debate,
Th' affairs that most affect their sacred State.
Hither the Princes of the Heav'nly Court,
Follow'd with Throngs unnumber'd, now resort.
There met, a solemn *Jubilee* they Vote,
In Honour of the Wonders lately wrought.
Straight a *Procession* publick was enjoyn'd,
And thus perform'd t' adore *th' Eternal* Mind.

Trumpets march'd first, and chiefly that whose Sound,
Shall strike Convulsions thro' the trembling ground;
Break their dark Prisons down, and call away
Th' awaken'd Dead, on the great Judgment Day.
Next Heav'nly *Viols*, soft harmonious *Flutes*,
Resounding *Dulcimers*, and tuneful *Lutes*
And *Harps*, like that which hangs the glitt'ring Pride,
As Poets feign, of young *Apollo's* side.
With perfect Skill here chosen *Cherubs* play,
And Celebrate th' *Almighty's* Resting Day.
Then the blest *Voices* came with Hymns of Praise,
Angelick Musick, sweet Melodious Lays,

Such

Book II. *Prince* Arthur. 43

Such as bright Spirits in high Raptures fing,
Around the Throne of their Eternal King.
Now the firſt Rank of Potentates and Peers,
Mighty *Arch-Angels*, and high Thrones appears.
Crowns of ſubſtantial, maſſy Glory made,
Adorn'd with *Gems*, and *Flow'rs* which never Fade,
And *Greens* of Heav'nly growth all wreath'd between,
Are on the Heads of this bright Order ſeen:
Freſh Greens and Flow'rs, ſuch as their Gardens bring,
Bleſt with mild Rays, and Everlaſting Spring.
Vials of *Incenſe* in their Hands they bear,
And the ſweet Clouds in Wheels roll up the Air:
Odours not to be told, fann'd from them fly,
And wondrous Fragrancy Perfumes the Sky.
Each had his *Lyre*, which from his Shoulders hung,
With Golden Wire, like radiant Sun-beams, ſtrung.
Such was their Splendour, with ſuch Grace they trod,
In Looks and Motion each appear'd a God.
Hither thick Crowds of vulgar *Angels* made,
And to admire this glorious Order ſtaid,
And, as they paſs'd, humble Obeiſance paid.
Then lower Ranks in long Proceſſion paſs'd,
With Crowns and Badges of Diſtinction grac'd.
And all ſo Splendid, all ſo Rich and Gay,
That Heav'n before, ne'er ſaw ſo bright a Day.
Unfading *Roſes* of a Heav'nly Red,
On the bright Pavement were profuſely ſpread.
Elyſian Jeſs'mine, and bleſt *Am'rant* lay,
In od'rous heaps along the Milky way.
The *Fountains* all, ſuch Coſt was then beſtow'd,
With unexhauſted Springs of *Nectar* flow'd.
And now advanc'd before th' Imperial *Throne*,
Which lofty with exceſſive Brightneſs ſhone,

They from th' uneasie Lustre of the Light,
Protected with spread Wings their dazled sight.
In prostrate *Adoration* down they fell,
Opprest with Glory unsupportable.
Entranc'd, Transported, Ravish'd, there they ly,
And with blest *Hallelujahs* fill the Sky.
In Songs Sublime they praise th' *Eternal Mind*,
His Works from all the Ages past design'd,
His *Greatness*, *Wisdom*, *Empire* unconfin'd.
His *Justice*, that no Force or Prayer can move:
His spotless *Truth*, and Everlasting *Love*.
They Sing th' *Eternal Son's* Immortal Praise,
And to an equal height the sacred *Spirit* raise.
Then all arising from the sacred Quire,
O'erflowing with unbounded Joys, retire
To the blest Shades of the Celestial Bowers,
Where oft they choose to pass their happy Hours.
Their Hunger here delicious *Banquets* met,
With vast Profusion on rich Tables set,
Banquets Divine, not such as Mortals Eat.
High Dishes in long Pomp and Order stood,
Fill'd with choice Fruits, rare Meats, all Angels Food.
Ambrosial Juices, sweet *Nectarean* Wine,
Ravish'd their Tast, and made their Faces Shine.
The *Sons of God* thus chear'd, dissolve in Joy,
Whilst his high Praises their blest Tongues employ.
In Joys and Triumphs so the Day they spend,
Such Mirth and Show the Festival attend.
Then, when the Ev'ning came, or what instead
Of Evening there, does in its turn succeed:
Glorious *Illuminations* made on high,
By all the *Constellations* of the Sky,
In bright Degrees, and shining Orders plac'd,
Spectators charm'd, and the blest Dwellings grac'd.

Through all th' inlight'n'd Air rare Fireworks flew,
Which the Celestial Youth with Shouting threw.
Comets fly up with their red sweeping Train,
Then fall in Starry Showers, and glitt'ring Rain.
In th' Air ten Thousand *Meteors* blazing hung,
Which from Heav'n's gilded Battlements were flung.
Here furious, flying *Dragons* hissing came,
Here harmless *Fires* play in a lambent Flame.
Such universal Joy in Heav'n they shew'd,
And in such hallow'd Mirth the day conclude.
In such Delights they pass their time above,
And so shall we, if like them, we Obey and Love.

In all the Joys that happy Minds attain,
Blest *Adam* first began to live and reign.
He to fair *Eden's* Paradise resorts,
Where every Sense its proper Pleasure courts.
The joyful Spring by soft *Favonius* fan'd,
Diffus'd her Riches with a wanton Hand.
From new-blown Flowers luxurious Odours fly,
And Heav'nly *Landschapes* meet his ravish'd Eye.
The twining Branches weave him shady Bowers,
And Hony-Dews fall in delicious Showers.
Birds with their Songs their Soveraign salute,
From Boughs that bend beneath their Golden Fruit.
Pure *Streams* to him their Crystal Waters bring,
And the glad *Fish* leap up, to see their King.
The harmless *Beasts* their humble Homage paid,
And the sole Monarch of the World obey'd.
Uninterrupted *Peace* his Mind possest,
And Joys unutterable fill'd his Breast.
He view'd his great *Creator's* glorious Face,
Clearly reflected from fair Nature's Glass:

On her bright *Form* he saw th' Impreſſions ſhine,
Of *Wiſdom* Infinite, and *Pow'r* Divine,
Whence all things, as free Emanations flow,
As Streams their Being to their Fountain owe.
Which binds faſt Nature's vaſt unſhaken Frame,
Left it diſſolve to Nothing, whence it came.
Whilſt in his Thoughts the pleaſing Objects move,
He feels his Breaſt all fir'd with Heav'nly Love.
His Eyes thus fixt, the great Seducer's Skill,
Could not engage his Thoughts, or move his Will.
A day ſerene ſmil'd on his God-like Mind,
Free from black Clouds, and undiſturb'd with Wind·
No *Guilt*, no *Frown* from Heaven diſturbs his Soul;
Calm as deep Rivers in ſtill Evenings roll.
No Storms of *Paſſion*, ſuch as us moleſt,
Annoys the Peaceful Region of his Breaſt.
No boiling *Luſt* ſwell'd the o'erflowing Blood,
To bear down Reaſon with th' impetuous Flood.
His ſpotleſs Mind knew yet no other Fire,
Then thoſe pure Flames, which Heav'nly *Minds* inſpire.
O happy Man! above deſcription bleſt,
Had he maintain'd the Station he poſſeſt.
Upon the Cryſtal *River's* flowry ſide,
Which winding did in ſlow Meanders glide
As loath to leave the bliſsful Place, there ſtood ⎫
A *Tree* that roſe above th' *Heſperian* Wood, ⎬
Its Fruit ſeem'd pleaſant, but forbidden Food. ⎭
For he who with enormous Bounty pours
On Man, freſh Pleaſures in inceſſant Showers;
That nothing can diſturb his flowing Joys,
Unleſs Variety ſuſpends his Choice:
Bids him not Eat the fatal Fruit, to prove
His due *Obedience*, and his conſtant *Love*.

The grand *Apostate* for high Crimes displac'd,
From Heav'n, by fierce *Almighty* Vengeance chas'd,
Till down th' unfathom'd Precipice he fell
Confounded to the fiery Gulph of Hell:
With Rage and Envy sees Man's happy State,
Whence he for ever lost had fall'n so late.
Himself undone urg'd with infernal Spight,
And dire Revenge, makes Ruin his delight.
That he from Heav'n might this fair Province gain,
That *Sin* and *Death* might wider Sway attain,
And he his baleful Empire might extend,
Conceal'd beneath the specious Air of *Friend*,
He does to Man the fatal Tree commend;
As such whose Worth transcends the greatest price,
The Flower and Beauty of his Paradise.
Pleasing to Tast, but much more to the Mind,
Which those that Eat, should boundless *Knowledge* find.
Then points up to the fair forbidden Meat,
Bids him be Wise, and boldly take and Eat.
He tempts him with the flatt'ring Hopes of Bliss,
Great as his God's, and lasting too, as his.
This gaudy Scene of Glory charm'd his Eye,
And his proud Thoughts at God-like Greatness fly.
The bright *Illusion* turn'd his giddy Head,
And with vast Hopes his vain Ambition fed.
Thus gazing at the Glory of a God,
The Precipice was hid, on which he trod.
The splendid *Phantome* now advances nigh,
And in his reach appears *Divinity*.
Which straight he grasps at, and to hold the more,
Empties his Hand of what it held before.
But sooner might he grasp unbody'd Minds,
And with clos'd Arms clasp in the raging Winds.

The glorious Shadow from his Hands does slide,
Mocks his Embraces, and defeats his Pride.
He Eat, but did no other Pleasures find,
Than the sad *Terrours* of a guilty Mind.
His cheated Hopes can no new *Knowledge* boast,
But of the *Ill* he feels, and *Good* he lost.

Thus fell lost Man, straight troubled *Nature* moan'd,
And shaking, with a strong Convulsion groan'd.
Ev'n *Paradise* look'd Sad, the *Herds* repin'd,
And lofty *Cedars* shook without a Wind.
The *Roses* fade, the Golden *Apples* turn'd
Pallid, and all the Sick *Creation* mourn'd.
To the thick Trees in vain fall'n *Adam* made,
To hide his blacker *Guilt* beneath their Shade.
Close Trees may so their well mixt Branches spread,
That Sun-beams cannot pierce their shady Head;
But *God's* clear Eye needs not so gross a Ray,
His Glory sheds a more Illustrious Day.
But had he been from his bright Eye conceal'd,
The crying Guilt had to his Ear reveal'd
Apostate Man, that Voice to Heav'n does rise
Loud, as the Thunder-claps, for which it cries.
What a black Train of *Woes* and hideous *Fears*,
Headed by one bold Crime, to Man appears!
The Serpent's Venom spreads through all his Veins,
And *Sin's* Contagion unresisted reigns.
A Death-like *Damp* shoots through his poison'd Blood,
And fear's cold Chains arrest the beating Flood.
A dreadful Face of Things confounds his Eye,
He cannot stay secure, nor can he fly.
Black Thoughts of *Vengeance* seize his guilty Heart,
And *Conscience* wounds him, with her poison'd Dart.

Amidst

Amidst the Trees he starts at every Noise,
Grows Pale, and thinks he hears th' *Almighty*'s Voice.
The trembling Branches make him tremble more,
Now feebler, than the Fig-leaves, which he wore.

Man's Soul, by this rude Shock from's *Center* driv'n,
Stands so a-skaunt, and so remote from Heav'n,
Tis scarcely warm'd by its weak, Oblique Ray,
And has at best but a Cold, darksome Day.
Fall'n from its bright Etherial Seat on high,
Down to the lowest Regions of the Sky,
It feels th' attractive *Earth*'s Magnetick Force,
And round this low-hung Ball directs its Course.
As when a *Planet*, once all fair and bright,
Sickens, and shines with pale and faded Light;
By some fierce *Storm* bred in its Bowels rent,
As Clouds are by the Thunder in 'em pent.
The mighty Orb disjoynted cracks, and all
The broken Parts in Noisy Ruin fall.
The hideous, burning *Hull* does floating lie,
And with the wondrous Wreck affrights the Sky.
Sometimes it blazes with a dismal Light,
And then grown dim, seems lost and drown'd in Night
Then sinking does the Starry Sky forsake,
Contented some inferiour Seat to take:
Where Heav'n new moulds the Heap, and from th' Abyss,
Calls forth perhaps a *Moon*, or *Earth*, like this.
So *Man* seduc'd by the *Impostor* fell,
From *Heav'ns* bright Coasts, to the black Verge of *Hell*.
There he his Lustre lost, and God-like Grace,
Shews the sad Ruins of a Heav'nly Face.
Where *Peace* dwelt undisturb'd, and smiling Light,
Confusion now, *Chaos* and horrid *Night*.

H   Black

Black, frowning *Clouds*, and murmuring Thunder roll,
O'er the vext Region of his guilty Soul.
Fierce, driving *Storms*, and bleak Tempeſtuous Wind
Beat on the waſteful Deſart of his Mind.
Revenge, Deſpair, Grief, Jealouſie, and *Fear,*
Have in their Turns, ſupreme Dominion here.
Reaſon dethron'd, muſt the Commands obey
Of this wild Rout, that holds the Sovereign Sway.

Mean time, th' *Almighty* does his Summons ſend,
Thro' Heav'n for all his *Angels* to attend.
High in the midſt of the Etherial Skies,
A Mount of rocky Diamond did riſe:
Inſuperably ſteep, and too ſublime
For the tir'd Wings of Cherubims to climb.
O'er-looking Heav'ns wide Vales and ſpacious Plains
It ſtands, and unmoleſted Peace maintains.
Here the *Almighty*'s bright *Tribunal* ſtands,
Whence his *Decrees* are ſent, and high *Commands.*
Hence he gives *Laws* to all the Worlds below,
And hence eternal *Right* and *Juſtice* flow.
Hence *Puniſhments* proceed, and juſt *Rewards,*
Hence *Orders* come to all th' Angelick Guards,
To keep the Peace of Heav'n, and next ſecure
On Earth th' afflicted, from th' Oppreſſor's Power.
And now the Thrones and Powers the Vally fill,
And ſtand adoring round the ſacred Hill.
Adam's Rebellion they had newly heard,
And God's fierce Wrath in dreadful Signs appear'd.
Lightnings and *Thunders* iſſue from his *Throne,*
Lightnings ſcarce heard of, Thunder ſeldom known.
Tremendous Murmurs, and a mighty Sound
Of wondrous Ruine from the Hill rebound.

T' ex-

Book II.   Prince Arthur.

T' expreſs incens'd *Omnipotence*, conſpire
Whirlwinds, thick *Darkneſs* and conſuming *Fire*,
United Terrors, which with Fury broke
From the bleſt Mount, whence thus th' *Almighty* ſpoke.

The *Man* I made, and with my *Image* grac'd,
And next to your Angelick Order plac'd,
Revolting to th' Apoſtate Prince of Hell,
Againſt my Throne has yielded to Rebel.
The *Death* I threaten'd, now I muſt inflict,
So *Juſtice* bids, nor is its Rule too ſtrict.
You're here from all the Regions of the Sky,
To hear the *Rebel* doom'd, and ſee him *Dye*.

He ſpake, and thro' all Heav'n a Terror ſtrook,
The *Spheres*, and all the Frame of Nature ſhook.
The *Moon* grew Pale, the *Sun* all Dim appear'd,
And all the *Sons of God* ſtood Mute, and fear'd.
Th' *Almighty* his Vindictive Arm makes bare,
Stretch'd out his Hand, and did for *Death* prepare.
Mercy Shreek'd out, and trembling on her Face,
Fell down, and did with Tears his Feet Embrace,
Offspring Divine, in Heav'n the moſt belev'd,
By whom ev'n Fate unchangeable is mov'd.
Her Looks ſo moving, ſuch Celeſtial Grace,
So mild, and ſweet an Air dwell on her Face,
So tender and engaging all her Charms,
That oft th' *Almighty's* Fury ſhe diſarms.
Her Language melts *Omnipotence*, Arreſts
His Hand, and thence his Vengeful Lightning wreſts.

Then thus ſhe ſpake:
Shall the ſucceſsful, ſly *Impoſtor* boaſt,
That by his Power the new *Creation's* loſt?

H 2   Shall

Shall he thus Triumph in his impious Deed,
And all our Hopes defeat from *Adam's* Seed?
Muſt this fair *Race* be loſt, ſo lately made,
And Hell made Bold your Empire to invade?
Adam has ſinn'd, and Heav'n's high Grace abus'd,
But ſinn'd betray'd, and by Hell's Fraud ſeduc'd.
Can't *Wiſdom* Infinite, Expedients find,
To puniſh *Guilt,* and yet preſerve Mankind?
Compaſſion, with ſtern *Juſtice* mixt, will draw
Honour to Heav'n's juſt Government, and Awe
All from offending the Eſtabliſh'd Law.

At this, the Eternal *Son* roſe from his Place,
The bright Effulgence of his *Father's* Face,
His fair and expreſs Image, full of Grace.
In whom Divine, Subſtantial Glory dwelt,
And who Almighty Life and Vigour felt.
Th' Eſſential *Wiſdom,* th' Everlaſting *Word,*
The Univerſal *Heir,* and Soveraign *Lord.*
And thus he Silence broke, mine be the Task
To do what Juſtice and Compaſſion ask.
To Reſcue *Man,* my Self will *Man* become,
Aſſuming Subſtance from a *Virgin's Womb.*
A willing *Sacrifice,* I'll Death Embrace,
Juſtice t' Attone, and Ranſom *Adam's* Race.

The *Father* ſtraight aſſented, *Mercy* ſmil'd,
To ſee the *Serpent* of his Prey beguil'd.
Juſtice well-pleas'd, accepts the offer'd Price,
And Heav'n's aton'd by its own *Sacrifice.*
The Heav'ns with loud rebounding Shouts did ring,
And the glad Angels in new Anthems ſing,
The *Interceſſor,* and *myſterious King.*

The

The rolling Years their Circles fill apace,
And well-breath'd Time runs its appointed Race.
Till it brought on the Hour when all should see,
The *Son* make good to Man, his blest Decree.

That our expected Hope might be enjoy'd,
Divinity appears with Man alloy'd.
His native Glory darts destructive Light,
And bright Oppression pours on Mortals Sight:
He therefore draws a humane Veil between,
That temper'd Lustre might not Kill, when seen.
Here two Extreams of Distance infinite,
In one ineffable, mysterious Knot unite.
God lives conceal'd, within a Mould of Clay,
And does in Dust himself, and's Glory lay.
He that in all th' expanded Skies wants room,
Lies now encompass'd with a Virgin's Womb.
Immensity is wrapt in Swadling Bands,
The Prince by whom the World's wide Fabrick stands,
Supported in his Mother's Arms we see;
And vast *Eternity* begins to be.
He leaves his starry Seat, and glitt'ring Crown,
And lays his dazling Robes of Glory down:
Then in an humble travelling Dress is seen,
Seeking, as unknown Strangers do, an Inn.
Lord of the World, to whom proud Monarchs owe
Their Crowns and Scepters, he that does bestow
Honours and Wealth profusely on the Great,
Can't for his own Repose, find out a Seat,
But must from Men, to kinder Beasts, Retreat.
No other Court receives the new-born King,
Who to debase himself, did choose to bring,
No other Pomp, but naked Innocence;
Nothing for Ornament, or for Defence.

He that the Wants of all the World supplies,
Himself oppress'd with Pain and Hunger, Cries.
He Man's Assistance asks in vain, to whom
For Aid and Comfort all th' aflicted come.
Angels that did the Royal *Stranger* know,
The greatest Signs of Joy and Triumph show.
The Out-guards of their Camp saw marching round,
Celestial Splendor rising from the Ground;
And gave th' Alarm, the shining Squadrons fly
To th' Out-lines, and the Frontiers of the Sky:
To see the wond'rous *Mediator* Born,
Whom they adore, though stupid *Hebrews* scorn.
Some with spread Wings shoot swiftly thro' the Air,
And to the Shepherds first the Tydings bear,
That a great *Shepherd* was at *Beth'lem* Born,
Whose Deeds and Triumphs should that Name Adorn.
Tho Angels Sing, obdurate Men are mute,
Nor will their *Saviour*, and their *King* salute.

Yet some few famous Sages come from far,
Conducted by a brighter Morning Star,
Left all the Wealth and Wonders of the East,
To see a greater *Sun* and *God* rise in the West.
To find the Prince to *Herod* they resort;
For where should Kings be found, but in a Court?
But the directing *Star* that led their Way, ⎫
Stands still, and points down with a streaming Ray, ⎬
To a mean Stable where the Stranger lay. ⎭
Where they with humble Adoration View,
The Infant *Intercessor*, known to few.
Whom they present with Odoriferous Gums,
Choice Spices, and *Arabia's* rich Perfumes.

The Sun of Righteousness begins to rise,
And Streaks with radiant Lines the Purple Skies.
Here did he from his healing Wings display,
The tender Dawn of *Everlasting* Day.
Pale Terrour thro' the Courts of Darkness flew,
And Hells sad Regions double Sorrow shew.
Th' infernal Spirits wandring in the Air,
As Thunder-struck, in Anger and Despair,
With Shreeks and hideous Yellings fly the Sight,
And the keen Horrour of the Heav'nly Light.
Like obscene Birds of Night, they haste away
And shun in Clefts and Caves the Rising Day.
The Prince of *Darkness* now begins to fear,
The Dissolution of his Empire's near.
Th' ambiguous *Oracles* with Fear struck Dumb,
Proclaim'd by Silence, the *Messiah* come.

Troubled and Sad th' Infernal Counsel sate,
Thoughtful how best t' avert th' impending Fate.
Various Projections, deep Designs were laid,
How best the dreaded Foe they might invade.
They first the Fury *Jealousie* dispatch,
To *Herod*'s Court who might Occasion watch,
To kindle strong Suspicions in his Breast,
That th' Infant from him should his Scepter wrest.
She did so well perform her Hellish Part,
Herod soon yielded to her subtil Art.
For while the Sages leave their Eastern home,
And to admire the wondrous Infant come.
Herod, afraid his ravish'd Crown to lose,
The Royal Infant's hated Life pursues.
What to pale Tyrants dreadful won't appear,
When *Love* and *Innocence* can move their Fear.

'Tis

'Tis true,
A *King*, he is, whose *Empire's* vast extent,
Shall pass all Bounds, and last when Time is spent.
Submissive Monarchs shall their Scepters lay
Before his Feet, and his Just Laws obey.
Kingdoms opprest shall his strong Aids invoke,
And thrust their Necks beneath his gentle Yoke.
The *Roman* Eagles shall the Conqueror own,
And *Cæsar* Court him to ascend his Throne.
Admir'd by all, he shall in Triumph go
Where fruitful *Nile*, or fam'd *Hydaspes* flow,
Unchekt by *Africk* Heats, or *Scythian* Snow.
Nations invited by his Fame, shall come,
More than e'er made their Court to conquering *Rome*,
In splendid Embassies to sue for Peace,
And Worlds unknown his Empire shall encrease.
The Earth shall banish'd *Justice* now regain,
And *Love* and *Truth* attend the happy Reign.
Soft *Peace* and *Joy* the chearful Earth shall Crown,
And Savage Beasts shall lay their Fierceness down.
The Lyon, Wolf, and Lamb, no more their Prey,
And little Infants shall promiscuous *play*.
The years in Golden Harness smiling pass,
And keeping beauteous Order run their Race.
Nor shall his Kingdom cease, or Subjects die,
For when Time finds its empty Channel dry,
And all its disappearing Streams shall sleep,
Lost and ingulph'd in vast Durations Deep:
Then shall this *King* his full Dominion gain,
And in Eternal Peace, and Triumph Reign.
But 'tis not Worldly Empire he design'd,
His Scepter is his *Grace*, his Throne the *Mind*.

Kings

Kings unmolested may their Scepters sway,
And Peaceful Subjects without Strife obey.
They may unrivall'd, and unenvy'd reign,
And all their Pomp, and Regal State maintain.
The great *Redeemer* has his Court unseen,
And reigns in *Light*, and Heavenly *Love* within.

But from the false *Usurper's* Cruelty,
Officious Angels, warn their Prince to fly.
He and his happy Parents leave their Home,
And all to *Egypt's* safer Borders come.
Egypt, tho' for its Monsters famous grown,
Is now by treach'rous *Palestine* out-done.
For here they find a more secure Abode,
Egypt once *Jacob* sav'd, and now his God.
The wandring God returns, the Tyrant dead,
To rich *Judæa's* Soil from whence he fled.
Where he begins his Kingdom to assert,
And his mirac'lous Virtue to exert.
The *Blind* receiv'd their Sight, their Feet the *Lame*,
And the *Dumb* spake to celebrate his Fame.
Loud *Storms* and *Winds* were husht at his Command,
And fierce wild *Beasts* did tame and harmless stand.
The wondring *Dead* arise, and hasty come,
Obsequious to his Call, from out their Tomb.
With fresh-created Fish and Loaves, he fed
Th' admiring Crowd, that lay around him spread.
To the *Decrepit* he new Force appoints,
And with strong Nerves new-brac'd their wither'd Joynts.
His Breath oft cool'd fierce *Feavers* raging Flames,
And his sole Word the deadly *Poyson* tames.
Round him in Crowds the sick and feeble throng,
The sick grow easie, and the feeble strong.

I

Fresh

Fresh healing Vertue he diffus'd around,
And dying Men rose leaping from the Ground:
The Languishing reviv'd, th' Afflicted cheer'd,
Took healthful Looks, and smil'd when he appear'd.
Demons at his Command vext Men forsake,
And to th' Infernal Caves and burning Lake,
Their hasty Flight, with piercing Screeches take.

Such *Miracles* did his high Office prove,
And Universal Admiration move,
Of all the chiefest was his wondrous *Love*.
He whom rebellious Men might justly fear,
In all his chosen Terrors would appear,
With Military Pomp, and Trumpets sound,
His shining Host of Cherubs pour'd around;
Arm'd with keen Lightning, and the sharpest Sword,
That all his Magazins of Wrath afford,
To lay all Waste before him, and Efface
All Footsteps of Apostate *Adam*'s Race,
He, unexampled *Love*! Attempts to win
Man from the Curse of *Death*, and Curse of *Sin*,
With Pity, more than that of Mothers Hearts,
With *Mercy*'s Charms, and *Love*'s persuasive Arts.
His high Design was with his Heav'nly Light,
To chase away th' Impenetrable Night,
That cover'd this lost World, and re-inspire
Man's frozen Breast, with fresh Celestial Fire.
Th' *Almighty*'s faded Image to repair,
That its bright Lines might shine distinct and fair.
To raise laps'd Minds to that high State of *Love*,
Of *Light* and *Bliss*, the Blest enjoy above.
To pull all bold Usurping Passions down,
And settle Reason in its ancient Throne.

To break Sins heavy Chains, its Slaves releafe,
And fix 'twixt Earth and Heav'n a lafting Peace.

The *Jews* amus'd with Worldly Empire's Charms,
Hoping fome Monarch with Victorious Arms,
With *Roman* Pomp and Grandeur would arife,
The great *Redeemer*'s, humble State defpife.
Infpir'd from Hell, his Meffage they refufe,
Deride his Perfon, and his Deeds accufe.
He that Supplies on all in want beftow'd,
Feafting with Miracles the hungry Crowd:
Finds from th' obdurate *Hebrew* no relief,
But with the Twelve Companions of his Grief,
He walk'd on his Eternal Purpofe bent,
Scatt'ring his Heav'nly Gifts where'er he went.
Yet did unwelcom through their Regions ftray,
From thofe ungrateful Cities thruft away,
Whence he had *Devils* and *Difeafes* caft,
Him, and his proffer'd Heav'n, they from them chas'd.
At laft his fpotlefs *Innocence* traduc'd,
He ftands before the *Roman* Throne accus'd.
On *Cæfar*'s King, *Pilate* in Judgment fits,
Condemns him, yet his Innocence acquits.
To pleafe th' inexorable *Jews* he fheds
Blood, and Heav'n's dreadful Curfes on their Heads:
That done, he wafh'd his guilty Hands in vain,
The Blood he fpilt, alone could Purge that Stain.

No Form of Cruelty his Foes omit,
They give fharp *Stripes*, and on his *Face* they fpit;
Which now adoring Angels blufh to fee,
Not for its Splendor, but Deformity.
To pleafe united Cruelty and Scorn,
On's wounded *Head*, they fix a Crown of Thorn:

They

They dress him in a Purple *Robe*, that gone,
His Blood with richer Purple dyes his own.
A *Reed* his Hand must for a Scepter sway,
Which with a Rod of It'n shall that Contempt repay:
They bow in Scorn before him, whilst he sate
A Pageant Prince, the mockery of State.
What various Shapes of Cruelty are shewn,
Under, and on his *Cross* he's made to groan:
And yet he bears a heavier Load within,
The pressure of the World's united Sin.
Stretcht on the cursed *Tree* his Body hangs,
Groaning its Life away in dying Pangs.
Forsaken both of Earth and Heav'n, his Breath
He wasted in the Pains of lingring Death:
Whilst on his *Soul* the blackest Horrors dwell,
That feels the Pains, without the Guilt of Hell.
The barb'rous *Hebrews* for whose sake he dy'd,
Stand by, and see their Sov'raign *Crucify'd*,
Without the slight Compassion of a Tear,
Scarce in the Crowd, does one sad Face appear.
Their Insolence dares mock his dying Moans,
Sport with his Torments, and deride his Groans:
Though solid Rocks touch'd with Compassion rent,
The more obdurate *Jew* does not relent.

For *Man* he dies, that Heav'n may be aton'd,
He dies, the *Universe* afflicted groan'd;
Heav'n's everlasting Frame shook with the Fright,
And the scar'd *Sun* shrunk back, and hid his Light.
Thro' th' Earth's dark Vaults a shiv'ring Horror fled,
That whil'st Convuls'd threw up th' awaken'd Dead:
Thin pallid *Ghosts* come sweeping o'er the Grass,
And howling Wolves glare on them as they pass.

Hoarse

Book II.   *Prince* Arthur.   61

Hoarſe Thunder rolls in Subterranean Caves,
Chaos to hearken ſtills his raging Waves.
Ev'n *Hell* gap'd horrible, ſuch was the fright,
And thro' the Chaſm let thro' prodigious *Night*:
Night that extinguiſh'd the Meridian Ray,
And with its gloomy Deluge choak'd the Day.
Sad Moans were heard, Shreeks, Howlings, Midnight Cries,
And Globes of Fire hung blazing in the Skies.
A fierce Convulſion thro' the *Temple* went,
The Pillars trembled, and the *Veil* was rent.
The *Heav'n's* and *Earth* both ſuffer'd when he dy'd,
As *Nature's* Self, were with him Crucify'd.
Down by their Sides the ſilent *Angels*, laid
Their Golden Harps, and neither ſung nor play'd;
Their drooping Wings, and Looks dejected ſhow
Sadneſs, as much, as thoſe bleſt Realms can know.

Thrice the ſwift Sun, his radiant Chariot drove
O'er the blue Hills, and out-ſtretch'd Plains above:
As oft the Moon had ſhot her paler Light,
In Silver Threads thro' the brown Veſt of Night:
When the *Reviving Saviour* leaves his Tomb,
And, as new-born, breaks from the Earth's dark Womb.
The Chains of Death ſhook off, he from the Ground,
Do's with new Force, *Antæus* like, rebound:
He comes in Triumph from the conquer'd Grave,
And this bleſt proof of *Reſurrection* gave.
Oft to his mournful Friends their Lord appear'd,
And their ſad Minds with Heav'nly Pleaſures cheer'd:
He then the Plan of his wiſe Kingdom laid,
Who ſhould ſubmit, and who ſhould be obey'd.
To theſe he gave a Power to looſe, and bind,
And with fixt Bounds that Sacred Power confin'd:

He

He set the Rights his Subjects should enjoy,
Which Princes must Protect, but not Annoy:
And by wise Laws fixt all things that relate,
To the Support of his new founded State.

That done, pursu'd by their admiring Eyes,
Born on a shining Cloud he did arise,
In Heav'nly Pomp Triumphant thro the Skies.
The Clouds dividing in Obsequious haste,
Smil'd, gilded by his Glory, as he pass'd.
Great *Michael, Raphael,* and the rest that boast,
The chief Commands in the Celestial Host,
Great Princes, Thrones, and high *Seraphick* States,
With splendid Equipage pour'd from the Gates;
Sublime in high Celestial Chariots rode,
Far out of Heav'n, to meet th' ascending God.
The Pow'rs and high Dominions with their Train,
Shone glorious bright on all th' Etherial Plain.
On a fair Hill that the wide Vale commands,
The numberless Angelick Army stands,
Drawn up in shining Lines, and Warlike Bands.
The Trumpets all salute him passing by,
And in the Air display'd the Banners fly.
And now arriv'd at Heav'n's Eternal Gate,
Attended with his long Triumphal State,
The blest Inhabitants due Honours give,
And all in Arms, their conquering Prince receive.
Dispos'd in glorious Ranks each Order Shines,
And all the way the bright Militia Lines.
On's *Chariot* Wheels the thronging Cherubs hang,
With whose loud Shouts the Heav'n's high Arches rang.
Thus did he to th' *Eternal*'s Palace ride,
The Guards stood to their Arms on either Side:

Entring

Book II.   *Prince* Arthur.   63

Entring he took his Place, and Brightly shone
On the Right Hand, of his great *Father*'s Throne:
Where he shall our great *Intercessor* stay,
Till the last Summons to the Judgment Day.

He ceas'd, and *Hoel* in his Arms embrac'd,
His God-like Friend, and cry'd, I'm highly grac'd
With this Divine Discourse, what Thanks to you,
Illustrious Prince, what Thanks to Heav'n are due?
Blest *Peace* came wafted on the raging Waves,
And your late Wreck, me and my Kingdom saves.
Kind Heav'n for me hath call'd forth Joy and Light,
From those fierce Storms, and that outrageous Night,
That forc'd your Vessels on th' *Armorick* Shore,
Your Loss I mourn, but Heav'n's Designs adore.
Long have I stray'd in gloomy Darkness lost,
Deep Gulphs, thick Woods, and trackless Mountains crost;
In endless Mazes, and in endless Night,
Without a Glimpse of Day, or Ray of Light.
The Gates of *Light* thrown open, you display
The first reviving Beams of Heav'nly *Day:*
Which darts acrofs the Shades in shining Streaks,
And on my Mind in tender Dawning breaks.
How much I wish to see this Light Divine,
Rise to its Noon, and in full splendor shine?
You've open'd Heav'n's Eternal Springs, whence flow
Those sacred Rivulets, which you bestow
On the parch'd Region of this barren Breast,
Now with pure Streams of Living Waters blest.
I drink them in with Joy, but thirst for more,
And for this thankful, still more Aid implore.

He ceas'd, the Prince who to oblige him strove,
Thus spake, all Seasons offer'd I'll improve,
To give more *Light*, and kindle greater *Love*.

My

My Toil and Sufferings when review'd, will please,
Caus'd by the stormy Winds and angry Seas,
If I can thus assist your Heav'nly Course,
Thro' gloomy Night, thick Mists, and Tempests force,
Thro' all the Snares of Hell, till you attain
Th' Eternal Haven, where blest *Spirits* Reign.
Now to the Foot of Heav'n's steep Precipice,
Ready to plunge into the deep Abyss,
The Red-fac'd *Sun* had roll'd the sinking Day,
Shooting along the Plains a level Ray.
The loving *Turtle* to his Airy Nest,
Flies with his moaning Mate, to Coe, and rest.
The timorous *Hare* steals from the Brakes to feed,
And from the Yoke the lab'ring *Ox* is freed.
With strutting Teats the *Herds* come lowing home,
And *Beasts* of Prey o'er Hills and Forrests roam.
And now the Princes, that had pass'd the Day
In various talk, to *Conda* came, to stay
Till the appearance of the Morning Ray.

Prince Arthur.

BOOK III.

NOW the Victorious *Sun* the *Night* invades,
Chasing from Hill to Hill, the flying Shades.
Up rose the Princes, and were soon prepar'd
To take their Way, attended with their Guard.
In the same Chariot friendly they abide,
Maintaining pleasing Converse, as they ride.
The *British* Captains, and th' *Armorick* Train,
On either Side their generous Courser's rein.
They past not far, when *Hoel* thust addrest,
With pleasing Looks, his Pious, British Guest:
Your lofty Subject now, brave Prince, resume,
How shall your *Lord* from Heav'n to Judgment come,
What follows, what precedes the general Doom?

    The *Briton* then began:
Before the Son of *God* appears on high,
Prodigious Signs are seen thro' all the Sky.
New-lighted *Comets* shake their Fiery Hair,
Or trail their flaming Trains along the Air.
Vast circling Flakes of Fire the World amaze,
And intermixt, prodigious *Meteors* blaze.
The Sky shines terrible with Lightning's Flame;
And Thunder shakes the Universal Frame:
Th' impetuous Roar, o'erturns Heav'n's lofty Towers,
And Starry Fragments fall in burning Showers:

Rent Clouds, pour Seas of raging *Sulphur* down,
Whose livid Flames th' extinguish'd Sun-beams drown.
Cross the red Air the flaming Torrents fly,
Gushing from all the fiery Springs on high.
The melting *Orbs*, and Firmaments conspire,
To make up one Tempestuous Sea of Fire..
The glowing *Sphears* dissolve with Heat, and all
In mighty Floods of liquid Crystal fall.
The lofty Digues gape wide, that stood around,
And from the dark Abyss did Nature bound;
Chaos comes pouring thro' the hideous Crack,
And Nature's Ruins, and th' amazing Wreck
Of burning Worlds, lie floating on his Waves:
Scarce its high Bank th' Empyreal Region saves.
Heav'n's spacious *Balls* are on each other hurl'd,
Ruin with Ruin crush'd, and *World* o'erturn'd with *World*.
Confusion, Noise, and Horror fill the Air,
The Earth, loud Cries, Distraction, and Despair.
Fierce Storms of raging Vapours, that aspire,
Mixt with hot Steams, from subterranean Fire,
That Lakes of Sulphur burning all beneath,
That kindled *Naphtha*, and hot Metals Breath;
The Earth's grip'd Bowels with Convulsions rack,
And with loud Noise their trembling Prisons crack.
Imprison'd Thunder roars for wider room,
Proclaiming loud the World's approaching Doom.
The *Globe* distorted, burst, disjoynted, rent,
Gives to the burning Exhalations vent:
Thro' gaping Clefts, the flaming Tempest flies,
And Hurricanes of Fire confound the Skies.
Great Cities, Mountains, Rocks, and shatter'd Hills,
Vast abrupt Tracks of Land, and sinking Isles,
Sap'd by the Flame, that underneath destroys;
Fall down with mighty Cracks, and dreadful Noise;

Prodigious

Prodigious Ruine filling all the Caves,
And dashing high the subterranean Waves.
  Ætna, Vesuvius, and the fiery kind,
Their Flames within blown up with stormy Wind;
With dire Concussions, and loud Roar complain
Of deadly Gripes, and fierce consuming Pain.
The lab'ring *Mounts* belch drossy Vomit out,
And throw their melted Bowels round about.
Broad Sheets of Flame, Pillars of Pitchy Smoak,
And glowing Stones, the Airy Region choak.
Down their scorcht Sides metallick Torrents flow,
And form a dismal, flaming Sea below:
The fiery Deluge rolls along the Ground,
Dreadful for Colour, horrible for Sound.
Huge Stones, and vast unmelted Cakes of Oar,
The thick, unweildy Tide encumber more.
  Horrour in Triumph, smear'd with Smoak and Blood,
Rides cross the Ridge of the tremendous Flood.
It burns new Channels riding o'er the Plain,
And turns o'er Cities with its pond'rous Train.
Down to the Deep it rolls its massy Waves,
Out-roars the Ocean, and its Waters braves:
Plung'd in the Seas it unextinguish'd lies,
And o'er the Waves the glowing Wedges rise.
Th' affrighted Seas the burning Horrour fly,
And the bare Shores beneath the Deluge fry.
Into the Air th' exhaling Ocean goes,
Where *Waters* slept, a Lake of *Sulphur* glows,
All the hot Seeds, and hidden Stores of Fire,
From subterranean Prisons freed, conspire
With their bright Arms to lay all *Nature* waste,
And to the general *Conflagration* haste.
A *fiery Chaos* Reigns with lawless Power,
And unresisted Flames the World devour.

These Signs first giv'n, amidst the Starry Sphears,
With all the Pomp of Heav'n the *Judge* appears.
Before his Chariot Wheels, that roll on high,
Whirlwinds, and Clouds discharging Thunder fly,
And curling Lightnings run along the Sky.
Immortal *Thrones*, pour'd out from Heav'n's bright Gates,
Dominions, Powers, *Seraphic* Potentates,
Crown'd *Saints*, and *Martyrs* rang'd in glorious Rows,
Attend his Chariot, and his State compose.
The dazling Pomp stretches across the Sky,
From utmost East to West, and passing by
The Heav'nly Orbs, comes on descending slow,
Into the Airy Region here below.
O'er all the Sky, Heav'n's mighty Army shines,
And here it halts in deep embattel'd Lines.
In bright Celestial Armour clad, they stand,
Their Swords of temper'd Flame drawn in their Hand:
They mark a *Camp* of spacious Circuit out,
And cast up Crystal Ramparts round about.
On some fit Eminence, they raise on high
Their Lord's August Pavilion in the Sky:
His bright, sublime *Tribunal* here they place,
On which he sits, with awful, God-like Grace.
Such Flames of Fire, wheeling in Clouds of Smoak,
Issue from thence, as from Mount *Sinai* broke.
Array'd with Majesty, and cloath'd with Light,
He Glory darts too fierce for Angels Sight.
In *Hallelujahs* they his Greatness sing,
And the shook Sphears, with loud *Hosannahs* ring.
Thus on the Throne, the Saviour sits prepar'd,
To judge the World, to punish and reward.

And

And now th' unnumber'd Armies ready ſtand,
Graſping revenging Firebrands in their Hand,
And only wait their Leader's high command.
The Signal giv'n, a general Shout, ſhall ſhake
The Heav'n's around, greater than Armies make
Ruſhing to Battel, or was heard in *Rome*,
When conquering *Cæſar* came in Triumph home.
Their furious Arms devouring Tempeſts throw
On all the guilty, trembling World below.
They pour down mighty, fiery *Cataracts*,
Flaming *Bitumen*, and *Sulphurous* Lakes;
Red Showers of fiery Arrows hiſſing fly,
And flaſhing Lightning flames around the Sky.
Fires from above, combin'd with Fires below,
O'er all the Earth in ruddy Torrents flow.
Vengeance Divine, waſtes Nature's burning Store,
And drowns the Earth in *Fire*, all drown'd in *Guilt* before.
The Heat diſſolves the *Fabrick* of the World,
The broken parts fall down, confus'dly hurl'd:
Chaos reſtor'd does in wild Triumph reign,
And ruin'd Worlds his hideous Throne ſuſtain.

Some great *Archangel* now ſprings forth on high,
And with the loudeſt Trumpet of the Sky,
Summons th' aſtoniſh'd, gazing World to come,
To *Judgment*, and the Univerſal *Doom*.
The dreadful Noiſe ſhakes Heav'n's Etherial Mounds,
And in loud Ecchoes from the Sphears rebounds:
In Ecchoes terrible, and piercing ſhrill,
That the low World with dire Amazement fill.
The guilty *Fiends* ſhreek out at theſe Alarms,
That in the Air fly thick in murmuring Swarms:

Their

Their *Prince* himself trembles, and dares not stay,
But spreads his broad, dun Wings, and shoots away.
They sink confounded to th' Infernal Deep,
Or into Clefts, and hollow Mountains creep.
They find the fatal Hour's arriv'd at last,
That shall revenge their bold Rebellions past:
When to their Torments they shall be restrain'd,
And lie beneath, on flaming Billows chain'd.
When *Hell* no more its Pris'ners shall release,
And *Sin's* black Empire must for ever cease.

   No less the dreadful Sound, and awful Sight,
Confound proud *Tyrants*, and their Guards affright.
What Horrour now distracts each guilty Soul,
In their sad Breasts, what storms of Vengeance roll;
How will they bear this dismal Scene of Woe,
Where will they stay secure, or whither go?
Terrour, Distraction, Anguish, fierce Despair
Drink up their Vitals, and their Heart-strings tear.
Ten Thousand poison'd Darts strike thro' their Reins,
And wound them with unsufferable Pains.
The Vulture bred within their Bowels gnaws,
And *Conscience* gripes them with her Harpy's Claws.
Such Wounds, such Stings, such Pangs must now be born,
Of everlasting *Death*, the sad Forlorn.
What strange Confusion in their Looks appears,
What wild Amazement, Guilt and deadly Fears!
What howling Lamentation, what dire Cries,
What doleful Shrieks, and Yellings fill the Skies!

   Besides, the Trumpet shakes the trembling Ground,
The startled *Dead* awaken at the Sound:
The *Grave* resigns its ancient Spoils, and all
Death's Adamantine Prisons burst, and fall.

The

The *Souls* that did their forc'd Departure mourn,
To the same *Bodies* with swift Flight return:
Whose scatter'd Parts God calls together, they,
To their appointed Meeting haste away.
The Crowding Atoms re-unite apace,
All without tumult, know, and take their place.
Th' assembled *Bones* leap quick into their Frame,
And the warm *Blood* renews a brighter Flame.
The quicken'd Dust feels fresh and youthful Heats,
While its old Task, the beating *Heart* repeats.
The *Eyes* enliven'd with new Vital Light,
Open, admiring whence they had their Sight.
The *Veins* too, twine their bloody Arms around
The Limbs, and with red, leaping Life abound.
Hard twisted *Nerves* new brace, and faster bind
The close knit Joynts, no more to be disjoyn'd.
Strong, new-spun Threds Immortal *Muscles* make,
That justly fixt, their ancient Figure take.
Brisk *Spirits* take their upper Seats, and dart
Thro' their known Channels thence, to every part.
The Men now draw their long-forgotten *Breath*,
And striving break the unweildy Chains of Death.
Victorious *Life* to every Grave resorts,
And rifles Death's unhospitable Courts:
Its Vigour thro' those dark Dominions spread,
From all their gloomy Mansions frees the Dead.
Now ripe Conceptions thro' the Earth abound,
And new sprung Men stand thick on all the Ground.
The Sepulchres are quick, and every Tomb
Labours with Life, and grows a fruitful Womb.

But how the *Dead* are chang'd, their Bodies more
Unlike each other, than their Souls before!

How

How monstrous foul the *guilty* Dead arise,
Each struck with Horrour from his Neighbour flies!
How much deform'd they look, all stain'd with *Sin*,
Black and mis-shap'd without, but more within.
Ugly and Fiend-like, from their Graves they crawl,
And on the Ground, like bloated Vermin, sprawl:
And like them too, their Bodies have their Birth,
From putred Damps and Vapours in the Earth.
So Serpents that entangled lay asleep,
From out their Beds disturb'd, and waken'd creep:
They hiss, and cast their fiery Eyes around,
And with their loathsome Bellies mark the Ground.
For flight their Poysonous Volumes they display,
And urg'd with Fear and Anguish, haste away.
So this foul Brood are forc'd their Graves to leave,
And to the Ground their grov'ling Bellies cleave:
Earthy and Black, confin'd so long to Night,
They dread the Horrours of the chearful Light.
Amazing change! see, some of these were they,
Whose Heads were crown'd, whose Hands did Scepters sway.
These did rich *Purple*, and fine *Linnen* wear,
And every Meal fed on delicious Fare.
That hideous *Thing*, that for a Covert seeks,
With hollow Eyes, fall'n Jaws, and ghastly Cheeks,
That monstrous Thing, was once, when kept with Care,
Proud of its *Beauty*, and look'd wondrous *Fair*,
Set off with all the Ornaments, that please
The Eye, and pamper'd with Luxurious Ease.
But how the guilty Crowd, wreckt with Despair,
With dismal Cries fill all the ecchoing Air;
When they the *Trumpet*'s dreadful Summons hear,
And find the Universal *Judgment* near!
Back to their Graves, the ugly Monsters fly,
And in those Coverts would for ever lie.

They call aloud for Death, and wish they might
Melt to thin Air, be drown'd, and lost in Night.

  But when Blest *Minds* their *Bodies* meet, no Pair
Can look more Beautiful, and charming Fair.
The happy *Souls* shoot swiftly thro' the Sky,
And to the Graves and Sepulchers they fly:
Where they their long-forsaken *Bodies* greet,
Which, like old Friends, they with fresh Pleasure meet.
Bodies, that seem, they are so Pure and Bright,
All thicken'd *Glory*, close compacted *Light*;
Purg'd and refin'd from all that's course and gross,
As melted Gold throws off the baser Dross.
Smiling they rise, such Charms, so sweet a Grace
They shew, as dwell not on a Mortal Face.
These rising *Stars* their Heav'nly Beams display,
Bright Harbingers of Everlasting Day.
Such Beauties, such mild Glories shall we see,
In the glad Spring of Immortality.
Yet these blest Sons of Light, that Angel-like,
Would Mortal Eyes, with deadly Lustre strike,
Were those, that once their Excellence disguis'd,
Liv'd here opprefs'd, and like their Lord, despis'd.
Welcom to them this long-expected Hour,
Safe by their *Judge's* Favour, from his Power:
High Tides of Joy into their Bosoms run,
And Everlasting *Life* they feel begun.
This shall past Griefs in deep Oblivion drown,
Compleat their Triumphs, and their Virtues Crown.
These in the Spring, great Care and Toil bestow'd,
And water'd with their Tears, the Seed they sow'd:
The Harvest now their happy Hours employs,
In reaping Pleasures and Immortal Joys.

                        I.   Bright

Bright *Cherubims* descending thro' the Air,
To these blest Men with speedy Flight repair,
Then to the gen'ral Doom aloft they fly,
And on their Wings convey them thro' the Sky.
In all the way encouraging their Charge,
Telling of all the Joys of Heav'n at large.
Plac'd in the Presence of their *Lord*, they stand
In their appointed Seats, at his Right-hand.

Whilst other *Angels* from the Deep of Hell,
Drive up the *Fiends* that in those Regions dwell.
With Swords of keenest Flame compelling some,
And dragging others to the gen'ral Doom.
In Anguish and Despair, the yelling Fiends,
Curse, Gnash, and Bite th' Eternal Chain that binds
So close, and strait, then turn their Heads away,
From the fierce Terrour of so bright a Day.
And impious *Men*, in no less Horrour, fly
To all the Shades, and Coverts they descry:
Mountains and Rocks their fruitless Cries invite,
To fall, and hide them from the *Judge*'s Sight.
For rise they must, and lose their vain Desire,
Caught up in Whirlwinds, and in Storms of Fire.
Before the *Judge* the Pris'ners stand in sight,
And take the Left-hand, as the Just the Right.

Th' Eternal *Books* before the *Judge* are brought,
Where all Mens long-forgotten Deeds are wrote.
And first are read the Vertues of the *Just*,
Their *Zeal* for Heav'n, their *Courage*, *Hope*, and *Trust*:
The *Prayers*, the *Tears*, the *Alms* themselves conceal'd,
Before applauding Angels are reveal'd.
The righteous *Judge* their Innocence declar'd,
Allots the glorious Kingdom, he prepar'd
For pure and holy Minds a blest Reward.

Their Guardian Angels at their Lord's Command,
Crown the glad *Saints* with an Officious Hand.

Who now in perfect Blifs, their time employ,
Difcourfing, to promote their mutual Joy,
How firft they left the pleafurable way,
Where wanton Streams of foft Delights, convey
Charm'd *Souls*, that with the treach'rous Tyde muft go,
To the dead Lake of *Pain*, and endlefs *Woe*.
How firft they lik'd the dark and lonefome Road,
Which leads to Blifs, and the bleft Minds Abode.
How when in Shades they mourn'd, a Heav'nly Ray
Darted a welcome, tho' imperfect Day.
How *Vertue*'s guidance they implor'd and gain'd,
And what bleft Converfe with her they maintain'd:
How thro' dark Pathes fhe did their Feet conduct,
Correct the Wanderers, and the reft inftruct.
How by her Aids they bore tempeftuous Shocks,
Climb'd o'er oppofing Hills, and hanging Rocks;
Till they at length the Peaceful Realms did gain,
Where *Joys Divine*, and endlefs Tranfports reign.
How fweet and fair Crown'd *Innocence* appears,
No more toft on the Waves of Hopes and Fears?
On Mortal Face fuch Beauties never fhone,
Like thofe of *Virtue*, feated on her Throne.

Next this, th' *Apoftate Angels* are accus'd,
That open Force, or fecret Arts they us'd,
To fet their Leader, on th' *Eternal*'s Throne,
Subvert *Chrift*'s Empire, and advance their own.
That *Man* by them feduc'd, did firft Rebel,
Relinquifh'd Heav'n, and to their Party fell.
That they the curft Defection did fupport,
And new-born Men, to new Rebellions Court.

L 2   That

That they with indefatigable Care,
Fresh Heats fomented, and renew'd the War.
Whence Plagues and Desolation wide, and vast,
And uncontroll'd Destruction laid all waste:
Hence *Noah*'s universal Deluge came,
And hence the World lies now o'erwhelm'd in Flame.
For these black Crimes they're sentenc'd to the Pains,
Of fiercer Fire, and doom'd to heavier Chains.

    Next *Cain*'s Rebellious Off-spring are accus'd,
As Heav'n's inveterate Foes, who long abus'd
Goodness Divine, whom Everlasting *Love*,
And Life *Eternal*, had no Charms to move.
They would no reconciling Terms embrace,
Alike by Threats unchang'd, or Acts of Grace.
They did with Wine and Noise the Method find,
To Calm a Conscious, self-revenging Mind.
To lay asleep th' uneasie Judge within,
Till they with Care and Pains, grew bold in Sin.
For when the sacred *Spirit*, did convey
Into their Breasts, a secret Heav'nly Ray,
Which did, where cherish'd, soon bring on the Day:
With hasty Care they choak'd the new-sprung Light,
Calling to Aid the Shades of Hell, and Night.
Divine Compassion's Force they never felt,
Nor would in Flames of *Love Eternal* melt.
Their Hearts untouch'd did all Heav'n's Stroaks repel,
Temper'd, and harden'd in the Forge of Hell.
No Overtures of *Peace*, no Offers made,
Tho' of an endless Kingdom, could perswade
The unrelenting Rebels, to lay down
Their impious Arms, to take a Heav'nly Crown.
They still asserted with their latest Breath,
Their fixt Confed'racy with Hell, and Death.

'Tis

'Tis on them charg'd, that others too that fell,
Drawn by their Arts, embark'd for Death and Hell.
They led them to the flow'ry Banks, and show'd
The flatt'ring Tide, where smiling Pleasures flow'd.
Where the charm'd Voyagers did careless ride,
Bewitching *Syrens* singing on their Side:
Till the false Flood betray'd them thither, where
It falls into the Gulph of black Despair.

Here secret Crimes are publish'd, and his Name
Who lov'd the *Sin*, but fear'd th' attendant *Shame*.
The sly *Adulterer*, who till the late
Approach of Night, and silent Shades did wait,
For the Caresses of the *Harlot*'s Bed,
And at the early Dawn of Twilight fled;
Is here upbraided, for his careful Flight
Of Mens, whilst he contemn'd th' *Almighty*'s Sight.

Th' *Audacious* Wretch, who did Heav'n's Laws deride,
And all its Thunder and dire Threats defy'd;
Who did cloy'd Nature to fresh Guilt excite,
Beyond her own ev'n Vicious Appetite:
Anti-Platonic that could Pleasure take
In naked *Vice*, and sinn'd for sinning's Sake;
Who could, abstracted from Enjoyment, sport
With *Guilt*, and *Vice* ev'n in Idea court.
Who did himself, so much he lov'd the Fame,
The secret Triumphs of his Lusts proclaim,
Strives in the Crowd to hide his guilty Head,
Whilst his high Charge, and black Indictment's read.
Th' astonish'd Wretch Sinks, Trembles, Dies to see
Enrag'd *Omnipotence*, and frowning *Majesty*.
Such deadly Torments on his Bowels feed,
Such Agonies he feels, as far exceed

All Shapes of Horrour, Mortals ever saw,
Poets invent, or troubl'd Fancies draw.
That There's a *God*, he gives a full Assent,
On the most sure, but saddest Argument:
He can his *Being*, and his *Power* attest,
From the Almighty Vengeance in his Breast.
Thus he at last believes, and trembles too,
On the same grounds that tortur'd *Spirits* do.
The Droll'ry which derided Heav'n's just Cause,
He hears repeated, but without Applause.
His Jests and bold Discourses, will not fit
This place, nor pass, ev'n with his Friends, for Wit.
Will he his feeble Arguments produce,
And make them here, renew their former Use?
Will he assert his Innocence, and plead,
'Twas only harmless *Nature* he obey'd?
That he to *Vice* did not his Mind enslave,
But only pleas'd the Appetites Heav'n gave.
Will he inform the Judge, it cannot be,
A Being Good, and Merciful, as He,
Can so much Rigour to his Errors show,
And make a Creature for Eternal Woe?
The Wretch's bold Objections will appear,
His wanton Fancy's wild Capriches here.
Able no more to stifle with their Night,
The natural Dictates of his inbred Light.
They can't the deadly Stings within controul,
Nor ease the Horrors of his tortur'd Soul.

And now less hardy Pris'ners are Arraign'd,
Which had not this obdurate temper gain'd.
Of such a Pendulous, Distracted Mind,
That oft to Heav'n, and oft to Hell inclin'd:

To make up *Peace*, they would with neither part,
But shar'd between them a divided Heart.
These travell'd on so long the happy Way,
Which leads to Life, and pure Etherial Day:
Till they reach'd Heav'n's bright Confines, could descry
The Peaceful World of Immortality.
But then, discourag'd at the steep Ascent,
And the strait Gate, thro' which the Trav'llers went,
Gave back, and did of their past Toil repent.
But how they now abhor the Cowardize,
Which made them almost Conquerors, miss the Prize:
Made them desert a prosperous Cause as lost,
Which could so many Spoils, and Triumphs boast.
Curst Sloth, that could perswade them to forsake
Christ's Camp, when such a *Kingdom* was at Stake.

Each hears his aggravated Crimes at large,
Devils accuse, and *Conscience* backs the Charge.
They can't excuse, or hide their *Crimes*, nor fly,
Nor what's the Refuge of the wretched, dy.
Now let their past Enjoyments Succour give,
Let *Wit*, and *Wine* their deadly Fears relieve.
Let their dear *Riches* their Assistance lend,
Honour and *Pomp* th' ambitious Man defend.
Let them sollicite with their loudest Cries,
Those Gods, they serv'd, to save their Votaries.
Blest Heav'n, that Man with such a swift Career,
Pursues those Toys which are so useless here.

The *Judge* will all his Terrours now assume,
And thus pronounce the Pris'ners dreadful Doom.
For ever cursed Souls from me depart,
As you did oft my Cause, I you desert.

Go,

Go, burn in Everlasting Fire, prepar'd
For *Devils*, take that sad, but just Reward.
Sink to the Bottomless Abyss of Hell,
Where Agonies, and endless Sorrow dwell:
Go to those Mansions of Despair, and lie
In never-ceasing Torments, go, and die.

The Rebels this expected Sentence past,
With Thunder and Tempestuous Fire are chas'd,
To *Hell's* black Gulph, thro' all th' Etherial Waste.
Where they shall see no chearful Ray of Light,
Doom'd to the Horrours of Eternal Night.
Th' *Almighty's* Arrows Fester in their Heart,
Drink up their Blood, and gall with deadly Smart.
His Wrath consumes the Wretch, his Power sustains,
And, like fierce Poison, o'er their Vitals reigns.
They waste their Souls in Cries, and howling Moans,
And spend *Eternity* in fruitless Groans.

Now the abstrusest Paths of *Providence*,
Which gave the wisest Men so great Offence,
Are so unriddl'd, and made easie here;
The Night dispell'd, they shine as Noon-day, clear.
Justice, that did till now her Graces shrowd,
And walk'd on Earth, encircled with a Cloud;
That did such by, and uncouth Ways frequent,
Perplex'd with Windings, frightful for Ascent;
See this bright *Goddess* to her Throne restor'd,
Unveils her Majesty to be ador'd.
Her Cloud thrown off, her Form is all *Divine*,
No Lustre now, her Glory can out-shine.
Such are the Beauties of her Charming Face,
Fair *Mercy's* Self, looks not with sweeter Grace.

Rivals

Book III.   *Prince* Arthur.   81

Rivals no longer, they are here combin'd,
And in so strict a Bond of Friendship joyn'd;
They seem distinguish'd only by their Name,
Their *Charms* alike, their *Votaries* the same,
And both are Worship'd with an equal Flame.

Justice to all in such due Measures shown,
The Judge returns to his Celestial Throne:
And as he goes, crown'd Saints, and Seraphs sing
Loud Songs of Praise to their Triumphant King.
He enters Heav'n attended with his Train,
Who in the new *Jerusalem* shall reign.

The City stands on pure expanded Fields
Of rising *Ether*, which wide Prospect yields,
O'er all the Gulph, and out-stretcht Vales below,
O'er all th' Inferiour, spacious Orbs can show.
The Walls are Marble of the richest Vein,
And their high Towers, o'er-look the Azure Plain.
Of polish'd *Gold* the glorious Structures rise,
With gilded Spires, and Turrets in the Skies.
From Heav'nly Quarries on their Front appear
Rich *Stones*, like Winter Stars, but far more clear:
Immortal *Rubies*, *Diamonds*, *Saphires* met,
In beauteous Mixture, and bright Orders set.
Rare Works, where Cost immense, and Art combine,
Built and adorn'd by th' Architect Divine,
To be for Holy *Minds* a blest Abode,
Th' Imperial Seat, and Residence of *God*.
The Streets are all of fine, Etherial *Glass*,
Pure, like the spotless Minds, that thro' them pass.
Thro' these Eternal, living Rivers flow,
Trees on their Banks, in goodly Ranges grow,
Which with their golden Fruit, immortal health bestow.

            M   Twelve

Twelve Gates of Orient *Pearl* unshaken stand,
Shut, and unbarr'd by the Almighty's Hand.
A steepy Gulph is plac'd beneath the Walls;
And down as low as Hell's Abyss, it falls;
Lest Hostile Fiends should leave their burning Lake,
And bold Excursions to these Regions make.
The *Air*'s Serene, and fit for happy Minds,
Secure from Thunder, and th' Assaults of Winds.
No Clouds, but those of curling *Incense* rise,
By playing *Zephirs* tost about the Skies;
Which with their gentle Breath sweet Odours blow,
Which from Blest Woods, and Heav'nly Gardens flow.
No noxious Damps, the Region's so sublime,
From Hell's Infernal Caves, can hither Climb.
No foul terrestrial Steams pollute the Air,
No Breaths ascend, but those of *Praise* and *Prayer*.
Essential Glory from th' *Almighty*'s Face,
With its resplendent Efflux, lights the Place.
All Heav'n's fair *Orbs*, thinn'd and beat out in Light,
Would not spread out a Day, so pure and bright,
As that, the *Saints* Illustrious Order sheds,
From the encircling Glory round their Heads.
The vanquish'd Sun would there seem Dark, his Light
Whence our course Day proceeds, would there make Night.
So Glorious are the Dwellings of the Saints,
Out-done by nothing, but th' Inhabitants.

On lofty Thrones the Heav'nly Princes sit,
In Robes as white as *new-fall'n* Snow, and writ
In Golden Characters, their Foreheads bear
Their *Saviour*'s Name, their Breasts his *Image* wear.
Immortal Vigour shines on ev'ry Face,
They look with Mild, but with Majestick Grace.

Thick

Thick Beams of Light stream out from ev'ry Head,
Each *Saint* does his own Heav'n about him spread,
His radiant Feet on pointed Glory tread.

Safe on the Shore with Pleasure they behold,
How the thick Waves are on each other rowl'd.
What Dangers of a strange amazing Shape,
What fatal Rocks, they scarcely did escape.
They hear the Winds grow loud and turbulent,
See Clouds swoln big, with Thunder in 'em pent,
With which the lowring Sky is over-cast,
Hang down upon the Seas which they have past.
Viewing these Woes themselves did once endure,
They stand surpriz'd, as if not yet secure.
Amaz'd at all the Glory they possess,
Wonder almost suspends their Happiness.
They on so sweet, and rich a *Climate* thrown,
Forget their Dangers, now for ever gone.
Th' *Almighty* they enjoy, at whose Right-hand
Fulness of *Joy*, and *Life Eternal* stand.
Down from his Throne, as Light does from the Sun,
Rivers of fresh Delight for ever run.
With ravish'd Eyes they drink in Heav'nly Beams,
Which from his Face flow down in Glorious Streams.
They gaze so on the *Beatifick* Sight,
Till they become all Intellectual *Light*:
So long they his substantial Brightness view,
Till they all grow *Divine*, and God-like too.
So quick they feel the mighty Influx come,
The most Capacious, thirsty Souls want room:
They widen and extend themselves, to hold
Those Floods of *Joys*, which to their Breasts are roll'd;
Till they a vast, unmeasur'd Bliss possess,
And strive beneath th' unweildy Happiness.

If but a Glimpſe of Heav'n, whoſe Glory ſtreams
Thro' the thick Clouds in weak, refracted Beams,
Can pleaſe ſo much, what Joys have thoſe above,
Where perfect *Knowledge*, kindles perfect *Love* ?
Tranſports Ineffable their Minds employ,
Delug'd in Glory, loſt in Tides of Joy.

Here *Innocence* will all its Luſtre ſhow,
The mournful Looks thrown off, it wore below.
Sorrows for ever baniſh'd hence, repair
To the low, guilty Regions of the Air.
There no black Clouds of *Diſcontent* appear,
Which ſpread themſelves o'er theſe dark Vallies here:
No *Groans* are heard, no *Tears* fall down the Face,
To interrupt the *Joy*, of this bleſt Place.
No croſſing *Arms*, or ſad dejected *Eyes*,
Seek out the ſecret Corners of the Skies.
If Courſe, Terreſtrial Pleaſures, court the Senſe
With ſuch ſtrong Charms, that few can make defence;
When backward Nature's forc'd by Wit, and Art,
All her delicious Treaſures to impart.
When the ſhort Days in all Delights are ſpent,
Which ſoft, luxurious *Aſia* can invent:
What are the Nobler Pleaſures, which tranſport
The bleſt, that reign in this Celeſtial Court?
Which no Decay, or Intermiſſion know,
Debas'd, when liken'd to the beſt below.
The Clouds all broke, the Tempeſt chas'd away,
The ſmiling Skies diſcloſe a chearful Day.
They've chang'd the Deſart's dry and barren Sand,
For all the Riches of a fruitful Land:
Where with Immortal Food they're ever fed,
And drink pure Pleaſures at the Fountain's Head.

Hatred,

Hatred, Distress, and Grief, are banish'd hence,
The sad Companions once, of Innocence.
No dying *Martyrs* Flames, or private Cries
Of *Innocents* opprest, disturb the Skies.

   Here our Delights are mixt with base Allay,
We have at best but a Tempestuous Day:
Our Sweets are still attended with a Sting,
And great Enjoyments, greater Sorrows brings.
Delights, those Beautiful Illusions, play
Around us, and, when grasp'd, they glide away.
Here tempting Joys, our fond Embraces fly,
Choice, Foreign Flow'rs, they only Blow, and Dye.
They shew themselves, but will not with us dwell,
But, like hot Gleams, approaching Storms foretel.
Pure unmixt Pleasures on us never flow'd,
But stream, like watry Sun-beams, thro' a Cloud.
But those above, see no unlovely Day,
Their *Joys* no Mixture know, nor fear Decay.
In those blest Realms they know no thoughtful Care,
Ever to Triumph is th' Employment there.
There's no Vicissitude of *Day*, and *Night*,
No *Tears*, or *Ages*, measure Heav'n's Delight;
Time has quite finish'd, and gone thro' its Round,
It did their Grief, but can't their Pleasure Bound.
Its Streams here disembogu'd for ever ly,
Lost in th' Abyss of *Immortality*.
They no sad Fears of future Sorrows know,
Compleatly Happy, and for ever so.
For *Ever!*
We strive in vain to hold this Boundless Space;
Too wide and vast, for Mortals to Embrace.
Our Arms may clasp the Earth with greater Ease,
And spread themselves a-shore round all the Seas.

When Ages have their wideſt Circle run,
Heav'n wears not, ſtill its *Joys* are but begun.
The Hero's here forget their toil and pain,
And in Eternal *Peace*, and Triumph reign.

No more the Scoffer mocks their pious Care,
As Native Dulneſs, and ungrounded Fear.
How different Fate he and the Impious kind,
Chain'd in the dark infernal Priſons, find?
Near the wild *Deep* where reſtleſs Atoms fight,
And th' unfrequented Coaſts of ancient *Night*,
Where Nature ne'er on Pregnant Matter ſate,
To hatch warm Life, and its ſtraight Bounds dilate:
There ſtands the vaſt, unbottom'd Gulph of Hell,
Where *Sin* and *Death*, in all their Terrors dwell.
Beyond the Verge of Day, theſe Regions lie,
As low and black, as Heav'n is bright and high.
Horror, and *Night* hang diſmal o'er the place,
And grizly Forms fill all the gloomy ſpace.
Dead Seas of pond'rous *Darkneſs* lie around,
And the ſad Realms, from Light's grey Frontiers bound.
Darkneſs which blunts the ſharpeſt pointed Ray,
And unannoy'd, repels th' Invading Day.
The ſluggiſh Air is choak'd with ſoultry Gleams,
With poiſonous Damps, and ſuffocating Steams;
Which from wide Lakes of boiling Sulphur riſe,
Laden with Groans, and Everlaſting Cries.
No ſuch malignant Breaths, ſuch deadly Reeks,
The delving Miner that hid Treaſure ſeeks,
E'er let out from a ſubterranean Cell,
As thoſe which break from the black mouth of Hell.
A fiery Sea burns fiercely all beneath,
Blown up, and kindled by th' *Almighty*'s Breath.

In flaming Heaps the livid *Ocean* rolls,
And scalding Waves involve despairing Souls.
The boiling Floods terrific Colours shew,
Some deeply Red, and others faintly Blue.
These with the Shades contend, but can't dispel
The Darkness which surrounds the burning Cell:
Or if they do, they dart pale, dismal Light,
Worse than the Horrors of the blackest Night.
The troubled *Whirlpool* belches Burnings out,
And throws red Seas of Sulphur round about.
Columns of *Smoke*, with spiral Flames of *Fire*
Inwreath'd, from wide-mouth'd Furnaces aspire.
Hence the black Region is annoy'd with Fumes,
Stench, Reeks, and Flame, which kills, but not consumes.
So when a *Mount*, hot with metallick Seeds,
In its rich Sides a secret Burning feeds;
Soultring within, it casts up Pitchy Smoke,
And the dead Air ascending Vapours choak.
In mighty Floods the wide *Volcano*'s throw
Their melted Treasures out, and overflow
With glowing Torrents, all the Neighb'ring Ground,
Which lies beneath a burning Deluge drown'd.
Thro' all the Air the liquid Riches fly,
And Floods of Fire dash thick against the Sky.

All *Hope* for ever banish'd flies this Place,
And fixt *Despair* sits Pale on ev'ry Face.
Grief, Anguish, Terrour, Shame, Confusion here,
In Forms more terrible than Death, appear.
Here hateful *Sin* throws off its flatt'ring Charms,
And shews a Monster in the Sinner's Arms.
It now no more can please awaken'd Eyes,
Stript of stoll'n Beauties, and the fair Disguise

Of promis'd Good, it does it self disclose
Its hideous Shape, and ghastly Visage shows.
Th' affrighted Sinner seeing, fain would fly
Th' Embraces of such foul Deformity:
He would forget their past Endearments now,
And from the Monster strives in haste to go:
But 'twill not be; those Friends on Earth must dwell
For ever, sad Companions too, in Hell.

    This fiery Gulph, was as their just reward,
For *Lucifer*, and his black Host prepar'd;
Where now the *Fiends*, once fairest Sons of Light,
Lie plung'd in Flame, chain'd in Eternal Night,
These wretched Minds, once pure and free from Stain,
In the bright Palaces of Heav'n did reign.
Array'd with dazling Brightness, there they dwelt,
Blest with their great *Creator's* sight, and felt
The beaming Influx breaking from his Face,
And shar'd the Pleasures of that Blissful Place.
Till with the task of blest Obedience tir'd,
They to th' *Eternal's* Sacred Throne aspir'd.
Incens'd with such Ambitious Aims, their *Lord*
Strikes thro' the Rebels with his flaming Sword.
Headlong he casts them from the Seats above,
No longer now, the Creatures of his Love.
Flaming, and Thunder-struck, the Traytors fell,
And sunk down to the fiery Jaws of Hell.
As when strong-rising Flames resistance find,
Beat downwards, by a fierce, impetuous Wind:
The liquid Pyramids, with labour bend
Their tops, and sink, still struggling to ascend.
So did these *Beings* of a Heav'nly Race,
Fall from the Regions of their Native Place;

Still

Still working up, they sunk in Pain and Toil,
For downwards thrown, their Natures still recoil.
So difficult's an *Angel*'s Fall, and thus
Sinking's to them, what rising is to us.

But who has Strength t' oppose th' *Almighty*'s Hand,
Who can against his deadly Terrours stand?
He with a single Word, an angry Frown,
Subdu'd this *Host*, and cast them headlong down.
Confounded, and amaz'd they sink, and all
Heav'n's Plagues, and Wrath, pursu'd them in their Fall.
Here they must lie far from the Coasts of Bliss,
Chain'd in the Dungeons of the dark Abyss:
Where now they feel what *Guilt's* Demerits are,
Weltring in Fire, and tortur'd with Despair.
How much they curse the sad Exchange, black *Night*,
And endless *Death*, for Heav'nly *Joy* and *Light*.
Sunk deep in liquid Fire they lift their Eyes,
Red both with Heat and Anguish, to the Skies:
Then rave aloud, to think what Joys they've lost,
To think how dear their bold Rebellion cost.
Nor is the Change of these two Dwellings such,
So great, but they themselves, are chang'd as much.
See how deform'd they are, to what before,
Stript of the Glory that in Heav'n they wore;
How much they look too like their guilty State,
How foul, and how unlike themselves of late.
Such fatal Changes one bold Crime can make,
Heav'n's lost, nay more left for a burning Lake.

Man's Crime th' Infernal Gates did open lay,
And rais'd, and pav'd, a broad and easie Way;
Leading a-cross the Gulph from Earth to Hell,
Where now, lost *Men*, with impious *Spirits* dwell.

A Way that's throng'd with mighty Crowds of those,
That for *Delight* and *Ease*, this Passage chose.
In Sports and Mirth they journey on, and find
All the Delights which please a *Vicious* Mind.
The Way's so wondrous smooth, so prone and broad,
They rather fall, than travel down this Road.
But how surprizing is their Journey's End,
To what dire Seats does this smooth Passage tend?
Down to th' Infernal Gulph they sporting glide,
Born on enchanting Pleasure's wanton Tide.
A sad exchange they meet, outrageous Seas
Of Sulphurous Fire, for Luxury and Ease.
In Darkness chain'd, on flaming Billows tost,
Too late they find themselves for ever lost;
Hopeless they rave, and curse the easie Way,
That did their Feet to these sad Realms betray.

  Hither the *Damn'd*, the final Sentence past,
With *Cherubs* bright, revenging Swords are chas'd:
Pursu'd with everlasting Wrath, they take
Their woful Refuge, in the burning Lake.
Transfixt on unextinguish'd Fire they lie,
Burn without waste, without expiring die.
Those Agonies, those Terrors here they know,
That from a self-revenging *Conscience* flow.
Grip'd with the sad Remembrance of their Sin,
They feel the *Stygian* Viper gnaw within.
With deadly Stings, th' *Almighty* wounds their Hearts,
And in their Breasts sticks deep his fiery Darts.
Along their Veins tempestuous Vengeance rolls,
Pouring Despair, and Horrour on their Souls.
Who can with everlasting Burnings dwell,
And bear the Guilt, and Punishment of Hell?

What Strength or Courage can support the Load
Of Wrath, inflicted by th' *Almighty God?*

Hear how the *Damn'd* devour'd with Plagues, begin
To curse aloud their *Judge, Themselves,* their *Sin.*
Transported with their Anguish, Grief, and Shame,
They gnash their Teeth, and bite the raging Flame.
Then sunk in deep Despair, such Sighs they breath,
Such dismal Groans, which but to hear, is Death.
A secret Fire their Breasts, like *Ætna,* feed,
And like that too, do their own Thunder breed.
Their Hellish Nature its own Punishment,
Is a worse Plague, than Furies can invent.
Their *Lusts,* like Vultures, tear their inward parts,
And never-ceasing Torments, rend their Hearts.
Their vicious *Appetites,* not yet destroy'd,
Still crave the Pleasures, they on Earth enjoy'd:
Though those are gone, the fierce, untam'd Desire
Remains, and burns worse than their Lake of Fire.
But what's the most afflicting Plague of Hell,
With all these Woes, they must for ever dwell.
For *Ever!* fatal State, for *Ever!* who
Can bear the Doom of *Everlasting Woe?*
What deadly Pangs, what fierce Convulsions rend
Their Breasts, who know their Pains shall never end?
How the despairing *Damn'd* cry out, Is this
The Place we chose, instead of Heav'nly Bliss?
Is this black *Prison,* these tormenting *Chains,*
This Lake of *Fire,* and these Eternal *Pains,*
The dismal Recompence our Crimes afford,
And must we thus curst, tortur'd, and abhor'd,
In these consuming Flames, these Torments ly,
To all the Ages of *Eternity?*

Curft be the fatal *Crimes*, which we obey'd,
Which ftole our Hearts, and have our Lives betray'd.
Curft be the tranfient falfe *Delights* that fhew'd
The Charms, which we fo greedily purfu'd;
Till down the fteepy Precipice, we fell
Into this deep Abyfs of *Death*, and *Hell*;
Curft be the treacherous *Joys*, that leave us now
Doom'd to Defpair, loft in Eternal Woe.

He ended, *Hoel* highly pleas'd, expreft
The grateful Senfe, which fill'd his joyful Breaft.
Methinks he cry'd, I view th' Infernal Caves,
And fee the *Damn'd* float on the raging Waves
In the dire Lake, where flaming Brimftone rolls,
And hear the difmal Groans of tortur'd Souls:
Then looking up, I fee the Bleft above,
Diffolv'd in Raptures of Eternal *Love*.
I feem to view their bright, triumphant Throngs,
And hear their *Harps*, and fweet Harmonious *Songs*.
Then he the *Briton* various queftions asks,
Who with great Joy performs the pious Tasks,
He teaches facred *Myft'ries* yet behind,
And ftamps the *Chriftian* Image on his Mind.

Prince Arthur.

BOOK IV.

IN such *Divine* Discourse, on things sublime,
The Royal *Pair* with Pleasure pass'd their Time.
Now the day wears, the Sun-beams faintly bound,
And taller Shadows stretch along the Ground.
Advanc'd, the rising Eminence they gain,
Which gave full prospect o'er the fertile Plain,
Where the Imperial Seat of *Hoel* stands,
And all the Soil and Towns around, commands.
Fair *Liger* the *Armoric* Region's Pride,
Does thro' the Vale in smooth Meanders glide,
And rolls his Silver Volumes by its side.
Here the *Nannetian* Heroes did of old,
For Arms and Wisdom fam'd, the Scepter hold.
Arthur the Structure's height, and Pomp admires,
The lofty Walls, strong Towers, and glitt'ring Spires.
He views the rich and fruitful Region round,
Where wanton *Nature* sate in Pleasure crown'd,
Scattering with lavish Bounty on the Soil,
Riches and Joys, without the Owner's Toil.

To Martial Sports by thirst of Honour led,
The active Youth o'er all the Fields are spread.
Some of robuster Limbs advance their Name
In wrestling Rings, the fam'd *Olympick* Game.

Some

Some rein their manag'd *Steeds* with Manly grace,
Some swift in *running*, strain to win the Race.
Some hurling pond'rous *Balls* their Fellows brave,
Some twang the *Bow*, and some the *Colours* wave.
But all desert their Games, and Warlike sport,
And round the Kings, run shouting to the Court.
Which was an ancient, stately *Pile*, that stood
On the sweet Banks of *Liger*'s peaceful Flood.
Alighted here, th' *Armoric* Prince exprest,
All signs of welcom to his Royal Guest.
He leads him to a fair and spacious Room,
Hung with rich Pieces, from the finest Loom:
Rare Workmanship, where fam'd *Sydonian* Art
Did all her Force, and happy Strokes impart.
Each piece fresh Pleasure, and new Wonder feeds,
Fill'd with th' *Armoric* Kings Heroick Deeds :
Their great Exploits in single Combate done :
The Towns they conquer'd, and the Fields they won.
Pleas'd with the Skill, and Story, *Arthur* stands,
And much of this, and much of that, demands.

   Mean time, within a *Supper* they prepare,
With great Magnificence, and Regal Fare.
Strong, brawny Servants sweat, and panting strode,
O'er-burden'd with the *Meats* unweildy Load.
The Iv'ry *Tables* groan beneath the weight,
Of high pil'd *Dishes*, all of massy Plate,
In decent Order set, and Princely State.
All things appear, which curious search can find,
Or in the *Finny*, or the *Feather'd* Kind :
Which *Hills*, or ransack'd *Forests* can impart,
Profusely heap'd, set off with costly Art.
Of Polish'd Gold capacious *Goblets* shine,
With sparkling *Stones* enrich'd, and sparling *Wine*.
                                        Delicious

Delicious *Fruit* crown'd with fresh *Laurel* stood
In lofty Pyramids, a golden Wood.
Great *Lights* in silver Sconces plac'd on high,
Shine round the Room, and more than Day supply.
The Kings both sate, the *Britons* take their place,
The other side th' *Armorick* Captains grace.
Chearful and highly pleas'd, they sit, and eat,
And now the Art they praise, and now the Meat.
Choice *Instruments*, some Strung, and some of Wind,
Were heard, in sweet melodious Consort joyn'd,
The lively *Hoboy*, and the sweet-mouth'd *Flute*,
The sprightly *Violin*, and warbling *Lute* ;
With the sonorous *Viol*, mingling sound,
Soft Ayres, and Heav'nly Harmony compound.

But that which *Arthur* with most pleasure heard,
Were noble Strains, by *Mopas* sung the Bard,
Who to his *Harp* in lofty Verse began ;
And thro' the secret Maze of *Nature* ran.
He the great *Spirit* sung, that all things fill'd,
That the tumultuous Waves of *Chaos* still'd.
Whose *Nod* dispos'd the jarring Seeds to Peace,
And made the Wars of hostile *Atomes* cease.
All *Beings* we in fruitful Nature find,
Proceeded from the great *Eternal* Mind ;
Streams of his unexhausted Spring of Power,
And cherish'd with his Influence, endure.
He spread the pure *Cerulean* Fields on high,
And Arch'd the Chambers of the Vaulted Sky :
Which he, to suit their Glory with their Height,
Adorn'd with *Globes*, that reel, as drunk with Light.
His Hand directed all the tunefull *Sphears*,
He turn'd their *Orbs*, and polish'd all the *Stars*.

He

He fill'd the *Sun*'s vaſt Lamp with golden Light,
And bid the ſilver *Moon*, adorn the Night.
He ſpread the Airy Ocean without Shores,
Where *Birds* are wafted with their feather'd Oars.
Then ſung the Bard how the light *Vapours* riſe
From the warm Earth, and Cloud the ſmiling Skies.
He ſung how ſome, chill'd in their Airy flight,
Fall ſcatter'd down in pearly Dew by Night.
How ſome, rais'd higher, ſit in ſecret Steams
On the reflected Points of bounding Beams;
Till chill'd with Cold, they ſhade th' Etherial Plain,
Then on the thirſty Earth deſcend in *Rain*.
How ſome, whoſe parts a ſlight Contexture ſhow,
Sink hov'ring thro' the Air, in fleecy *Snow*.
How part is ſpun in ſilken Threads, and clings
Entangled in the Graſs in glewy Strings.
How others ſtampt to *Stones*, with ruſhing ſound
Fall from their Cryſtal *Quarries*, to the Ground.
How ſome are laid in Trains, that kindled fly
In harmleſs *Fires* by Night, about the Sky.
How ſome in *Winds* blow with impetuous Force,
And carry Ruine where they bend their Courſe:
While ſome conſpire to form a gentle Breez,
To fan the Air, and play among the Trees.
How ſome enrag'd grow turbulent, and loud,
Pent in the Bowels of a frowning Cloud;
That cracks, as if the Axis of the World [hurl'd.
Was broke, and Heav'n's bright Towers were downwards
He ſung how Earth's wide *Ball* at *Jove*'s command,
Did in the midſt on Airy Columns ſtand.
And how the Soul of *Plants*, in Priſon held,
And bound with ſluggiſh Fetters lies conceal'd,
Till with the Spring's warm Beams, almoſt releaſt
From the dull weight, with which it lay oppreſt,

Its

Its Vigour spreads, and makes the teeming Earth
Heave up, and labour with the sprouting Birth:
The active *Spirit* freedom seeks in vain,
It only works and twists a stronger Chain.
Urging its Prison's sides to break away,
It makes that wider, where 'tis forc'd to stay:
Till having form'd its living House, it rears
Its Head, and in a tender *Plant* appears.
Hence springs the *Oak*, the Beauty of the Grove,
Whose stately Trunk, fierce Storms can scarcely move.
Hence grows the *Cedar*, hence the swelling *Vine*
Does round the *Elm* its purple Clusters twine.
Hence painted *Flowers* the smiling Gardens bless,
Both with their fragrant Scent, and gawdy Dress.
Hence the white *Lilly* in full Beauty grows,
Hence the blue *Violet*, and blushing *Rose*.
He sung how *Sun-beams* brood upon the Earth,
And in the *Glebe* hatch such a numerous Birth;
Which way the genial warmth in *Summer* Storms
Turns putrid Vapours to a Bed of *Worms*.
How *Rain*, transform'd by this prolifick Power,
Falls from the Clouds, an animated Shower.
He sung the *Embryo*'s growth within the Womb,
And how the Parts their various Shapes assume.
With what rare Art the wondrous Structure's wrought,
From one crude Mass to such Perfection brought;
That no part useless, none misplac'd we see,
None are forgot, and more would Monstrous be.

Such was the splendor of King *Hoel*'s Feast;
Which ended, *Arthur* straight retires to rest.
Hoel not so, but with the *Britons* sate,
Asking of *Albion*'s past, and present State.

O Much

Much he inquires of their inteſtine Jars,
Much of the *Picts*, and of the *Saxon* Wars.
At laſt, requeſted *Lucius* to relate,
Prince *Arthur*'s Story, and King *Uter*'s Fate:
Lucius began, the reſt attentive wait.

  How ſad a Task do your Commands impoſe,
Which muſt renew unſufferable Woes?
Which muſt our Grief with freſh Affliction feed,
And make your generous Heart with pity bleed.
Whilſt I the diſmal Scene of Ills diſcloſe,
And bleeding *Albion*'s ghaſtly Wounds expoſe:
The cruel Foes in telling would relent,
And with their Tears, the Spoils they caus'd, lament.
Pity would *Picts* and *Saxon* Breaſts invade,
And make them mourn, o'er the dire Wounds they made,
But ſince you're pleas'd to hear our Country's Fate,
I'll pay Obedience, and our Woes relate.

  Great *Empires*, like their Founders, Mortal are,
And the ſad marks of Age, and Sickneſs bear.
Their ſtrong Foundations mouldring wear away,
And ſapp'd by Time's devouring Teeth, decay.
Triumphant *Rome*, with Pomp and Grandeur crown'd,
Proudly ſurvey'd the Conquer'd World around.
The Cold and Burning *Zone* obey'd her Arms,
And either *Pole* trembled at her Alarms.
Where Storms can beat, or angry Billows foam,
Where Sails can fly, or ſavage Beaſts can roam,
Proud *Tyber*'s ſwelling Tide no Banks withſtood,
Which o'er the *Globe* roll'd her Victorious Flood.
To ſo ſublime a pitch of Power and Fame,
Rome's wiſe and valiant Sons advanc'd her Name.

Sons,

Book IV.   *Prince* Arthur.   99

Sons, that she bore when vigorous Youth did crown
Her Limbs with Beauty, and with Strength full grown:
Enervated with *Age* and *Vice* at last,
She found her Strength, and Youthful Vigour waste.
Decrepit grown, a puny wither'd Race,
Feeble of Head and Arms, her Womb disgrace.
Of all her *Romans*, *Rome* remains bereft,
Old Names alone, with modern Vices left.
The Noble *Scipios*, and brave *Cæsars* gone,
A starv'ling Brood puts their great Titles on.
Her *Legions* now can no new Triumphs sing,
Her molting *Eagles* hang their sickly Wing.
To break her Yoke the *Provinces* rebel,
Those she invaded, now she can't repel.
Fierce *Northern* Storms chastise old *Tyber*'s Pride,
And to its Banks chase the retreating Tide;
Loud, foaming Torrents, from high *Scythian* Hills,
From bleaky *Continents*, and frozen *Isles*,
In one vast Sea combin'd, come pouring down.
And *Rome*'s fair Cities, and rich Valleys drown,
A barb'rous Flood of *Vandals*, *Goths*, and *Huns*,
Their Banks broke down, the Provinces o'er-runs.
As a tall *Oak* that Young and Verdant stood
Above the Grove, it self a Nobler Wood;
His wide extended Limbs the Forest drown'd,
Shading its Trees, as much, as they, the Ground.
Young, murmuring Tempests in his Boughs are bred,
And gathering Clouds frown round his lofty Head.
Outrageous Thunder, stormy Winds, and Rain,
Discharge their Fury, on his Head, in vain.
Earthquakes below, and Light'ning from above,
Rend not his Trunk, nor his fixt Root remove:
But then his Strength, worn by destructive Age,
He can no more his angry Foes engage.

O 2

He spreads to *Heav'n* his naked, wither'd Arms,
As Aid imploring, from invading Harms.
From his dishonour'd Head the slightest Storm
Can tear its Beauties, and his Limbs deform.
He rocks with every Wind, while on the Ground
Dry Leaves, and broken Arms lie scatter'd round.
So *Rome* decay'd.
Britannia's warlike Youth on this Pretence,
Is call'd off from her own, to *Rome*'s defence.
Till the exhausted, weak, deserted Isle,
Tempted fierce Neighbours, to an easie Spoil.
Britannia of her Valiant Son's bereft,
Expos'd to every Ravisher is left.
The savage Foes, that did her Anger dread,
And from her Arms, to Wilds and Mountains fled,
Now leave the Coverts, where they sculking staid,
And roaring out, th' unguarded Land invade.
A cruel Rout of Northern *Scots* and *Picts*,
The direful Marks of barb'rous Rage inflicts.
Their Arms from Blood and Ravage never cease,
Where once they basely crouch'd, and fawn'd for Peace.
Wide Ruine, Desolation, Rapine, Spoil,
Rage in the Bowels of th' unhappy Isle.
So *Wolves*, the faithful *Mastiffs* gone, grow bold,
And fiercely leap into th' unguarded Fold:
The trembling *Flock* they seize with eager Claws,
And tear their mangled Limbs with ravening Jaws.
Till they stand panting with th' uneasie load,
O'ercloy'd with Carnage, and opprest with Blood.

Britannia thus dishonour'd, spoil'd, distrest,
And by her proud, insulting Foes opprest,
Is forc'd of stronger Neighbours, to implore
That Aid and Help, she us'd to lend before.

Urg'd

Urg'd by her Fate, and hard Neceſſity,
She dreads th' Expedient, that ſhe's forc'd to try.
Hard fate of Princes, who to prop their State
Oppreſt and ſinking, heap on greater weight!
Fatal Diſtemper, where we ſeek for Eaſe
From Drugs, more dang'rous than the ſharp Diſeaſe.

A Warlike Race in *frozen Climates* bred,
Leaving their *Wilds*, by Valiant Captains led;
A fertile Soil, and milder Regions ſought,
And won the happy Seats for which they fought.
Bold by Succeſs, which waited on their Arms,
They ſtill advanc'd in thick, victorious Swarms.
Till Seas as wild, oppos'd their Torrent's Force,
And watry Banks reſtrain'd their rapid Courſe.
They ſtretcht their Seats along the *Belgian* Coaſt;
No Soil, can more of Nature's Favour boaſt:
No Region's bleſt with more indulgent Beams,
With fatter *Glebe*, with more, or ſweeter *Streams*.
The warlike *Saxons* here their Empire rear'd,
With Plenty crown'd, and by their Neighbours fear'd.

King *Vortigern*, unable to oppoſe
The barb'rous *Picts*, and fierce *Albanian* Foes,
With humble Language, and rich Preſents pray'd
This mighty Nation to afford him Aid.
The *Saxon* Princes with his Prayer comply'd,
Britannia was too fair, to be deny'd.
As Friends they landed on our naked Coaſts,
And ſtill pour'd on their freſh, unnumber'd Hoſts.
They chas'd indeed the barb'rous *Picts* away,
But ſeiz'd, themſelves, the *Kingdom* as their Prey.
The *Lyon's* Title to the Crown they plead,
As Friends receiv'd, as Conquerors obey'd.

No more let *States*, vext with Inteſtine Wars,
Call in great *Princes* to compoſe their Jars.
What *Britons* by their ſad Deliverance won,
Was, by a ſtronger Foe, to be undone.
'Tis true, oppreſt, they did their Wrongs reſent,
But 'twas too late their Counſels to repent.
Britannia's weak, precarious Kings obey
The proud *Protector*'s Arbitrary Sway.
Our Forts, and Navies, and the chief Commands,
Were, on Pretence of *Caution*, in their Hands.
Th' inſatiate Leeches do for ever crave,
And for their Service, ask us, all we have.
Our Strength is ſpent, and barb'rous Avarice
Draws all our Wealth into her deep Abyſs.
Rapine and Murder all our Cities fill,
Our haughty Friends take leave to Spoil and Kill.
Theſe dire *Protectors*, arm'd with Lawleſs Power,
The *Plowman*'s Hopes, and *Merchant*'s Gains devour.
What we prepare, the ravenous Harpies eat,
And from our frighted Children tear their Meat.
We ſtarve and die, while they poſſeſs our Food,
Grow Sleek with Eaſe, and Fat with Spoil and Blood.
Villains diſhonour *Virgins* in our ſight;
And bloody *Ruffians* break our Doors by Night.
To ſeek redreſs, and of our Wrongs complain,
Was but to add Deriſion to our Pain.
How bitter then were ſad *Britannia*'s Moans,
What deep-fetch'd Sighs were heard, what deadly Groans?
Betray'd and ruin'd by a treacherous Friend,
We ſaw the Error, which we could not mend:
We curſt our Folly, but we curſt too late,
And all that our Miſtake ſhould imitate.
We wiſh'd Ten Thouſand Woes and Plagues might light
On their curſt Heads, who ſhould again invite

Victorious

Victorious Kings, with *Foreign* Arms to bless
Their *Native* Country, and their Wrongs redress;
They'll readily assist your Cause, and fight,
To do, to injur'd *States*, and *Princes*, Right:
But still they keep, what, by their Arms, is won;
Great *Monarchs* conquer for themselves alone.
They want a fair Pretence to seize the Prey;
They come as Friends, but will as Masters stay.
Thus *Albion* far'd, may *Heav'n* her Sons restrain,
From splitting on this fatal Rock again.

In vain we strove to break the servile Yoke,
Our Impotent Attempts new Wrongs provoke.
At last, no greater Evils left to fear,
We took fresh *Hope*, and Courage from Despair:
Fury from Ruine sprung rag'd in our Veins,
And *Death*'s seem'd lighter, than the *Saxon* Chains.
Each free-born *Briton* thought the Choice more brave,
To die their *Victim*, than to live their Slave.
We that could ne'er the *Tyrant*'s Yoke endure,
Boyl with Revenge, now Slaves to Foreign Power.
Kings *Uter*'s Breast swells with distracting Rage,
Whose wounded Soul, no Language could asswage;
Asham'd his Country's Freedom to out-live,
He takes the Councils, Grief and Fury give.
His *Knights* together call'd attentive wait,
While *Uter* sits on his high Chair of State.
His troubled Looks reveal'd his inward wound,
And Storms of Fury on his Forehead frown'd.

Who thus began; you see what Tides of Woe,
What angry Seas o'er all your Country flow.
Th' insulting *Saxon* claims our Land, and draws
From greater Power, the Justice of his Cause.

Thro'

Thro' all our Towns our Foes triumphant ride,
Wearing their awful Title by their side.
They shed your *Blood*, and helpless *Maids* deflow'r,
Exhaust your *Treasure*, and your *Land* devour.
A faithless Nation, that no Rule of Right,
Reveres as sacred, but superiour Might.
We oft our Fate in bloody Fields have try'd,
But *Heav'n* has Vict'ry to our Arms deny'd.
Egyptian Plagues lay waste our ruin'd Land,
No *Moses* here, holds his controlling Wand.
Humbly invok'd, *Heav'n* will perhaps relent,
And of its fierce, accustom'd Wrath repent.
Perhaps the *Saxons* Crimes with louder Cries,
For greater Vengeance importune the Skies:
Let us howe'er make one strong Effort more,
Our Country's Peace, and Freedom to restore.
We'll take the Field, 'twill gain us greater Fame,
To perish there, than here, with Grief and Shame.
How much my Soul disdains th' Inglorious Chain?
I'll fall with *Honour*, or with *Honour* reign.

 Tumultuous Passions, *Wrath*, *Revenge*, and *Shame*
Invade our Breasts, and our gall'd Souls enflame.
Strait, with one Voice, we all for Arms declare,
And every Breast already feels the War.
Resolv'd to make the vanquish'd *Saxons* fly,
Or in the just and brave Attempt to dy.
With Fury urg'd, we part from *Uter*'s sight,
Resolv'd for Freedom, and our Native Right.
Thro' all our Towns we spread the loud Alarm,
And animated all our Men to Arm;
To vindicate their ravish'd Country's Cause,
To banish Foreign *Gods*, and Foreign *Laws*.

'Tis ſtrange, how ſoon the *Britons* Blood was fir'd,
What Life and Hope their drooping Hearts inſpir'd.
They ſaw fair *Liberty* extended lie,
The *Saxon* Whips and Torments lying by:
They view her ſquallid Face, exhauſted Veins,
And beauteous Limbs eat in with ruſty Chains.
They heard her mournful Groans, and piercing Cries,
Her interrupted Sobs, and dying Sighs.
They ſaw from gaping Wounds, the guſhing Blood
Enrich the Pavement, with a noble Flood.
While Pity, Mercy, Hope in Sorrow drown'd,
To finiſh the ſad Scene, ſtood weeping round.
The *Britons* rave, reſolving her Defence,
And vow her Reſcue at their Blood's expence.
In *Albion* this fair Emp'reſs ſtill obey'd,
An unconteſted Scepter ever ſway'd.
As univerſal Soul the Life diffus'd,
And Warmth to all the heaving Maſs infus'd:
She ever gave to all true *Britons* Hearts
More Vigour, than their own warm Blood imparts.
'Tis quick'ning *Liberty*, that gives us Breath,
Her Abſence more, than that of *Life*, is *Death*.
Such love to Liberty the *Britons* ſhow,
Such were her Charms, and may they ſtill be ſo.
May never *Briton*, ceaſing to be Brave,
Submit his Neck, content to be a Slave:
May thoſe be doubly curſt, that would betray
Their Country's Freedom, to a Foreign Sway.

Our Men enrag'd, in numerous Bodies meet,
Arm, Arm, was heard the Cry in every Street.
The *Plowman* haſtens to a nobler Toil,
Unyokes his *Ox*, and leaves untill'd the Soil.

Abandons all his Hopes, and ruſtick Care,
Lays down his *Goad*, and ſhakes the warlike *Spear*.
The *Tradeſman* quits his *Shop*, and takes the *Field*,
And makes his thirſt of *Gain*, to thirſt of *Honour* yield.
Arm'd *Tenants* crowd about their valiant *Lords*,
And full of Courage, wave their threatning Swords.
Near *Sorbiodunum*'s ſtately Walls, a Town
For Strength and Beauty, of the firſt Renown;
Whoſe ſpacious Plains rich Seas of waving *Corn*,
And lowing *Herds*, and woolly *Flocks* adorn;
Our Univerſal Rendezvous was ſet,
Where all our Squadrons, and Battalions met.

Mean time the Cautious *Saxon* was alarm'd,
And to diſpel the gathering Tempeſt, arm'd.
Octa the famous *Hengiſt*'s Son, a bold
And warlike Prince, did then the Scepter hold.
Hengiſt that did the firſt our Land invade,
And brought to *Albion* his deſtructive Aid.
The Fifth from mighty *Odin*, whoſe great Name,
Had tir'd the flaggy Wings of weary Fame.
The Stock, from which a Race Illuſtrious ſprings
Of numerous Hero's, and Victorious Kings.
That founded *Empires*, and that living led
Their Conquering *Armies*, and their *God*, when dead.
They ſoon the Hills by their long Marches gain,
And with their Troops o'erſpread the ſpacious Plain.
We with their haſty March alarm'd, prepare
To guard our Camp, and wait th' approaching War.
Our Parties now in rude Rencounters, try'd
Their Courage, ſtill th' advantage on our ſide.
Th' advancing Hoſt at laſt appear'd in ſight,
But Toil and wearing Day, deferr'd the Fight.

Now

Now *Night* advancing, draws her Sable Train
Along the Air, and shades th' *Etherial* Plain.
King *Uter* with his Lords in Council sate,
Things of th' important Juncture to debate.
Where Measures were concerted to oppose
With warlike Arts, and Force, th' impending Foes.
Their *Provinces* the great Commanders share,
And from the Council to their Posts repair:
Where they their Troops dispose, and Orders give,
How the Invading *Saxon* to receive.
Encamp'd we lay on advantageous Ground,
With strong Entrenchments, and high Works around.
Our chearful Troops great Joy and Courage show,
And from the Works defie the powerful Foe.
All things dispos'd with Military Care,
We wait in Arms, th' approach of *Day* and *War*.

Now did the Morn disclose her smiling Ray,
And from the *East* let forth th' important Day.
To bloody Labour all things did invite,
And sounding *Trumpets* Martial Heat excite.
Heav'n's starry Roof resounds with warlike Noise,
With *Horses* Thunder, and their *Riders* Voice.
The *Saxons* and the *Britons* stand prepar'd,
Those, to attack, and these, their Posts to guard.
King *Octa* leads his numerous Army on,
And at their Head in dazling Armour shone.
Drawn on the Right our rang'd Battalions stood,
Our Left a River guards, the Rear, a Wood.
Octa here makes his warlike Columns halt,
Detaching *Horsa* to begin th' Assault:
Whose chosen Troops a furious Onset make,
With no less Brav'ry, ours sustain'd th' Attack.

P 2   They

They mount our Works, and our high Ramparts scale,
And with projected Fires our Men assail:
Our Troops unbroken stout Resistance make,
And always forc'd th' invading *Saxon* back.
As when a *Mold* repels th' invading Seas,
Protects the Ships, and gives the Harbour Peace;
The foaming Tempest on high Billows rides,
And Storms with watry Troops, its lofty Sides:
Th' unshaken Structure all their Fury braves,
And stops the Current of th' insulting Waves.
The angry Seas break on th' opposing Shore,
And beaten back with Indignation roar.
No less unmov'd our valiant *Britons* stood,
Against the Insults of the *Saxon* Flood.
Fresh Bodies still pour'd on, their loss supply,
But still Repuls'd, they from our Trenches fly.
Enrag'd, about our Lines King *Octa* flew,
To find where best he might th' Assault renew:
To see what place lay most expos'd, and where
Our Troops did on the Works but thin appear.
As when a *Wolf*, pinch'd by Nocturnal Cold,
And Hunger-starv'd, scours round the lofty Fold;
He licks his rabid Jaws, and seems possest
Already of his Prey, and bloody Feast:
He offers oft to enter, while the *Lambs*
Affrighted, tremble round their bleating Dams.
So *Octa* thirsts for Blood, and scouring round,
Surveys our Lines, and well observes the Ground.
Now with fresh Rage his Troops our Walls ascend,
Which we with Show'rs of Darts and Stones defend.
What *Shouts*, what noise of *Arms* the Air confound?
What *Ruine*, what slain *Heaps* deform the Ground?
The Earth grows slipp'ry all distain'd with Blood,
Which fills the Ditches with a Crimson Flood.

The

Book IV.   *Prince* Arthur.   109

The *Dead* make Bulwarks, which the Living climb,
That in the Air, rife, like our Walls, fublime.
O'erpower'd and weaken'd by the Men they loft,
And faint with Toil, the *Britons* quit their Poft.
Thrice the invading *Saxon* forc'd our Lines,
And to their Arms, thrice Victory inclines.
The valiant *Uter* that had ftill withftood
Their fierceft Troops, all fmear'd with Duft and Blood;
Who ftill to Pofts of greateft danger flew,
And with unerring Arms their Squadrons flew:
Who fpread frefh Life and Vigour where he came,
And in our Breafts renew'd the Martial Flame.
For where we faw his fhining Arms appear,
Our Men reviv'd, and ftraight forgot to fear;
Obferving his diforder'd Troops retir'd,
His boiling Soul diftracting Paffion fir'd.
He fpurs his furious Steed, and thundring thro'
The thickeft Ranks of the Victorious Foe;
Stay, foolifh *Britons*, ftay, he cries from far,
Save yet your Country, and renew the War:
Come follow me your *King*, I'll lead you on,
And chafe the *Saxons* from the Pofts they've won.
The *Britons* Hearts were touch'd with gen'rous fhame,
Love to their *Country*, and to Martial Fame,
With noble Ardour does their Souls inflame.
Their Leaders Rally all their Troops that fled,
And Charge the Foe, King *Uter* at their Head.
With unrefifted Fury they attack
The *Saxon* Troops, refolv'd to force them back.

Now what *Deftruction*, what wide *Ruine* reign,
What heaps of flaughter'd *Saxons* load the Plain?
Now arm'd with hiffing Death thick *Arrows* flew,
And out-ftretcht Arms as fatal *Javelins* threw.

Then

Then what vast Havock did the *Sword* employ?
What Troops did *Uter's* single Hand destroy?
What sever'd *Limbs* lay scatter'd on the Ground,
What Streams of Blood gush from each ghastly Wound,
What *Shields* and *Spears* in the red Deluge drown'd?

Here first brave *Arthur* did his Courage prove,
His Age then fitter for the Field of Love.
God-like his *Face*, and God-like was his *Mind*,
To virtuous Deeds, and warlike Games inclin'd.
The Down of Manhood on his Face appears,
And blooming Beauty grac'd his youthful years:
Yet *Wise* and *Manly*, far beyond his Age;
His early Deeds the Hero did presage.
Till now the Woods and Forests were his Joy,
Where he the Savage-kind strove to destroy,
That did the Herds, and bleating Flocks annoy.
He chas'd the *Fox*, the rav'nous *Wolf* and *Bear*,
His Country's *Pest*, dy'd by his fatal *Spear*.
The People blest him, as a Saviour sent,
And thought kind *Heav'n*, some great *Deliv'rer* meant.
He ne'er before had brac'd the *Helmet* on,
Nor in the Field in polish'd *Armour* shone.
His *Sword* had ne'er been stain'd with humane Gore,
Nor had he grip'd the *Shield*, or *Gauntlet* wore.
His Country's Cause, and Military Fame,
Invite the Youth to chase a nobler Game.
No more his Thoughts his rural Sports pursue,
Tyrants and savage *Men* he'll now subdue.
For warlike Toil he leaves the gameful Wood,
And flesht his Courage first in *Saxon* Blood.
The greatest Captains the brave Youth esteem'd,
He fought like *Mars*, though *Mercury* he seem'd.

Like

Book IV.   *Prince* Arthur   111

Like some fair *Cherub*, or the *Beamy* God,
He wav'd his flaming Sword, and thro' their squadrons rode.
His youthful Veins Heroick Ardor fir'd,
And more than humane Force his Breast inspir'd:
For the great *Deeds* his fatal Arms atchiev'd,
Were by th' amaz'd Spectators scarce believ'd.

At last amidst the Foe advanc'd too far,
Alone he long sustain'd th' unequal War.
Surrounding Throngs the fainting Youth opprest,
And Showers of Death flew pointed at his Breast:
His weary Arm supports his *Shield* with Pain,
And his bruis'd *Armour* Streams of Blood distain.
Here the young Hero had been crush'd, and all
Our Hopes and Joy had perish'd in his Fall;
Had not brave *Malgo* a *Dimetian* Chief,
Forc'd the thick Foe, and flown to his relief.
Then, when the warlike Youth was most distrest,
And *Elfrick*'s Sword, was falling on his Crest
With dreadful Sway; *Malgo* its Fury broke,
And on his Shield receiv'd the mighty Stroke.
The Prince thus guarded from the fatal Blow,
Bold *Malgo*'s Spear transfixt th' audacious Foe.
Groveling in Death he murmur'd on the Ground,
And pour'd his Life out, from his gaping Wound.

Here *Vortipor* advancing did attack
Their plying Troops, and forc'd the *Saxon* back:
While *Octa*'s wavering Men began to yield,
And to pursuing *Uter* quit the Field.
As when a *Lyon*, that with Fury ran
To seize by Night, some weary Caravan,
That lay encampt on an *Arabian* wild,
Repuls'd by Fires, and of his Prey beguil'd;

With

With hideous Roar he raves at his Defeat,
Oft stands, looks back, and makes a sowre Retreat.
King *Octa*'s Soul like Indignation fir'd,
That raving, with his vanquish'd Men retir'd.
But, oh, how soon was this serener Day
By Clouds, and rising Tempests chas'd away?
How short a space could we our Conquests boast?
How soon were all our Hopes of *Freedom* lost?

Won by the potent Charms of *Saxon* Gold,
Carvil his Prince, and Native Country sold.
He in indulgent *Uter*'s Bosom lay,
And did the Secrets of his Breast betray.
He on his Conduct, and his Faith rely'd,
In Peace and War alike his treach'rous Guide.
He held the most important Trusts of State,
Nor could his Treasons *Uter*'s Love abate.
Unhappy Prince, that still his Foes believ'd,
Only by Ruine to be undecciv'd!
To Friends ingrate, his Foes he entertain'd,
Thus lost the one, but not the other gain'd.
Wisely undone, he knew his Friends to late,
By his own Prudence manag'd to his Fate.
Our Prayers and Warnings tir'd his Ears in vain,
Perfidious Councils only could obtain:
Rough *Truth*, and loyal *Bluntness* gall'd his Ear,
That only soft, melodious Sounds could bear.
His firm and loyal Friends, tho' hardly us'd,
Look'd on enrag'd, to see their Prince abus'd.
Tho' some grown cold, ceas'd to lament his Fate,
For Will and Choice, Compassion still abate.
Pity a Prince whose Virtues shone so bright,
Should let so dark a Cloud obscure their Light!

Book IV.   *Prince* Arthur.   113

To him and us this Weakness fatal prov'd,
That Men suspected were imploy'd and lov'd.
So *Carvil* was:
Who labour'd after *Octa*'s late Retreat,
To more than balance his, with our Defeat.
The Traytor during all the bloody Day,
Found not the Means, our Army to betray.
But when the *Sun* drew off his radiant Train,
And left the Empress of the Night to reign:
Then *Carvil* open'd his black Scene of Guilt,
Wherein such Seas of *British* Blood were spilt.
He by confiding Hands to *Octa* sent,
To let the *Saxon* know his dire intent,
To give him Entrance to our Camp by Night,
Whither his Arms he did with speed invite.
Octa, whose Arts and purchas'd Treasons won,
More Towns and Battels, than his Sword had done:
So fair a Season offer'd, not delay'd,
But straightway march'd our Army to invade.
Carvil mean time his Creatures had prepar'd,
To yield the Posts, their Duty was to guard.

    Revolving *Cynthia* with her doubtful Light,
Had now o'erpass'd the Noon of wearing Night:
When *Octa*'s chosen Troops approach'd the Gate,
Where to admit their Arms the Traytors wait.
The furious *Saxon* straight our Camp invades,
Beneath the Covert of the silent Shades:
Their unexpected Arms our Men assail,
Dissolv'd in Sleep, and wearied with their Toil.
What Carnage now the raging *Saxons* make,
Our Camp converted to a bloody Lake.
They first the brave *Dunwalio* resting found,
His *Cuirass*, *Helm*, and *Javelin* lying round,
And with their *Spears* transfixt him on the Ground.

Q   His

His generous Soul flew upwards with Disdain,
To be massacred, not in Battel slain.
Moriffo next with clatt'ring Swords alarm'd,
Wak'd with the Noise, but naked and unarm'd;
His Side pierc'd thro' by *Horsa*'s Javelin, fell,
Enrag'd he should his Life, so cheaply sell.
Then *Offa*'s Spear pierc'd *Capor*'s Bosome through,
His Soul to *Heav'n* thro' the wide Passage flew:
Leaving his Body drown'd in purple Gore;
None serv'd his Prince, or lov'd his Country more.
Edwal, a Leader of unblemish'd Fame,
Who from the Banks of fair *Sabrina* came,
Fell by *Morino*'s Spear, and by his Side
Brave *Adomar*, by *Balda*'s Javelin dy'd.
Then *Meirick* in his Breast a fatal Wound
Receiv'd, and lay extended on the Ground.
Next *Catel*, who excell'd in youthful Charms,
Was slain by great *Romondo*'s conqu'ring Arms,
The glitt'ring Steel did thro' his Bowels pass,
The Youth expir'd, and with him *Admel*'s Race.
And now what Slaughter reign'd, what Heaps of Dead,
What Ruine o'er the bloody Camp was spread?

Thro' the brown Shades at last, they found the way
To the *Pavilion*, where King *Uter* lay:
Who soon, awaken'd with the Clamour, rose,
And form'd his Troops th' Invaders to oppose.
Long their unequal Force he did repel,
Till, pierc'd by *Cerdick*'s fatal Spear, he fell.
Urg'd to retire, *Arthur* our Prayer withstood,
Tho' faint with Labour, Wounds, and loss of Blood.
We prest him our remaining Hopes to spare,
And not of *Albion*'s Fortune to despair.

Book IV.   *Prince* Arthur.   115

He does at laſt to our Entreaties yield,
And with reluctant Steps forſakes the Field.
We thro' the Wood retreated, where the ſhade
With *Cynthia*'s Rays, uncertain Twilight made.
When the ſucceeding Day declin'd, we came,
To *Alda*'s Gates, a Port of ancient Fame:
Where we the Night in various Sorrows ſpent,
Now *Uter*, now our Country we lament;
Juſt *Catel*'s now, now great *Dunwallo*'s Fate,
And faithful *Edwal*'s Fall, freſh Grief create.

While our ſad Minds endur'd ſo rude a Storm,
Entring the Room, great *Gabriel*'s God-like Form,
Mild Glory, and *Celeſtial* Day diffus'd,
Advanc'd, he theſe kind words to *Arthur* us'd.
Now *Albion* ſinks beneath the *Saxon* weight,
So *Heav'n* decrees, 'tis ſo ordain'd by Fate:
But after Ten times the revolving Sun,
His crooked Race, has thro' the *Zodiack* run,
The Clouds diſpell'd, propitious *Heav'n* ſhall ſmile,
On *Uter*'s Houſe, and this reviving *Iſle*.
Octa ſhall feel juſt *Heav'n*'s revenging Stroke,
And *Albion*'s Youth ſhall break the *Saxon* Yoke.
Mean time, brave Prince, whom univerſal Love
Attends beneath, and Grace Divine above:
To *Neuſtrian Odar*'s Court with ſpeed repair,
Go, *Albion*'s Hopes, and my great Truſt and Care;
Go, *Albion*'s Hopes with Triumph to return,
And Reſcue thoſe, which ſhall your abſence mourn.
That ſaid, his Heav'nly Glory he withdrew,
And to th' immortal Seats, of happy Spirits flew.

Now the fair Morn ſmiles with a Purple Ray,
Clearing before the Sun the Eaſtern Way.

Q 2   Whoſe

Whose radiant Train pours from the Gates of Light,
And the new Day does to new Toil invite.
We the Celestial Message to obey,
On a stout Ship, that in the Haven lay
Ready to Sail, embark and haste away.
The Sky serene, a fresh and prosp'rous Gale,
Sprang from the Shore, and swell'd out ev'ry Sail.
Albion's white Cliffs and Towers we quickly lost,
Standing our Course strait to the *Neustrian* Coast:
Where when the Sun twice starting from the East,
Had ran his Race, and reach'd the falling West,
We safe arriv'd at fair *Cartinia*'s Port,
And took our way from thence to *Odar*'s Court.
Odar, a Prince indulgent, valiant, good,
Ally'd to *Uter* by the Mother's Blood,
The barb'rous *Goths* Incursions, then withstood.
His beauteous Queen, with Joy the Prince receiv'd,
Her Words our Grief, her Gifts our Wants reliev'd.
Here we to ease our troubled Minds remain'd,
Till *Arthur* perfect Strength and Vigour gain'd:
Then taking leave, we straight direct our way
Unto the Camp, where *Odar*'s Forces lay.

And as we pass'd to mitigate our Grief,
And to our Woes to give Divine Relief,
From his blest Tongue such *Heav'nly* Language flows,
As did the Greatness of his Mind disclose.
We thought some God-like *Cherub* to us spoke,
When from his Lips these high Expressions broke.
Heav'n's Off-spring, with Divine Contentment blest,
Enjoy the Empire of a guiltless Breast.
Tho' spoil'd by prosp'rous Robbers, still they find,
The large Possessions of a peaceful Mind.

Content

Book IV.   *Prince* Arthur.   117

Content alone can all their wrongs redress,
Content, that other name for *Happiness*.
Free from Desire, they are as free from Want,
And from the Cares, that envy'd Greatness haunt.
'Tis equal, if our Fortunes should augment,
And stretch themselves to the same vast Extent
With our Desires, or those Desires abate,
Shrink, and contract themselves, to fit our State.
Pois'd on their own unshaken Base they view,
All the Vicissitudes, that Time can shew.
They, like tall Mountains, are advanc'd so high,
That the low Clouds do all beneath them fly.
Hence while loud Storms inferiour Seats molest,
They undisturb'd, enjoy soft Peace and Rest.
These Men that suit their Wishes to their State,
And, pleas'd still with themselves, enjoy their Fate:
Whose modest *Passions Reason*'s Nod obey,
Are greater *Kings*, than those who Scepters sway.
They can the Triumphs of a Court despise,
And the rich Toys, that charm deluded Eyes.
They rather chuse to tame their Thirst, than have
All the Supplies their Feaverish Drought can crave.
Desires for *Freedom* first make humble Suit,
And modestly demand th' unlawful Fruit :
But when set loose, they know not where to stay,
But lawless thro' the World's Dominions stray.
So subterranean *Vapours*, that contain'd
In some close *Cavern*, are with Ease restrain'd;
When once releas'd, ungovernable grow,
And prove fierce Storms, which no Resistance know.
Th' unhappy Man, slave to his wild Desire,
By feeding it, foments the raging Fire.
His Gains augment his unextinguish'd Thirst,
With Plenty *Poor*, and with Abundance *Curst*.

But

But greater Minds, which can themselves subdue,
Preserve their Peace, and still their Joys renew.
They never by a Vile, or Impious Course,
Protect their Wealth from rising Tempests force.
They face the Storm, and stand its fiercest Shocks,
Bold as the Winds, unshaken as the Rocks.
No Tempest that invades th' ambitious Breast,
Can the calm Region of their Mind molest.
So Winds, which Rivulets disturb, will play
In harmless Breezes, on the wider Sea.

Sowre *Discontent*, that quarrels with our Fate,
May give fresh smart, but not the old abate.
Envenom'd with its Sting, each harmless loss,
Grows wondrous sharp, and proves a deadly cross.
Th' uneasie *Passion*'s disingenious Wit
The *Ill* reveals, but hides the *Benefit*.
It makes a Toy press with prodigious weight,
And swells a Mole-hill, to a Mountain's height.
So melancholy Men lie down, and groan,
Prest with the Burden of themselves alone.
Crusht with Phantastick Mountains, they despair,
Their Heads are grown vast Globes too big to bear.
A little Spark becomes a raging Flame,
And each weak Blast, a Storm too fierce to tame.
So peevish is the quarrelsome Disease,
No prosp'rous Fortune can procure it Ease.
Their Breasts are ne'er from inbred Tempests free,
Restless as Winds, and troubled as the Sea:
The Pleasure now they seek would bring Content;
But when enjoy'd, 'twas somewhat else, they meant:
Some absent *Happiness* they still pursue,
Dislike the present Good, and long for New.

The

Book IV.   *Prince* Arthur   119

The Man now thinks he sees his Blifs, and flies
With greedy Arms to grasp the gaudy Prize;
But then, enquiring what his Hopes have won,
Vain Man, he finds the cheating Shadow gone.
Oft does the fair *Illusion* by him stand,
But when pursu'd, gives back, and mocks his Hand.
Sometimes he sees the beck'ning *Phantome* here,
Which, when he follows, does elsewhere appear.
The Wretch, though tantaliz'd, and always crost,
Yet still pursues, though still that Labour's lost.
The God-like *Arthur* with such pious Words,
Divine Instruction, and *Delight* affords.

And while his Language, with a Heav'nly Flame
Thus warm'd our Breasts, to *Odar*'s Camp we came;
Where to the *Neustrian* King the Prince addrest,
Who all the highest Signs of Love exprest.
The Royal *Exile* he embrac'd with Tears,
And by these tender words himself endears.
King *Uter*'s Fall, your loss, and *Albion*'s Fate,
Wound me with Grief too mighty to relate.
Long to Misfortunes, and great Wrongs inur'd,
I pity those that have like Ills endur'd.
You are a Stranger here, but not your Name,
Your early Worth is told aloud by Fame.
Arthur's preserv'd to be the *Saxons* dread,
And rear opprest *Britannia*'s drooping Head.
While you are safe, *Britannia* must revive,
And *Uter* still in valiant *Arthur* live:
While you survive, King *Octa*'s Fears remain,
And *Albion* hopes to break her pond'rous Chain.
Hero's are for Heroick Deeds design'd,
And noble Work, attends a noble Mind.

Mean

Mean time, while here your Choice is to refide,
No Succours, no fupplies fhall be deny'd.
And if your *Britons*, banifh'd from their home,
Drawn by their Prince's Fame, fhall hither come;
Briton and *Neuftrian* fhall like Treatment find,
I'll be to both, without diftinction, kind:
And when mild Days fhall your Return invite,
My Arms fhall Aid you, to affert your Right.

    The Prince reply'd:
Divine Compaffion melts your Royal Breaft,
And makes your Bounty flow on all diftreft.
Like *Heav'n*, you Succours to th' Afflicted grant,
Comfort their Sorrows, and fupply their Want:
You crufh Oppreffors, to th' Oppreft are kind,
Such gen'rous Deeds reveal a God-like Mind.
O'er *Uter*'s Houfe the *Saxon* Power prevails,
And fad *Britannia* her dire Fate bewails.
The World's fupream *Director* fo ordains,
Hence in my Soul no murmuring Paffion reigns.
Pleas'd or *Contented*, ftill I meet my Fate,
Would not be *Impious*, though Unfortunate.
Your gen'rous Offer of Protection here,
With fuch engaging Language, fuch an Air,
As Love and Friendfhip feek out to endear;
Perfwade, that here my Refuge is defign'd,
Till *Albion* grows more Juft, and *Heav'n* more Kind.
Here your Example fhall my Mind prepare,
For all the high Concerns of *Peace* and *War*.
Till *Albion* call us back, I'll here remain,
And in your Service fhall grow fit to Reign.
Here in the Camp the pious *Briton* ftaid,
To whom the *Neuftrian* Chiefs great Honour paid.

Book IV.   *Prince* Arthur.   121

For his high Merit could not be conceal'd
His valiant Deeds the Hero soon reveal'd.
Loud Fame his God-like Virtues did proclaim,
And either Camp resounds with *Arthur*'s Name.
He still the Posts of highest Danger sought,
And Death and Vict'ry follow'd, where he fought.
When he advanc'd, the *Goths* unnumber'd Swarms
Fled from the Terror of his fatal Arms.
Like Love and Wonder *Camp* and *Court* express,
That did the Hero, this the Saint confess.
His Sword still won fresh *Laurels* in the Field,
And to his *Virtues* ev'n Court-*Vices* yield:
And 'tis more easie to reduce a Fort,
Or win a Battel, than reform a Court.
He the fixt Mounds of trembling *Europe* stood,
And still repell'd the *Goths* impetuous Flood.
When he appear'd, their Men, tho' fierce and bold,
Grow chill with Fear, as when at home with Cold.
Thro' the admiring World his Fame was spread,
The Christian's Joy, and barb'rous Nations Dread.
Where gagg'd with Ice, the Waves no longer roar,
But with stiff Arms embrace the silent Shoar:
Where naked Hills in frozen Armour stand,
Where raging *Sirius* fries the thirsty Land,
And rich *Pactolus* rolls his golden Sand;
Thither his Triumphs and Illustrious Name,
His gen'rous Deeds, and loud Applauses came.
His wondrous Virtues, wondrous Love engage,
That reach'd Perfection, long before his Age.
Odar embrac'd him, as an Angel sent
To guard his Throne, and threaten'd Fall prevent.
He own'd his bright Example did support,
Th' esteem of Virtue in the *Neustrian* Court.

R   Their

Their Peace at home proceeded from his Care,
And from his Courage their Succefs in War.
When we, our hopes of finking *Albion* loft,
Made by Divine Command the *Neuftrian* Coaft;
The *Gothick* Arms that Kingdom had o'er-run,
Surpriz'd their Forts, and faireft Cities won.
All Banks born down, fo high the Deluge rofe,
Before King *Odar* could its Courfe oppofe.
'Twas then the young Deliv'rer *Arthur* came,
To drive the *Goths*, and win immortal Fame.
He foon reduc'd the Cities, and reftor'd
A peaceful Country, to its peaceful Lord.

Mean time the *Britifh* Knights oppreft at home,
Drawn by his Fame, to find a Leader come.
So thick they Land, our Troops were numerous grown,
And *Arthur* led an army of his own.
Ten times the Sun had pafs'd his oblique way,
By turns contracting, and increafing Way,
Darting to either Pole a warmer Ray:
And now the *Britifh* Lords, who though oppreft,
The *Weftern* Region of their Ifle poffeft:
Whither retreating, they remain'd fecure,
And from their Hills defy'd the *Saxon* Power:
Encourag'd by his war-like Fame, invite
The Valiant *Arthur* to affert his Right.
To make a bold Defcent upon their Coaft,
And win the Regions back that *Uter* loft.

Ten chofen Orators were ftraight difpatcht,
The chief whofe charming Tongue was never matcht,
Was the great *Tylon*, whofe Immortal Worth,
Raifes to Heav'n the Ifle that gave him Birth.

A

A sacred Man, a venerable Priest,
Who never spake, and Admiration mist.
Of *Good* and *Kind* he the just Standard seem'd,
Dear to the *Best*, and by the Worst esteem'd.
A gen'rous Love diffus'd to Humane Kind,
Divine Compassion, *Mercy* unconfin'd,
Still reign'd Triumphant in his God-like *Mind*.
Greatness and *Modesty* their Wars compose,
Between them here a perfect Friendship grows.
His Wit, his Judgment, Learning, equal Rise,
Divinely Humble, yet Divinely Wise.
He seem'd Express on *Heav'n's* high *Errand* sent,
As *Moses* Meek, as *Aaron* Eloquent.
Nectar Divine flows from his *Heav'nly* Tongue,
And on his Lips charming *Perswasion* hung.
When he the sacred *Oracles* reveal'd,
Our ravish'd Souls in blest Enchantments held,
Seem'd lost in Transports of *Immortal* Bliss,
No simple Man could ever speak like this.
Arm'd with Celestial Fire his sacred Darts
Glide thro' our *Breasts*, and melt our yielding *Hearts*.
So Southern Breezes, and the Spring's mild Ray,
Unbind the *Glebe*, and thaw the Frozen Clay.
He triumph'd o'er our *Souls*, and at his Will
Bid this touch'd *Passion* rise, and that be still.
Wolves, *Tygers*, grizly *Lyons* did admire,
As *Poets* feign, the famous *Orphean* Lyre:
Charm'd with sweet *Tylon's* Voice, a Kind more wild,
More fierce and savage, grow divinely Mild.
Lord of our *Passions* he with wondrous Art,
Can strike the secret movements of our *Heart*;
Release our *Souls*, and make them soar above,
Wing'd with Divine *Desires*, and Flames of *Heav'nly Love*.

He still convey'd sublime, *seraphick* Sense,
In unaffected Strains of *Eloquence*.
Easie and wonderful is all he says,
Does both Delight, and Admiration raise.
His pious Soul did in sad Accents mourn
Britannia's Chains, and *Pagan* Gods return:
But hop'd, kind *Heav'n* would free, by *Arthur*'s Hand
Of barb'rous *Laws*, and *Gods*, th' afflicted Land.
With the great *Tylon* young *Pollander* went,
Fam'd for his Valour, and of high Descent:
With these wise *Galbut* and *Mordennan* joyn,
Whose Virtues vye with their Illustrious Line.
Valiant *Giralden* worn with War and Age,
Does in th' Important Embassy engage.
Gisan was added, a *Dobunian* Knight,
Bold in the *Senate*, and as Brave in Fight.
Hobar, Manfellan, Cadel, Milo, skill'd
In Arms and *Eloquence*, the number fill'd.
Such *Orators* they chose, fit to excite
The Pious *Arthur*, and his Arms invite.

 Thus *Tylon* to the Pious Prince addrest,
And found the Passage open to his Breast:
Britannia crush'd beneath the *Saxon* Yoke,
Does with her mournful Prayer your Arms invoke.
Enslav'd by Foreign Power, Distrest, Undone,
She sues for Aid to you, her valiant Son,
And hopes for Succour from your Sword alone.
Octa all Right, and ancient *Law* subverts,
And uncontroll'd Tyrannick *Power* asserts.
His Lawless Will grasps Arbitrary Sway,
And *British* Slaves, without Reserve, Obey.
The sacred Bounds and Lines, which *Right* and *Law*,
Round all those just and happy Kingdoms draw;
          Which

Which from the Waste of Tyranny they gain,
Where Uproar, Rage, and wild Confusion reign,
These broken down, *Octa* does open lay,
And throw the goodly *Island* up a Prey
To Furies, which in lawless Kingdoms stray.
Britannia by the Conqu'ror ravish'd first,
Then giv'n to Priests, and Soldiers raging Lust:
Wretched *Britannia*, sunk in deep Despair,
Beats her white Breasts, and tears her golden Hair.
Dying with Anger, Shame and Grief, she lies,
And Floods of Tears gush from her beauteous Eyes;
Which swell the silver Tide of mournful *Thames*,
And grieve old Ocean with the troubled Streams.
Hear, pious Prince, how to the *Neustrian* Shoar,
Complaining Waves roll the sad Treasure o'er:
How murmuring Winds waft o'er *Britannia*'s Sighs,
Can *Arthur* disregard his Country's Cries?
With words like these, and such a moving Art
As can't be told, he touch'd the Prince's Heart.
With so much Life, he spake sad *Albion*'s Moans,
We thought we felt her smart, and heard her Groans.
Nor did the Pious Prince their Prayer oppose,
But soon resolv'd to ease *Britannia*'s Woes.
To *Odar* he reveal'd his high Intent,
Who *Ships*, and *Men*, and *Arms* rejoycing lent:
Supplying all things our Descent requir'd,
And heaping Gifts, more than our selves desir'd.
Our *Ships* prepar'd, with chearful Zeal and Care,
We went on Board, and soon embark'd the War.
Our Anchors weigh'd, and Topsails loos'd, a Gale
Sprang up, and swell'd the Womb of every Sail.
Old *Ocean* pleas'd our bounding Vessels laves,
Which with sharp Keels cut thro' the foaming Waves.

The

Th' aftonifh'd *Saxons* fee, and fear from far,
The long Succeffion of the Sailing War.
They fpread thro' all the *Ifle* the loud Alarm,
And trembling *Octa* haftes his Men to Arm.
We Sail'd not long before the Sea ran high,
And gathering Clouds deform'd the lowring Sky:
The fearful Storm arofe, wherein we loft
Th' extinguifh'd Day, and on the Billows toft,
We drove, till forc'd upon th' *Armoric* Coaft.
He ceas'd, and now the Shades of wearing Night,
Did the pleas'd Audience to their Reft invite.

Prince Arthur.

BOOK V.

Ovely *Aurora* makes a mild Essay
With glimm'ring Dawn, to introduce the Day.
Her rosie Steps the *Sun* pursues, and spreads
His smiling Glories on the Mountains Heads.
The Princes rose, and *Hoel* thus exprest
His friendly Passion, to his Royal Guest.
Your Virtues shew you are by Heav'n design'd,
A great *Deliv'rer* of opprest Mankind.
You give to Realms with Wars molested, Peace,
And from their Chains tormented Slaves release.
Fair *Liberty*'s, and blest *Religion*'s Cause,
Reviving Hopes from your Protection draws.
Your prosp'rous Arms invading Plagues repel,
And monstrous *Gods*, and monstrous *Tyrants* quell.
King *Odar*'s Realm and mine you save, in his
You settle Peace, and Truth Divine in this.
And now Compassion arms your valiant Hand,
To free from barb'rous Rage, your native Land.
To vanquish *Pagan* Darkness, and display
Immortal Light, and pure *Etherial* Day.
My self will here abide, and Succours lend,
O'er all the Realm *Christ*'s Empire to extend:
Conan my Son shall on your Triumphs wait,
And when return'd, your glorious Deeds relate.

I'll

I'll now command that with inceſſant Care,
My Men aſſiſt, your Loſſes to repair.
Then I'll conduct you to the *Druids* Grove,
Which Men of Heav'nly Contemplation love.
Where ſolemn Walks and awful Shade invite
Compos'd Devotion, and Divine Delight,
Exclude the Sun's, to let in purer Light.
There with your pious Converſation bleſt,
New light will fill my Mind, new Joy my Breaſt.
The Orders giv'n the *Navy*'s Wants *requir'd*,
The Princes to the *Druids* Grove retir'd:
Where *Arthur*'s Language did the King inſpire,
With Holy Tranſports, and Seraphick Fire.

Mean time th' *Armoricans* and *Britons* meet,
All zealous to Equip the ſhatter'd Fleet:
Part to the *Groves* and woody *Hills* repair,
And with loud Labour fill the echoing Air.
Axes high rais'd by brawny Arms, deſcend
With mighty Sway, and make the *Foreſt* bend.
The Mountains murmur, and the nodding *Oaks*,
Groan with their Wounds, from thick redoubled Strokes.
The falling Trees deſert the neighb'ring Sky,
Where now the Clouds may unmoleſted fly.
A ſhady Harveſt lies diſperſt around,
And lofty Ruine loads th' encumber'd Ground.
Part the hewn Trees draw down with wondrous Toil,
T' enrich the Ocean with the Mountains Spoil.
So faſt they came, and in ſuch Order ſtood,
As th' *Orphean* Lyre had call'd th' obſequious Wood,
From their fixt Seats, to dance upon the Flood.
Part raiſe the *Maſts*, now to be ſhaken more
With furious Winds, than on their Hills before.

Part

Part shape new Ribs, and with industrious Care,
Ships broken Backs, and ghastly Wounds repair.
Part their bruis'd Sides anoint with unctious Pitch,
Part the carv'd Sterns, with Paint and Gold enrich :
Part Cables twist, part smear'd with Smoak and Sweat,
With vast Cyclopean Strokes huge Anchors beat.
While thus the *Britons* did their Ships repair,
Th' Infernal Prince enrag'd and wreckt with Care,
Swift, as exploded Lightning from the Skies,
A second time to *Lapland* Mountains flies :
Where the rough Monarch's noisy Palace stands,
Whose awful Nod, the raging Winds commands.
To him thus *Lucifer:* Kind Prince, to you
A second time I for Assistance sue.
The cursed Prince that by your high Command,
Your furious Subjects drove on *Hoel*'s Land ;
Aided by *Hoel* does his Fleet repair,
Ready to *Albion* to transport the War.
Let adverse Winds blow on the troubled Main,
Retard their Project, and their Ships detain :
Till *Octa* has prepar'd his Warlike Fleet,
The proud Invader on the Seas to meet.

He ceas'd ; The Emperor of the Winds replies,
When you shall ask what Rebel Power denies :
Your Realms you rule with uncontested Sway,
Your Post is to Command, mine to Obey.
That said, he calls his wandring Subjects home,
Eurus and *Notus* straight obedient come ;
Last, sluggish *Auster*, to his Den with wet
And flabby Wings, does heavily retreat.
To whom their Prince ; Let now your Labours cease,
Indulge your Wings, be reconcil'd to Peace :

S   Close

Close in your Darksome Prisons sleeping lie,
To gain more Breath to blow, more Strength to fly.
Then down their howling Throats black Sops he threw,
Of *Poppies* and cold *Night-shade* made, that grew
On the dark Banks, where *Lethe's*-lazy Deep
Does its black Stores, and drousie Treasure keep,
Rolls its slow Flood, and rocks the nodding Waves asleep.
The strong Enchantments quick Admission find,
And the wild Rout benumming Fetters bind:
They murmur in their sleep, and strive in vain
To spurn away th' unweildy leaden Chain.
Then calling *Boreas*, says, Fly *Boreas*, fly,
Blow o'er the Lands, and on the Billows lie:
Make haste, and to th' *Armoric* Coast repair,
Be thine the spacious Empire of the Air.
Unrivall'd, unmolested Reign alone,
Till all thy Force is spent, and all thy Breath is gone;
No Hostile, windy Powers contest thy Reign,
And uncontroll'd Dominion of the Main.

Scarce had he ended, when up *Boreas* springs,
And thro' the Air spreads out his furious Wings.
He o'er warm Climes diffuses *Northern* Spoils,
And the cold Treasures of the frozen Isles.
With blustring War he frights old Ocean's Court,
Buffets the Waves, and raises Storms in sport.
In vain th' impatient *Britons* spread their Sails,
Loud *Boreas* keeps them back with adverse Gales.
Proud *Lucifer* urg'd with his Rage and Spight,
Back to *Britannia* takes his Airy Flight;
To find the *Saxon* Monarch, and inspire
His trembling Soul with fresh Infernal Fire.

And

Book V.   *Prince* Arthur.   131

And now the Night does her black Throne ascend,
And dusky Shades her silent State attend:
While pale fac'd *Cynthia* with her starry Train,
Dart down their trembling Lustre on the Main.
The weary Lab'rers their stiff Limbs repose,
And Sleep's soft Hand their drowsie Eye-lids close.
All rest enjoy, but *Octa* anxious lay,
Wakeful, and longing for returning Day.
His dreadful Crimes affright his startled Soul,
And in his Breast black Tides of Horrour roll.
Dire Shapes, and staring Ghosts pass threatning by,
And Streaks of Fire across th' Apartment fly.
He hears the Shrieks of those his bloody Hand
Had murder'd, or that dy'd by his Command:
He hears the Widows Sighs, and Orphans Moans,
Himself had made, and tortur'd Pris'ners Groans.
The Grounds of pale Despair he sometimes draws,
From *Arthur's* Valour, and his Righteous Cause.
Sometimes he fears his injur'd Subjects Rage,
Their vengeful Arms, against him will engage;
Then starts, and thinks he hears Prince *Arthur's* Fleet
Is on the Coast, proclaim'd in ev'ry Street.

Then *Lucifer* does *Odin's* Shape assume,
And with Stern Grace enters King *Octa's* Room.
His vig'rous Limbs had dazling Armour on,
And round his Head his polish'd Helmet shone.
His conqu'ring Sword hung down with awful Grace,
And Scars of Honour seam'd his manly Face.
His warlike Hand grip'd his Vulcanian Shield,
With rare Devices pourtray'd on the Field.
With Martial State he strides along the Room,
And shakes at ev'ry Step his lofty Plume.

S 2   Advancing

Advancing to the Bed where *Octa* lay,
He spake: Son *Octa*, from celestial Day,
From the blest Groves, and mild *Elysian* Seats,
Thy Father *Odin* to thy Aid retreats.
To ease thy restless Mind of Anxious Cares,
Support thy Hopes, and dissipate thy Fears.
Stand thou unmov'd at *Arthur*'s proud Alarms,
Conquest attends thine, and thy *Saxons* Arms.
He'll sink beneath the Sea's insulting Wave,
Or landing, find on Shore a surer Grave.
Think on the Spoils and Trophies you have born,
And spreading Laurels on your Temples worn.
Let none that's sprung from my Victorious Race,
At Danger shrink, and my great Stock debase.
Go, haste thy Royal Navy to prepare,
Let *Ships* with *Ships* encounter, *War* with *War*.
On the wide Main th' Invader's Fleet oppose,
Better to meet, than here expect your Foes.
Go chase their scatter'd Navy o'er the Deep,
And thus in Peace, thy envy'd Empire keep.
He ceas'd; and with Majestick Pace retir'd,
And left King *Octa* with fresh Life inspir'd.

Who with the Sun arose, resolv'd to meet
With all his Naval Power, Prince *Arthur*'s Fleet.
He gave Command, the Captains straight resort
To their tall Ships, and leave the wanton Court.
A forward Zeal the busie Sailors shew,
Some mend old Ships, and some equip the new.
With flaming Reeds some their pitch'd Bellies dry,
Some hoist the Yards, and Canvas Wings apply.
Some from its Cradle launch a rocking Hull,
Some at the Cables strain, and howling pull

Vast

Book V.   *Prince* Arthur.   133

Vast Anchors up, some Stores and Arms entomb,
And stow with hidden War the Ship's dark Womb.
The Shores around, and all the Oazy Soil
Resound with Clamour, and the Sailors Toil.
Well Rigg'd and Mann'd, the Ships from ev'ry Port
To their appointed Rendezvous resort.
The Rivers disembogue, besides their Flood,
Into the Seas, a lofty, painted Wood.

And now the Moon, had twice the Silver Field
Of her fair Orb, with borrow'd Glory fill'd:
Since the uneasie *Britons* had remain'd
By adverse Winds, within their Port detain'd.
Boreas that had his Blasts profusely blown,
His Storms all spent, and bleaky Treasures gone,
With tir'd and flaggy Pinions now retreats,
To fetch Recruits from wild *Laplandian* Seats:
Auster does next with milder Blasts prevail,
And for the *Britons* blows a prosperous Gale.
Now each rough Hero of the Ocean stands
On the high Deck, giving Austere Commands.
Prince *Arthur* to Embark approach'd the Shoar,
Where the reposing Seas no longer roar:
But at his Feet obsequious Billows lay,
As Conscious of the Power they must obey.
Then their broad *Backs* subsiding they submit,
Proud to sustain their future Monarch's Fleet.
The lofty Ships on rolling Billows bound,
The Waves in soft Embraces clinging round.
As when the *Trojans*, in the *Mantuan* Song,
From *Africk* Sands, to *Latium* sail'd along:
Old Ocean rose up from his rocky Throne,
A Crystal Scepter, and a reedy Crown

His

His Power confeſt, his dewy Head he rear'd,
Above the Flood, and ſmiling on the Waves appear'd.
New-gather'd Banks of Quickſands he remov'd,
And kindly thro' the Deep, the Navy ſhov'd.
So the calm Ocean ſeem'd with equal care,
On its pleas'd Waves, the *Britiſh* Fleet to bear.
Unweildy *Porpoiſſes* ſpout Seas away,
And friendly *Dolphins* round the Squadrons play.
The floating Caſtles dance upon the Tide,
And on its foaming Ridge Triumphant ride.
In glorious Lines the painted Squadrons move,
As if the Poets Gods laps'd from above,
In gilded Clouds, were dancing on the Seas
In Maſquerade, with the green Deities.

Twice the great Ruler of the Day, had hurl'd
His flaming *Orb*, around th' enlighten'd World:
When at the early Dawning of the Day,
The Navies in each other's Proſpect lay.
The *Saxon* Squadrons cover all the Main,
And with their *Prows* divide the liquid Plain.
Plying to Windward, *Arthur*'s Men prepare
Their Navy, to receive th' advancing War.
Down on their Fleet King *Octa* bravely bore,
Whoſe long-wing'd Navy ſtretcht from Shore to Shore.
Both Fleets in Lines of War ſtood croſs the Deep,
And ready to engage, juſt Order keep.
They hoiſt their bloody Flags on either ſide,
And Death her Jaws does for her Feaſt provide.
Now the ſhrill Trumpets ſprightly Voice, and all
The Harmony of War, to Combate call.
The *Saxon* Sailors with a hideous Cry,
Affright the Deep, and rend the echoing Sky:

The

The barb'rous Yellings and out-rageous Sound
From Rock to Rock, and Shore to Shore rebound.
A furious Fight between the Fleets began,
And bold *Selingbert* first Attacks their Van.
Now bearded Darts, and fatal Javelins fly,
And Balls of Fire hifs thro' th' inlighten'd Sky.
Each on his Foe miffive Destruction pours,
And Death receives, and gives in feather'd Showers.
Thus milder Fate at distance sparing flew,
Till to a closer Fight *Selingbert* flew,
And on his Foe his maffy Grapples threw:
Which clenching fast their pond'rous, griping Claws,
The rude Embrace, both Ships together draws.
The *Saxons* flew on Board with furious Arms,
And on the Decks appear in numerous Swarms.
Vogan enrag'd, did fatal Wounds difpenfe,
With lavifh Hand, and made a brave Defence.
With Battle-Axes, Swords, unweildy Crows,
They clear the Decks of the infulting Foes.
Beat down with ghaftly Wounds, fome gafping lie,
Others their Arms caft down, for Mercy cry.
Into the Waves fome their pale Bodies throw,
And fly from Death above, to Death below.
Down the Ships fides Torrents of *Saxon* Blood,
With unknown Crimfon dye th' aftonifh'd Flood.
Upon the Decks, which flaughter'd Heaps deform,
Enrag'd *Selingbert* pours a fecond Storm,
Which like a Summer's Shower foon difappear'd,
By Valiant *Vogan* and his *Britons* clear'd.
Selingbert thus defeated, boils with Rage,
But forc'd at laft, his Ship to difengage;
He bears away, and quits th' unequal Fight,
Providing for his fafety, by his flight.

Octa mean time his Men for Fight prepares,
And fiercely down on *Arthur*'s Squadron bears.
The spacious sides of his high Ship consum'd
Whole Forests, and whole Mountains Spoils entomb'd.
It self a Fleet a-cross the Billows stood,
Engross'd the Winds, and press'd the lab'ring Flood.
The lofty, gilded Palace shone from far,
Presenting to the Foe a glorious War.
Bold *Octa*, and the Valiant *Arthur* meet,
Which struck a vast Concern thro' either Fleet:
On this important Action seem'd to wait
The *British* Hero's, and *Britannia*'s Fate.
Both sides with Shouts their fatal Weapons fling,
And wing'd with Death thick Showers of Arrows sing.
Unerring Darts in hissing Tempests fly,
And carry swift Destruction thro' the Sky.
Ships rush to Battle with enormous Shocks,
As Tow'rs with Tow'rs encounter'd, Rocks with Rocks.
So in the *Northern* Seas when Storms arise,
High Rocks of Snow, and sailing Hills of Ice
Against each other with a mighty Crash,
Driv'n by the Winds, in rude Rencounters dash.
The Sea afflicted foams, the Waves on high,
Toss'd by th' batt'ring *Islands*, lave the Sky.
The Crystal Towers break with a fearful Crack,
And on the Billows spead their foaming Wreck.
Vast Sheets of rocky Ice, and broken Isles,
Oppress the lab'ring Ocean with their Spoils.
On both sides now they call forth all their Rage,
Resolv'd in closer Combate to engage.
Then Death and Slaughter in sad Triumph reign'd,
And Seas of Blood the slipp'ry Decks distain'd.

Some

Some the Pale Dead into the Ocean heave,
Some in the Ships low Caves the wounded leave.
Prodigious Numbers fell on either Side,
Thin on the Decks they look'd, but thick upon the Tide.
For neither Chief e'er met a greater Foe,
Both wondrous Skill, and wondrous Courage show:
While Vict'ry poising equal Hope and Fear,
With doubtful Wings hung hov'ring in the Air.

 The wise Prince *Arthur*, whilst on Shore equips,
Their use till then unknown, a sort of Ships,
That since the Deeds of that Important Day,
Among lost Arts in deep Oblivion lay:
Till Captains that in after Ages liv'd,
The long forgotten Stratagem reviv'd.
Bitumen, Sulphur, and *Vulcanian* Spoils,
From lab'ring Mountains, and from unctious Soils;
Naphtha and Pitch, with Skill and Labour wrought,
With hidden Stores of Flame the Vessel fraught:
Like rolling Clouds where Lightning's Seeds remain,
Their swelling Wombs a fiery Birth contain.
Arthur so strange a Ship to *Octa* sent,
With such Infernal Treasures in it pent:
Which with its grappling Engines fixt, and fir'd,
The bold Commander to his Friends retir'd.
The Fire with unextinguish'd Rage, consumes,
The Subterranean Wealth the Ship intombs.
Vast sheets of Flame, and Pitchy Clouds arise,
And burning Vomit spouts against the Skies.
Tempests of Fire th' astonish'd Heav'ns annoy,
Fierce, as those Storms, that from their Clouds destroy:
As *Ætna* from its glowing Roots was torn,
And by its own wild Hurricanes, was born

From its old Seat, to float upon the Waves,
With *Vulcan*'s Magazins, and *Cyclops* smoaking Caves
The burning Plague adher'd to *Octa*'s side,
And the scorcht Ribs the hot Contagion fry'd:
The spreading Mischief's growth no Force restrains,
The Plague resisted more severely Reigns.
To the tall Masts the raging Flame aspires,
And neighbour sits to Heav'n's contiguous Fires.
Octa at last his flaming Ship forsakes,
And in stout *Horsa*'s Vessel Refuge takes.
He once more here his Royal Standard Rears,
Where on the Deck undaunted he appears,
With chearful Looks, dissembling inward Fears.
He strives the *Saxons* Courage to excite,
To press the Foe, and still maintain the Fight;
But strives in vain, assisted by the Wind,
The spreading Burnings no Resistance find.
Resistless Flames advance with lawless Power
From Ship to Ship, and thro' the Fleet devour.
Naked, and half-burnt Hulls with hideous Wreck,
Affright the Skies, and fry the Ocean's back:
Scorcht Bodies, broken Masts, and smoaking Beams,
Promiscuous Ruin, float along the Streams.
Deform'd Destruction, and wild Horrour ride
In fearful Pomp, upon the Crimson Tyde.
At last King *Octa*, dreading longer stay,
Commanding all to follow, tows away;
The *Saxon* Captains chearfully obey.

But *Lucifer* enrag'd at this Defeat,
Plots to protect, and cover their Retreat.
Summon'd to his *Pavilion*, straight repair
The *Dæmons*, that infest th' Inferiour Air:

With

With bloated *Fiends*, that in dark Caves abide,
And o'er the Subterranean Damps preside.
Last the slow *Powers* come from their misty Dens,
That rule the *Marshes*, *Lakes*, and stagnant *Fens*:
To whom their Prince, see, how King *Octa* tows
His shatter'd Ships, prest by Victorious Foes.
Go, and protect him from the fierce Pursuit,
And give him time, his Navy to recruit:
Let all your *Damps*, and lazy *Fogs* arise,
And with your sluggish Treasures cloud the Skies;
Let your thick *Mists* repel th' unwelcome Light,
And o'er the Ocean spread a friendly Night.

The humble Powers their haughty Prince obey,
Some from dark Caverns far remote from Day,
From each embowell'd Mount, and hollow Vault,
Crude *Exhalations*, and raw *Vapours* brought.
Some from deep Quagmires, Ponds, and sedgy Moors,
Drive the dull *Reeks*, and shove the *haizy* Stores:
To their appointed Station all repair,
And with their heavy Wings encumber all the Air.
The ponderous *Night*'s impenetrable Steems
Exclude the *Sun*, and choak his brightest Beams.
The hov'ring Clouds the *Saxon* Fleet embrace,
And wondrous Darkness stops the *Briton*'s Chase.
Octa, *Æneas* like, a misty Night
Around him cast, escapes the *Briton*'s Sight.
Now had the Sun diffus'd the early Day,
From his bright Orb, and chas'd the Fogs away:
To their known Shore the *Saxon* Navy flies,
And in their Ports and Rivers safely lies.

Arthur, who while the Shades prevail'd, had lain
Under an easie Sail, upon the Main;

T 2 Discovering

Discovering that the *Saxon* Fleet was lost,
Tack'd, and directly stood for *Albion*'s Coast.
He sail'd not long, before his Joyful Men
Could from the Masts, their native Country ken.
First the *Bolerian* Promontory rears
His Head, and as a lofty Wedge appears,
That down into the Deep, had from the Shore,
Run from *Danmonian* Mines and melted Oar:
Here when the Oazy Shore, by ebbing Tides,
Is naked left, around its glitt'ring Sides,
Pale *Tinny* Oar, and *Copper*'s brighter Vein,
Casts Glimmering Lustre o'er the liquid Plain.
Next they discover the aspiring Hills,
Whose Precious Sides *Metallick* Treasure fills:
In their dark Caves *Cyclopian* Lab'rers sweat,
And their vast Blows the eechoing Hills repeat.
With ghastly Wounds they rend the groaning Earth,
And from its Bowels wrest the massy Birth :
By racking Engines, and redoubled Blows,
She's forced her hidden Riches to disclose.
Under wide *Caldrons*, some whole Forrests pile,
And melt in purging Flames the wealthy Spoil.
Some in their hot *Ætnean* Forges sweat,
And glowing Wedges on huge *Anvils* beat:
Their mighty strokes shake all the bellowing ground,
The neighb'ring Mountains, and the Vales around,
With subterranean Toil and Noise resound.
They pass the crooked Shore, which Fame of old
Enrich'd with pond'rous *Pearl*, and scatter'd *Gold*:
They view the *Rocks* with *Gems* and Treasure blest,
In verdant *Samphire*, and *Eringo* drest.
Danmonian Crows, leaving the Neighb'ring Hills,
In numerous, noisy Flights, their Feet and Bills

With

With Native Crimson dy'd, o'erspread the Sky,
And o'er the Fleet in Ominous Circles fly.
Not far remov'd, it's sides a Mountain shows,
Where winding Shores a spacious *Bay* enclose:
His lofty Head, that flying Clouds invades,
From Shore to Shore the dusky Ocean shades.
Long this wild Seat, as ancient Fame obtain'd,
A fierce *Gigantick* Race of Men maintain'd;
Tall as the Hill, on which the Monsters dwelt,
Whose groaning sides their striding motion felt:
Torn from wild Beasts raw Skins, and grisly Hydes,
A horrid Dress, adorn'd their hideous sides.
Half roasted *Swine* their savage Jaws devour,
That stain their squallid Chins with flowing Gore.
In thorny Dens the outstrecht Monsters ly,
Half eaten Limbs, and mangled Bodies by:
With Rapes and Thefts, and endless Murders cloy'd,
A fearful Plague, the Region they destroy'd.
Weathering the Point with favourable Gales,
Along the Shore the Conquering Navy Sails:
Into the rough *Hibernian* Seas they came,
That howling Monsters, and dire Gulphs defame;
Which to avoid, close to the Shore they keep,
Where fair *Sabrina* to her Parent Deep,
Drawing her silver Train along does glide,
Diluting with fresh Streams the Briny Tyde.
Lovely *Sabrina* that for refluent Tydes,
Fair Cities, verdant Meadows, flow'ry Sides,
For Finn'd Inhabitants; and pleasant Streams,
Yields only to her fairer Sister *Thames*.
Passing these Seas, they view the fertile Soil,
Till'd by *Silurian* Farmers skilful Toil;
Where the vext Sea fair *Clamorgania* laves,
And rolls along the Sand its foaming Waves:

Here

Here *Rhemnius*, gliding by *Carphilli*'s Walls,
Proud of its *Roman* strength, into the Ocean falls.
Then *Ratostibium* from the hilly Lands,
Rolls down its rapid Tyde, and troubled Sands.
Next they descry an Isle of wondrous Fame;
Which the succeeding Ages *Barry* name.
In its high sides that to the Sea appear,
Dreadful to tell, th' astonish'd Saylors hear
Ætnean Labour, where the bellowing Rocks,
Shake with Gigantick Toil, and Thundering Strokes
Of groaning *Smiths*; sometimes a mighty sledge,
On a vast Anvil, beats a flaming wedge:
Now Bellows form'd of vast, capacious Hydes,
All *Boreas* blow from their *Æolian* sides.
Now the resisting Flames and Fiery Store,
By Winds assaulted, in wide Forges roar,
And raging Seas flow down of melted Oar.
Sometimes they hear long Iron Bars remov'd,
And to the sides, huge heaps of Cynders shov'd.
As we advanc'd the Coast in Prospect lay,
Which the *Dimetian* Lords did then obey:
Here th' opening Land invites, with outstretcht Arms,
The troubled Seas, free from the loud Alarms
Of the rough, windy Powers, to take their Ease,
And on its Bosom lye diffus'd in Peace.
The flowing Waters smooth their furrow'd Face,
And gently roll into the Land's Embrace:
To secret *Creeks* the weary Billows creep,
And stretcht on *Oazy* Beds securely sleep.
No happy Land, along th' *European* Coast,
Can such a fair and spacious *Haven* boast.
In this wide Station, the *Dimetians* pride,
The biggest *Ships*, and greatest *Fleets* may ride,
Safe from the Insults of the Winds and Tide.

Two

Two lofty *Caſtles* with their gilded Towers,
Inlighten, and defend the ſubject Shores.
Here the Victorious *Britons* ſafe arrive,
With all the Joy, long-wiſh'd for Harbours give.
In frequent Throngs, the glad *Dimetians* ſtand
Upon the *Coaſt*, thick as th' unnumber'd Sand.
Their Acclamations and loud Shouts rebound,
From trembling Hills, and ſhake the Shores around:
The Ships lay rocking, and their Maſts bend more
With *Britons* Breath, than with the Winds before.
The joyful *Britons* and their Friends debark,
And near the Shore a ſpacious Camp they mark.
The pious Prince at a fair Caſtle ſtaid,
That *Malgo* the *Dimetian* Lord obey'd.

Now her brown Wings the ſilent Night diſplays,
Light ſprinkled o'er with *Cynthia*'s ſilver Rays.
Silence and Darkneſs all to Reſt invite,
And ſleep's ſoft Chains make faſt the Gates of Light.
Prince *Arthur* ſleeps, by Summons from on high,
From trembling Joynts, his active Spirits fly
To the round Palace of th' Immortal Soul,
And thro' the Rooms and dark Apartments roll.
The buſie Crowd fills all the labouring Brain,
Bright Fancy's Work-houſe, where cloſe Cells contain
Of Forms and Images an endleſs Train,
Which thither thro' the waking Senſes glide,
And in fair *Mem'ry*'s Magazine abide.
Compos'd of theſe, light Scenes and Shows appear,
That ſtill employ the reſtleſs Theater.
Divinely mov'd, the Airy Figures take
Their ſeveral Ranks, and this bright Viſion make.
Prince *Arthur*, on a verdant Eminence
Converſing with King *Uter* ſtood, from whence,

He

He views with wondring Eyes, great Lords and States,
Crown'd Heads, Victorious Princes, Potentates,
Heroes and Heroines, a glorious Train,
That in long Order fill'd the subject Plain.
Prince *Arthur* on the Royal Scene intent,
Demands what this August Assembly meant:
For what end thither come, and who they were
That at th' Illustrious *Congress* did appear.

    King *Uter* then reply'd: Know pious Son,
That after various bloody Battels won,
You Beauteous *Ethelina* shall espouse,
The fairest Branch of all King *Octa*'s house.
A *Christian* Princess of a Pagan Line,
Whose Virtues equal with her Beauty shine.
You shall Triumphant mount the *British* Throne,
Which has not yet, so great a Monarch known.
Swell not with Pride, th' Imperial Seat you gain,
Brings envy'd Honour, but unenvy'd Pain.
Your People rule with equal *Laws*, and know
You're happy, when you make your Subjects so.
Let them a Good, Indulgent *Father* find,
Be mercifully *Just*, severely *Kind*.
Let your bright Virtues Imitators draw,
Glorious Examples have more Force, then Law.
Seek not an uncontroll'd and lawless Sway,
Subjects from *Love*, but Slaves from *Fear* obey.
And whom the People fear, they quickly hate,
Which Passions in their Prince the like Create:
Hence mutual Jealousies, and deep Designs,
Hence strong Distrust the mould'ring State disjoyns.
Diffusing good on all Mankind, you'll show
You imitate Heav'n's Government below.

The

Book V.   *Prince* Arthur.   145

The *Benefactor* will most Honour bring,
And the *Deliverer*'s greater than the *King*:
Believe no Foreign hostile Power, can move
Your Throne, supported by your Subjects Love.

The bright Assembly that surrounds the Hill,
And with their Numbers all the Vally fill,
Are *Albion*'s Hero's, who in future days,
Their own, and *Albion*'s Name, to Heav'n shall raise.
The Regal Orders that the rest outshine,
With glittering Crowns, are the Imperial Line,
That after you, on *Albion*'s Throne shall sit,
Their Names in Fate's Eternal Volumes writ.
The Kings that in the foremost Rank appear,
Who frowning and unpleasant Aspects wear;
Whose waning Crowns with faded Lustre shine,
Shall after you succeed, first *Constantine*,
Conanus, and the rest of *British* Line:
These look not with their Native Splendour bright,
But dimly shine, with delegated Light.
Heroick Deeds by great Forefathers done,
Cast all their Glory on them, not their own:
To narrow Bounds their scanty Empire shrinks,
And *Britons* Grandeur, with their Virtue sinks.
At last their Crimes, offended Heav'n provoke,
To crush their Nation with the *Saxon* Yoke.

Here *Arthur* sigh'd, that his degenerate Race,
Should with inglorious Deeds their Stock debase:

When *Uter* cry'd, Observe the *Saxon* Line,
Where mighty Kings the *British* Rank outshine:
Crowns on their Heads, and Scepters in their Hand,
All great in War, and born for high Command.

U   Their

Their Arms the *British* Empire shall Assail,
And aided by the *Britons* Crimes prevail.
This mighty Nation, quickly shall believe
The Christians God, and Heav'nly Light receive.
That's *Ethelbert* the first of *Saxon* Race,
That shall pure Faith, and Truth Divine embrace.
He shall destroy in their own Temples Flames,
Their senseless Gods, of barb'rous, Northern Names:
In vain their Priests on helpless Idols call,
They, and their Groves by the same Axes fall:
Fragments of broken Altars, and the spoil
Of ruin'd Gods, fill all th' applauding Isle.
All shall adore the great mysterious King,
And of his Cross the glorious Triumphs sing.
The Spring of Life gilded with Heav'nly Beams,
Purge guilty Minds, with pure Baptismal Streams.
From hence the Light shall break, which shall dispell
The *Pagan* Shades, that on the *Saxons* dwell.
Proud *Lucifer* subdu'd, flies in despair,
With all th' Infernal Powers about the Air,
That with their broad, extended Wings retreat,
To seek a safe, and unmolested Seat:
To fix on *Scythian* Hills their gloomy Throne,
Or on the Sands fry'd by the burning *Zone*.
As when the *Storks* prepare to change their Clime,
The long-neck'd Nation, in the Air sublime,
Wheeling, and towring up in Circles fly,
And with their cackling Cries disturb the Sky:
In lingring Clouds they hang, and Leisure give,
For all their feather'd People to arrive.
To th' Airy Rendezvous all hast away,
And their known Leaders noisy Call obey;
Then thro' the Heav'ns their trackless Flight they take,
And for new Worlds, their present Seats forsake:

So

Book V.	*Prince* Arthur.	147

So here the Fiends assembled in the Air,
Quit *Albion*'s Soil, and to wild Lands repair.

  Remark that Prince, that in the midst appears,
Seven bright Imperial Diadems he wears;
That's the great *Egbert*, whose heroick Might,
Shall the dismember'd Island reunite:
His Arms shall give him universal Sway,
And all the *Saxons* shall his Power obey.

  See there the great *Northumbrian* Monarch stands,
Edwine his Name that all the Isle commands:
A happy Prince, if his good Angel's Art
Diverts the *Mercian* Ruffian's bloody Dart.
Saxons and *Britons* shall obey his Arms,
Himself, the lovely *Ethelburga* Charms:
Her beauteous Eyes the mighty Monarch fire,
Her Words, his Soul with *Christian* Flames inspire.
Blest *Ethelburga* of unrival'd Worth,
That plants Religion in the barren North.

  See *Alfred* there, all shall his Praises sing,
A pious Souldier, and an humble King.
Hero and *Bard*, able in lofty Verse
His own great Deeds, and Triumphs to reherse.
Obey'd by all his unresisted Arms,
Shall to their Coasts repel the *Danish* Swarms:
Into the Seas swept by his potent Hand,
Those *Northern* Locusts leave th' afflicted Land.
The People his wise Laws shall cultivate,
From their rude Minds, and smooth th' unpolish'd State.
Upon the Verdant Plain, where *Isis* Streams
Hast to th' Embraces of her Sister *Thames*:

U 2   This

This mighty Prince shall a fam'd Empire Found,
Where Learning sits with branching Laurels Crown'd.
Where sacred Arts with all their Letter'd Train,
In lofty Schools shall unmolested Reign:
Banish'd from *Greece* and *Rome*, no safe Retreat
They'll find; till setled in this Peaceful Seat.
Ages to come, this Seat will *Oxford* name,
Of which no Time, or Place, shall bound the Fame.
Remotest Nations shall her Wonders know,
Far as *Great Britain*'s potent Navies go.
Learning, her Native growth, shall Strangers fetch,
And taught by her, their own rude Countries teach:
Th' admiring World shall *Albion* then adore,
Revere her Armies, but her Learning more.
As when the Wisdom of th' Eternal Mind,
Rude *Chaos* labour'd, and the Mass refin'd;
The scatter'd Rays that wander'd in the Air,
Did to the Sun's capacious Orb repair;
The shining Colonies pour'd thick around,
Here fixt, and did a glorious Empire Found:
So here the broken Beams of glimmering Arts,
Assembling all their Light from distant parts,
To make bright *Oxford*'s Luminary stay,
That o'er the World shall spread Celestial Day.

Remark *Elfeda* there, a Martial Dame,
That by her Arms shall win Immortal Fame.
At last the Princes of the *Saxon* Line,
From Heav'nly Love and Purity decline:
Their Christian Virtues, and pure Zeal abate,
And with them sickens their decaying State.
With Christian Names, their Pagan Crimes they keep,
And deaf to Heav'n's loud Threats securely sleep:

Till the fierce *Dane* sent by supream Command,
A vengeful Scourge does on their Borders Land.
The *Saxon*'s Guardian Angels call'd away,
Leave them to hostile Arms, an easie Prey,
Thus Heav'n afflicts a Land, when Impious grown,
And from their Throne pulls haughty Monarchs down.
This dreadful Curse, shall by relenting Heav'n,
Be soon from sad *Britannia*'s Empire driv'n:
The Cruel, slothful *Dane* shall soon decline,
To make way for a nobler *Norman* Line.

That Prince observe, that moves with so much Grace,
Is the great *William* of the *Norman* Race:
A mighty Prince, a Leader Brave, and Wise,
Whose towring Fame shall soar above the Skies.
Heav'n does for him *Britannia*'s Crown design,
From which great Stock, shall branch a numerous Line
Of mighty Princes, that shall Rule this Isle,
Enriching it with Conquer'd Nations Spoil.

The Valiant second *Henry*, see him there,
What Majesty does in his Looks appear?
Through wild *Hibernia* he shall force his way,
And add four Kingdoms to the *British* Sway.

Brave *Richard* see, who from the sacred Coast,
Shall drive the Barb'rous, Unbelieving Host.
In *Gaul* this Monarch's Arms shall be renown'd,
Dreaded in Battel, and with Conquest Crown'd:
Long time in Peace his Crown might be enjoy'd,
Could he the Arrow at *Chaluz* avoid.

Now, Son, your Eye to that brave Warriour turn,
Whose Beams so much the *Norman* Line adorn.
How

How great a Presence, what a Port he bears?
How much a mighty Conq'rour he appears?
That Prince is *Edward*, whose Victorious Arms
Judea save from *Pagan* Foes Alarms.
How he returns thro' the *Trinacrian* Isle,
Thro' high *Parthenope*'s delicious Soil,
Thro' loud Applauses of admiring *Rome*,
Reeking in hostile Blood triumphant home!
The beauteous Person next that Monarch seen,
Is *Eleonora* his Illustrious Queen.
In Storms she's with him on the Ocean tost,
To seek out horrid War on *Asia*'s Coast.
Midst barbarous Arms his Wife, Adviser, Friend,
She his prodigious Labours shall attend.
And when her Lord, so Heav'n permits, shall feel
Within his Veins, the Murd'rer's poison'd Steel:
She to the spreading Plague her Lips applies,
And gives that Ease, which *Asia*'s Balm denies.
Invading Death her healing Kisses charm,
And with new Life the sinking Monarch warm.
No other Prince that in this Age shall reign,
Shall equal Honour to brave *Edward*'s Gain,
But great *Adolphus*, of th' Illustrious Race
Of Heroes, which the House of *Nassau* Grace:
This mighty Prince shall gain th' Imperial Sway,
And wide *Germania* shall his Laws obey.
The God-like Virtues, and Heroick Fire,
That shall the brave *Nassovian* House inspire,
Shall make *Adolphus* shine in this high Sphear,
Preluding to the great Deliverer,
The pious *William*; yonder he's in Sight,
In whom *Nassovian* Blood, and ours unite.

There

There war-like *Edward* ſtands, that with his Hoſt,
Shall croſs the Ocean to the *Gallick* Coaſt:
Where he his Conquering Enſigns ſhall diſplay,
And make the haughty *Franks* his Laws obey.
There Queen *Philippa* ſhines, th' *Albanians* Dread,
Worthy of *Britain*'s Crown, and *Edward*'s Bed:
While Foreign Kingdoms *Edward*'s Arms ſubdue;
Hers thro' the North the vanquiſh'd *Scots* purſue.
See the Black Prince in Armour by her ſide,
Proud *Gallia*'s Terrour, and fair *Albion*'s Pride:
What Triumphs wait him in *Pictavian* Fields?
What never-fading Laurels *Croiſſy* yields?

That *Henry* mark, the glorious Conquerour,
That *Gallia* ſhall reduce by *Albion*'s Power.
Immortal Prince, if Arms can make thee ſo,
For thee in *Norman* Fields what Laurels grow?
How great he'll ſeem, his Arms diſtain'd with Blood,
Chaſing the *Franks* o'er *Sein*'s affrighted Flood!
At *Agencourt* what Wonders ſhall be done,
What Towns of Force, what Battels ſhall be won,
Before in Triumph he aſcends their Throne?

Our Blood the Royal Channel now regains,
Deriv'd thro' *Tudor* our brave Offſpring's Veins;
Which with the *Norman* joyn'd, the Confluent Tide
As long, as that of Time, ſhall downward glide.
From their Embrace to rule *Britannia* ſprings,
A glorious Race of Queens, and potent Kings.
See, the firſt *Tudor* that aſcends the Throne,
After the glorious Field at *Boſworth* won:
The Scepter he ſhall ſway with great Applauſe,
And Rule the Iſle with Wiſe and Equal Laws.

Young

Young *Edward* there, *Albion*'s Delight, appears
Learn'd, Pious, Manly, Wise above his years.
Then Liberty in all her lovely Charms,
Shall sit secure from Tyranny's Alarms:
Religion purg'd from *Rome*'s Adulterous Stain,
Shall in her pure, and Native Splendor Reign.
No greater Mind to *Albion*'s Crown succeeds,
Rever'd for Brave, and lov'd for Pious Deeds.
Blest *Albion*, if kind Heav'n would long permit
So great a Monarch, on thy Throne to sit!
But, oh, how short Delights attend him here,
Such Heav'nly Guests are shewn, and disappear:
Dear both to Earth and Heav'n, he'll soon remove
His Throne from hence, to Reign in Bliss above:
With what Complaints, with what despairing Cries,
Shall sad *Britannia* Mourn his Obsequies?

    There, see, the bright *Elizabetha* rise,
Inlightning with her Rays the *British* Skies.
Th' Indulgent Parent of her People, she
Loves, Feeds, and Guards *Britannia*'s Family.
Heav'n's and her People's Rights she shall protect,
And for *Britannia*'s Ease, her own neglect:
Her Sons she shall embrace with pious Care,
And from her Coasts send back th' *Iberian* War.
Blest times, when she that wears th' Imperial Crown,
Regards her Peoples Safety, as her own.

    Intently now on that great Monarch gaze,
So much distinguish'd by his brighter Rays:
This is the Man, the brave *Nassovian*, whom
I nam'd, the great Deliverer to come.
Succeeding Prophets under your great Name,
This our great Offspring shall aloud proclaim;

                                     Rais'd

Book V. *Prince* Arthur.

Rais'd from a noble Branch of *Tudor*'s Line,
From *Thamifis* tranfplanted to the *Rhine*.
Amaz'd Pofterity, will fcarce believe
The wond'rous Deeds, this Hero fhall atchieve.
Th' *European* World by *Rome* and *Gaul* oppreft,
By his long-wifh'd-for Arms fhall be releaft.
He'll far out-fhine his own Heroick Race,
Europe's Protectors, who fhall Tyrants chafe,
And Monfters vanquifh with *Herculean* Toil,
And refcue from their bloody Jaws, their Spoil.
The beardlefs Hero's firft victorious Arms,
Shall free his Country from the *Gauls* Alarms:
As he advances, Seas of *Gallick* Blood,
Shall with red Streams, fwell *Mofa*'s wondring Flood:
Their flaughter'd Ranks fhall lie along the *Rhine*,
And with ftrange Purple ftain th' aftonifh'd Vine.

For in this Age,
Juft Heav'n fhall caufe a haughty Prince to rife,
Cruel, as *Lucifer*, and like him wife.
Heav'n's Laws, and Power, the Tyrant fhall deride,
Breaking in Sport, the Oaths wherewith he's ti'd.
Th' infatiate Monfter pleas'd with humane Gore,
And urg'd with Hellifh Rage, fhall firft devour
His *Gallick* Slaves, and with a merc'lefs Hand,
Spread fearful Ruin o'er his fruitful Land.
Raging with Fire and Sword, he fhall invade
His Neighbour's Cities, to his Gold betray'd.
No Spoil, no Carnage, fhall his Fury cloy,
But drunk with Blood, he fhall around deftroy,
Like fpreading Fires, or Torrents roaring down,
From melting Snows, that all the Vally drown.
Like Hell, he fhall derive his chiefeft Joy,
From the divine Permiffion to deftroy.

X   Mifchief

Mischief and Ruin, he shall Conquest name,
And from Destruction raise a dismal Fame.
Regions laid wast, Orphans and Widows Cries,
Proclaim his Power, and barb'rous Victories.
So dire a Plague, shall Heav'n permit to reign,
To scourge the impious World, but to restrain
The savage Spoiler, shall this Prince employ;
Monsters grow up, for Heroes to destroy.
The valiant Youth sinking *Batavia* saves,
Their surest Digue against the *Gallick* Waves.
After opprest *Britannia* shall invite,
The fam'd *Deliverer* to assert her Right.
His Arms the lowring Tempest shall dispel,
Which threatning *Albion*, rolls from *Rome* and Hell:
Fair Liberty her drooping Head shall rear,
And blest Religion on her Throne appear.
His Reign fresh Life to *Albion* shall impart,
And teach her Sons War's long-forgotten Art.
Britons dissolv'd in soft, inglorious Ease,
In courtly Vices, and luxurious Peace,
He shall inspire with a new martial Flame,
And lead them on, to gain their Ancient Fame.
Now *Albion*'s Youth polish their rusty Arms,
And once more, *Gallia* dreads their loud Alarms:
Victorious *Britons*, as of old, shall come
Laden with Spoils, and crown'd with Laurels, home.

He ceas'd; but near the great *Nassovian* stood
A *Heroine*, by mien of Royal Blood.
Her Form Divine, and Seraph-like her Face,
Where Heav'nly Sweetness, strove with Princely Grace.
But a black Cloud on her fair Temples lies,
And on the ground she fixt her beauteous Eyes.

Prince *Arthur* on th' Illuſtrious Form Intent,
Ask'd who ſhe was, and what the Sadneſs meant,
That her dejected Eyes did overſpread,
What the thick Miſt that hover'd round her Head.

King *Uter* with Reluctance thus replies,
While flowing Tears guſh'd from his mournful Eyes:
Ah, Son, demand no more their Fates to know,
That muſt produce ſuch univerſal Woe.
Telling that Offspring's Story, I reveal
A Scene of Grief, I labour'd to conceal.
This Wonder to the World, as ſoon as ſhown,
Is taken up to her Celeſtial Throne.
Ah! what ſad Accents, what a mournful Cry,
What lamentable Sounds will fill the Sky,
When her high Herſe, ſhall from her Palace go
Thro' weeping Throngs, in all the Pomp of Woe?
So ſad a Cry did wondring *Nile* affright,
When *Egypt*'s firſt-born Youth were ſlain by Night.
What Strains of Sorrow will *Auguſta* ſhow?
What Floods of Tears, ſad *Thamiſis*, will flow
Into thy Stream, while gliding by the Dome,
Where freſh erected ſtands her lofty Tomb.
Son, mind her Preſence, what a God-like Air?
What Throngs of Graces in her Eyes appear?
No nobler Genius, no well faſhion'd Mind
E'er took a Turn more happily deſign'd,
From an Etherial Mould more labour'd and refin'd.
Mild as the bleſt above, without ſerene
As *Eden*'s Air, and calm as Heav'n within.
No lovelyer Star adorns the *Britiſh* Sphear,
Ah! might ſhe longer in her Orb appear,
That her Celeſtial Influence might Flow
In chearing Streams on all the Iſle below!

X 2   New

New warmth to *Albion* her kind Beams afford,
To *Albion* guarded, as before restor'd,
By the *Nassovian* Angel's flaming Sword.
My fairest Offspring ! ah, her rigid Doom !
She shall *Maria* be : Come, quickly come,
Bring me white Lillies, Roses newly blown,
Lillies and Roses, like *Maria*'s own :
These on her Herse I'll scatter, and perfume
With od'rous Herbs and Flowers, the precious Tomb.
Let me my Sorrow thus express, 'tis true,
A fruitless Deed, but all that Love can do.

   The Tides of Grief that here swell'd *Arthur*'s Breast,
Broke Sleep's soft Fetters, and dissolv'd his Rest :
The Airy Objects, that without did wait,
Now rush in by the Senses open Gate.
His waking Thought, the wondrous Scene reviews,
And various Passions in his Mind renews.

Prince Arthur.

BOOK VI.

Now in the East the Saffron Morn arose,
And call'd the Lab'rer from his soft repose.
Thro' all the Region flew Loquacious Fame;
And the glad tydings spread, where'er she came:
Prince *Arthur*'s Landed, is the general Cry,
Straight to their Arms the chearful *Britons* fly:
The great *Restorer* all prepare to meet,
And warlike Noise resounds in every Street.
His eager Friends impatient of delay,
Had long expected this Auspicious Day.
They knew he was Embark'd to bring them Aid,
And for his quick, and safe Arrival pray'd.
Oft on the Rocks and highest Hills they stood,
And all around the Subject Ocean view'd
With longing Eyes, hoping the sight to gain
Of *Arthur*'s Conquering Navy on the Main:
And when no Fleet, no *Arthur* they descry'd,
They chid the Winds, and interposing Tyde.
With less impatience staid th' *Ithacian* Dame,
Till to her Arms her wish'd *Ulysses* came.
The *Sestian* Maid not with such Passion stood,
To spy her Lover cutting thro' the Flood.
The Zealous Men while adverse *Boreas* reign'd,
And from the Coasts Prince *Arthur*'s Fleet detain'd,

When

When mild *Aurora* with her rosy Light,
Began to streak the dusky Face of Night,
Oft from their Beds, up to the Windows flew,
And thence the Fanes and flying Clouds would view,
To see if yet more favourable Gales,
Rose from the South, to swell Prince *Arthur*'s Sails.
Anxious they look around, but when they find
Their hopes retarded by an adverse Wind,
Their Sorrow in repeated Sighs exprest,
They to their Beds return, but not to Rest.

Thus they expected *Arthur*'s powerful Aid,
And such their Sorrow was, their Hopes delay'd.
But now, at last the Prince's Fleet arriv'd,
Raises their Courage, and their Hopes reviv'd.
The joyful Throngs Prince *Arthur*'s Praise proclaim
This every Tongue employs, ev'n Children aim,
That scarce have learn'd to speak, to lisp his Name.
Some praise his Stature, and his God-like Face,
His awful Presence, and Majestick Grace,
His Courage some, and Conduct in the Field,
And think great *Cæsar*'s Fame to his, must yield:
His Clemency and Pity some admire,
And all the Virtues, that his Mind inspire.
The Actions of his Childhood some repeat,
In which they still discover'd something Great:
And now, what they expected, he appears,
The Hero promis'd in his tender years.
Others relate the ancient Prophecies,
Wherein was told a Monarch should arise
Of mighty Power, and Universal Fame,
That should to Heav'n advance the *British* Name:
Things weigh'd, and well compar'd, they all consent
Arthur's the Conq'rour, that the Prophets meant.

Some tell their Friends, their Courage to support,
What mighty Guards surround the Prince's Court.
What Succours hir'd were from *Germania* brought,
Succours, as oft Victorious, as they fought:
Fierce *Alpine Allobrogs* with slaughter fed,
In Snows and everlasting Winter bred.
Men of stupendous Bulk, pamper'd and cloy'd
With Blood of Nations, which their Arms destroy'd.
Arm'd with broad, flaming Swords, and mighty Spears;
Their Caps were Wolves, their Coats rough Skins of Bears:
Who stretcht on Beds did n'er their Limbs repose,
But from the naked ground still vig'rous rose.
Of Aspect terrible, their squallid Face
Thick, matted Beards with bristly Terrour grace:
None e'er escap'd, that did their Arms provoke,
They Mow whole Squadrons with a single stroke.
This monstrous Kind of Men did Fame invent,
And *Arthur*'s Troops so dreadful represent,
To raise the *Britons* Hearts before deprest,
And strike a Terrour thro' the *Saxon*'s Breast.
With Joy transported all for Arms declare,
And all the Accoutrements of War prepare.
The *Shepherds* on the Hills forsake their *Flocks*,
And leave their brouzing *Goats* upon the Rocks.
Instead of Crooks, that did their Flocks command,
Long warlike Spears they brandish in their Hand.
The *British* Youth their Courage rais'd, rejoyce
To see the Banners fly, and hear the Trumpet's Voice.
The *Farmers* leave the Hopes their Fields afford,
To reap fresh Laurels with their Conquering Sword.
The noise of War does from the Hills rebound,
And midst the *Miners* Eccho's under ground:
Who straight alarm'd, at nobler Labour Sweat,
And into Swords their glowing Metal beat.

Their

Their Forges, Anvils and wide Bellows breath,
Are all employ'd in various kinds of Death.
Some shape the Halbert, and broad Fauchion's Blade,
And Darts by some, and Arrows Heads are made.
Some forming Battle-Axes heave the Sledge,
Some into Shields strike out a flaming Wedge:
To fashion Helmets some the Hammer ply,
Some labour, Pieces for the Leg and Thigh.
With Lances arm'd, some their hot Coursers rein,
And to the War Curvet along the Plain.
Some with their clenching Gauntlets grasp the Shield,
Shake their long Spears, and rush into the Field.
Across their Shoulders some their Quivers hung,
Their Arrows trim'd, and Bows for Death new strung.
As when black Clouds dark'ning the Summer Sky,
Loaded with Cryftal Tempests slowly fly,
Th' Artillery discharg'd, with mighty Sound
Th' exploded Hailstones, leap upon the ground,
Thunder amidst the Woods, and from the Hills rebound.
So with the *Britons* all the Region swarms,
So thick their Troops, so loud the noise of Arms:
The groaning Earth complains, and trembling feels
The trampling Hoofs, and Chariots fervid Wheels.

In order now, Celestial *Muse*, declare
What Troops, and who those ancient *Britons* were,
Who for their Country's Liberty combin'd,
And their Brigades with *Arthur*'s Forces joyn'd.
From Time's dark Prisons set the Hero's free,
And may their glorious Names Immortal be.

First warlike *Cadwall* the *Dimetians* Head,
His Forces from the neighbouring Region led.

Their Troops advance from the bleak Northern Shore,
On which th' *Hybernian* Sea's loud Billows roar:
And where *Octopitarum*, thro' the Waves
Wedging his Way, th' oppofing Ocean braves.
Fair *Mariduxum* pours her Squadrons forth,
Where the fam'd Sorc'rer *Merlin* had his Birth.
They came who dwelt round high *Plinlimmon*'s Sides,
Where *Stuccia* flows, and fwift *Turobius* glides.

King *Meridoc*, the *Ordovician* leads
Down from the *Britifh* Alps, whofe fnowy Heads,
Imaus like, ftand towring in the Air,
And midft the Stars eternal Winter bear:
And from the Soil lav'd by *Conovius* Flood,
And *Menai*'s Banks, where old *Segontium* ftood.
Great Numbers fwarm'd from *Mona*'s noble Ifle,
Deform'd for Afpect, but of fertile Soil:
Where once in fhady Groves erected ftood,
The *Druids* Altars ftain'd with humane Blood.
The Troops their March from *Mediolanum* take,
From *Helen*'s Way, and the *Tegeian* Lake;
Thro' which fair *Deva*'s Streams fo fwiftly pafs,
They uncorrupted fhun th' impure Embrace:
Here the fublime *Mervinian* Mountains rife,
And with fharp-pointed Tops transfix the Skies.

Next *Morogan* the bold *Silures* brought,
None for their Country's Freedom better fought.
They bravely *Valens* and his Troops withftood,
And dy'd *Sabrina*'s Streams with *Roman* Blood:
With like Succefs *Veranius* they defeat,
And forc'd his vanquifh'd Eagles to retreat.
This caufe, as much their Courage did provoke,
To free their Country from the Saxon Yoke.

Y They

They take in haſt their Swords and Bucklers down,
And march to meet the Prince from every Town.
From all the Cities on the verdant ſide
Of *Nidus*, and on *Loghor*'s Cryſtal Tyde.
They march from *Bovium*, and the neighboring Shore,
Thick, as the Waves, that there inſulting roar.
Down from the Hilly Lands the *Britons* came,
Which now th' Inhabitants *Brechinia* name:
Where the black Mount ſtands lofty in the Air,
And forky *Peak*, ſince call'd great *Arthur*'s Chair.
They march from *Bulleum*, *Haga*, and the Lake,
Where when broad Sheets of Ice diſſolving crack,
The ratling Noiſe rebounds from neighb'ring Hills,
And with loud Thunder all the Region fills.
From *Ariconium*, and the flowry Space,
Which wanton *Vaga*'s winding Arms embrace:
Where *Lugus* his tranſparent Boſom ſpreads,
And where *Liddenus* murmurs thro' the Meads.
Where thick *Heſperian Woods* with Apples crown'd,
Of golden Hue, enrich the Fields around:
Which the moſt generous *Britiſh Wine* produce,
Auſonia ſcarce affords a nobler Juice.
They leave the Fields fam'd for the pureſt Corn,
And the rich Plains that Wooly Flocks adorn,
Which bleſs the Farmer with a nobler Fleece,
Than what *Apulia* boaſts, or fertile *Greece*.
They leave the golden Vale, and happy Ground,
Which *Dorus* laves, and lofty Woods ſurround.
The warlike Youth from *Venta* came, and thoſe
That *Muno*'s Flood and *Iſca*'s Streams incloſe.
With thoſe that round the *Oazy Moor* are bred,
And near the Golden Rock's refulgent Head.
Out from her Gates her Youth fair *Iſca* pours;
Crown'd with gilt Spires, rich Domes, and lofty Towers.
Where

Where Golden Roofs, and checker'd Floors abound,
Deep Vaults, and spacious Chambers under ground.
A stately Theater the Town o'erlooks,
And noble Works convey the neighb'ring Brooks,
By Conquering *Romans* built, that far from home
They might enjoy the Sports and Pomp of *Rome*.
Such was the ample City's ancient Fame,
Now worn by time it scarce preserves its Name.
Those from *Gobanium* march, a Town that stood
On *Isca*'s and *Gevini*'s confluent Flood.
In cheerful Troops the stout *Cornavians* came,
From the rich Soil we now *Salopia* name:
From either side of fair *Sabrina*'s Tyde,
Whose silver-Streams the fruitful Land divide.
From *Usocona*, and the Towns that lay
On the fam'd *Roman* Military way:
From *Uriconium*, yet a Noble Town,
And old *Rutunium*, then of good Renown.
Galbut their Leader at their Head appears,
A lovely Youth, and Wise above his Years.
Descended from a Noble, ancient Race
Of Heroes, who the *British* Annals grace.
He by Forefathers Beams Illustrious shone,
Great by their Deeds, but greater by his own.
Zeal for his Country, and the *British* Cause,
The generous Youth to glorious Danger draws:
For this he crost the Ocean, to implore
Prince *Arthur*'s Arms, their Freedom to restore.
The Prince embrac'd him, as his Fav'rite Friend,
And did his Zeal and Vigilance commend.
He staid the dear Companion of his Toil,
Both on the Seas, and on th' *Armorick* Soil:
And when the *Saxon*, and the *British* Fleet,
(A dreadful day) did on the Ocean meet,

By *Arthur*'s fide upon the Deck, he ftood.
Diftain'd with fcatter'd Brains, and recking Blood.
The Youth at danger unconcern'd appear'd,
And nothing but his Country's Suff'rings fear'd,
He leap'd out firft on the *Dimetian* Strand,
And welcom'd *Arthur* to his Native Land:
Where taking leave, he to his Country came,
To Head his Men, and win yet greater Fame.

Devana fends brave Troops, a noble Town,
For lofty Works, and fplendid Structures known:
Where once the *Roman* Conquerors did refide,
And envy'd not *Italia*'s Wealth and Pride.
The bold Inhabitants on *Deva*'s Bank,
And they who *Danus*, and *Merfeia* drank;
With thofe that had their Seats, along the Soil
Which Briny Riches gives with cafie Toil;
Draw out and Mufter on the Neighb'ring Plain,
Refolv'd the *Britifh* Honour to regain.
Eothan their Captain was a Warlike Knight,
A brave Afferter of his Country's Right.
A noble, but ungovernable Fire,
(Such is the Heroes) did his Breaft infpire.
His honeft Rage, his Friends could fcarely Rule,
Hot for the Camp, but not for Counfel Cool:
Fit to aflift to pull a Tyrant down,
But not to pleafe the Prince that mounts the Throne.
Impatient of Oppreffion, ftill he ftood
His Country's Mounds, againft th' invading Flood:
Impetuous, as a Tempeft in its Courfe,
He not to Conduct trufted, but to Force.
Unskill'd in Court Intreagues, on which the wife
And crafty Statefmen, as his ftrength, relies;

He

He still expected that a loud Applause,
Should follow Brav'ry, and a Righteous Cause.
His Country prais'd him; no *Britannick* Lord,
Was as his People's Patron more ador'd.
And Now in Arms they throng about their Head,
None to the Prince such numerous Forces led.

The *Coritanians*, that the Soil possest,
By fair *Darventio*'s fruitful Waters blest,
And *Repandunum*, where clear *Trenta*'s Tide
Do's into *Dovo*'s silver Bosome glide.
Those near high *Peak*, in heavenly Waters drown'd,
And in the Dale, which craggy Rocks surround;
Their Zeal and Courage rais'd by loud Alarms,
Forsook their Seats, and Fields, and flew to Arms.
These valiant Men that Fame and Freedom sought,
To join the Prince's Arms *Canvallo* brought.
Noble *Canvallo*, who did with him bring
The Majesty, and Presence of a King.
Of lofty Stature, and a graceful Air,
By's own Sex fear'd, and favour'd by the Fair.
Th' Inglorious Pleasures of the wanton Court,
Which drain'd his Wealth, did not the Patriot hurt:
Fit for the Camp, or Business of the State,
But soft Enjoyments Love to both abate.
Alarm'd with Publick Danger, he arose
Like a rous'd Lion, from his long Repose.
Arm'd, and equip'd with great Magnificence,
He mounts his fiery Turk, bought at a vast Expence:
His princely Train, and splendid Equipage,
Wher'ere he goes the Eyes of all engage.

The *Atrebatians* from the happy Land,
Which then sublime *Gallena* did command:

Where

Where winding *Thamifis* does bless the Soil,
The Wealth and Glory of the *British* Isle:
In War-like Bands advance to *Arthur*'s Aid,
And rich *Bertudor*, as their Head obey'd.
Who still against the Pagan Interest strove,
Rich in Possessions, and his People's Love.
His happy Tenants, and the Farmers round,
His Hospitable House still open found.
Each Week ten Oxen from the Stall he drew,
A hundred Sheep, and forty Swine he slew;
Fat Venison, Fowl, and Fish, an endless Store,
To feed his Guests, his Servants, and the Poor.
He to the Woods, and Forests was inclin'd,
To hunt the Fox, and chase the flying Hind.
Pleas'd with his Friends, and with his rural Sport,
He wisely shun'd, the Dangers of the Court.
But for the Christian Cause, and publick Peace,
He quits the Forests, and his Wealth and Ease:
His Helmet brac'd, and on his Arm his Shield,
He march'd before his Troops into the Field.
And that my Verse may to his Name be just,
Of all the Lords *Bertudor* was the first,
That to the Camp, his valiant Forces brought,
Tho' not inur'd to War, and tho' remote.

The *Durotriges* from the western Coast,
Where the *Britannick* Ocean's Waves are tost:
Their Troops assembled, for the Prince declare,
And march from all the Towns, to meet the War.
From *Dornavaria*, and the Seats that stand
On *Froma*'s Stream, and wealthy *Blackmoor* Land;
From *Vendogladia*, and the Tow'rs that rose
On the fat Glebe, where pleasant *Stourus* flows.

Sakil

Sakil their Leader, an Illustrious Peer,
Was to his Prince, and to his Country dear.
He, their *Mæcenas*, cheers the *British Bards*,
Learns them to Sing, and then their Songs rewards.
So Heav'n to make Men good, does Grace bestow,
And then rewards them for their being so.
Him, as their Head th' *Athenian* Sons adore,
The Muses Fav'rite, but the People's more.
To form great Men, his Palace was the School,
His Life good Breeding's, and good Nature's Rule.
To him the needy Men of Wit resort,
And find a Friend in an unletter'd Court:
The Poets Nation, did Obsequious wait
For the kind Dole, divided at his Gate.
Laurus amidst the meagre Crowd appear'd,
An old, revolted, unbelieving Bard,
Who throng'd,and shov'd,and prest,and would be heard.
Distinguish'd by his louder craving Tone,
So well to all the Muses Patrons known,
He did the Voice of modest Poets drown.
Sakil's high Roof, the Muses Palace rung
With endless Cries, and endless Songs he sung.
To bless good *Sakil*, *Laurus* would be first,
But *Sakil*'s Prince, and *Sakil*'s God he curst.
Sakil without distinction threw his Bread,
Despis'd the Flatt'rer, but the Poet fed.
His Sword the Muses great Defender draws,
T' assert *Britannia*'s, and Religion's Cause.

Osron their Head, the bold *Brigantes* brings,
Subject of late, to the *North-Saxon* Kings:
Now for their Liberty they boldly speak,
And thro' the Foe, to joyn Prince *Arthur*, break.

Osron's

Ofron's Example all the Region fir'd,
With noble Heats, and Martial Thoughts inspir'd.
None in the Field did greater Courage show,
Whether he charg'd, or else sustain'd the Foe.
Yet none more fit in Council to preside,
And in a Storm, the lab'ring State to guide:
A mighty Genius of uncommon Mould,
As *Cæsar* Eloquent, as *Cæsar* Bold.
He could th' unstable People's Tumults stop,
And a declining Kingdom underprop.
Matur'd by Age, and business of the State,
The hoary Oracle in Council sate.
Where he the *British Nestor* was esteem'd,
And all his Language, Inspiration seem'd.
This finish'd Statesman, did the Prince perswade
To pass the Seas, the *Saxon* to invade.
And at his Landing quick Assistance brought,
And for his Country none more bravely fought.

The fartheft *Western* Soil, which with their Wave,
The *British*, and *Hibernian* Oceans lave.
From *Isca*'s Noble Stream, far as the Shore
Where round *Bolerium*'s Head the Billows roar,
By the *Danmonian Britons* was possest,
And with King *Cador*'s temperate Empire blest,
This war like People, at their King's Command,
Now take up Arms, and muster thro' the Land.
The good King *Cador* worn with War and Age,
No longer does the Foe in Arms engage.
Macor his Son supply'd the Father's Place,
Whose Virtues equal'd his Illustrious Race.
To serve Prince *Arthur*, and his righteous Cause,
His Sword the brave *Danmonian* Hero draws.

A.

Book VI.   *Prince* Arthur.

A beauteous Youth, whose Breast a strong desire
Of Fame, and Martial Glory did inspire.
Eager of War, he the *Danmonians* led,
And shone in splendid Armour at their Head.
His coming Joy to all the *Britons* gives,
And in his Arms, the Prince his Friend receives:
To whom to be endear'd, he always strove,
By all expressions of Respect and Love.
The Valiant Youth he did with Honours grace,
To his high Merit due, and noble Race.
Macor, mean time, Prince *Arthur* did adore,
None serv'd his Cause, or sought his Favour more.

Tracar, and *Ormes* in the Camp arrive,
Whose Presence to the rest, fresh Courage give.
Their Wisdom was by Fame aloud proclaim'd,
The *Britons* none with greater Honour nam'd.
Both fit about a Monarch to abide,
To aid his Counsels, and the State to guide.
None more admir'd for clear, unerring Sense,
For piercing Sight, and charming Eloquence.
Great Spirits both, but of a different Mould,
Ormes impetuous, Turbulent, and Bold;
But *Tracar* was compos'd, sedate, and cool,
His Passions subject to a stricter Rule.
Ormes was haughty, inaccessible,
And knew his Riches, and his Sense too well:
Tracar was courteous, easie of Access,
Of great Humanity, and mild Address.
Ormes was therefore honour'd not desir'd,
Tracar belov'd, and equally admir'd.
Ormes would still advance unbounded Power,
Tracar his Country's Liberty secure.

Z   *Tracar*

Tracar had Letters, *Ormes* Native Fire:
Both had by Birth, what Labour can't acquire.
Arthur to neither Rival Wit inclines,
But us'd them both, to serve his wise Designs.
Such Love the *Britons* to the Prince exprest,
Who when he found his Numbers thus encreast,
Advanc'd his Enfigns, and to *Isca* came,
Where the *Silures* dwelt, the chief for Fame:
Hither fresh Squadrons to the Prince resort,
Which from that time is call'd great *Arthur*'s Court.
Five times the Sun had his Diurnal Race
Compleated, when from this delightful place
The pious Prince his Enfigns mov'd, and came
To *Glevum*, seated on *Sabrina*'s Stream.
Decamping hence, his arm'd Battalions gain
Prince *Arthur* at their Head, the fertile Plain,
By easie Marches, where *Gallena* stood,
Which *Thamisis* laves with its noble Flood.

Thus stood the *Britons*, after his Defeat,
Octa with Grief did to his Coasts Retreat.
As when by chance a Royal Eagle spies,
From some high Mountain's Top, amidst the Skies;
A flight of Swans, obscuring all the Air,
Swift as the Lightning, which he's said to bear,
Upon the Prey his Airy Flight he takes,
And with sharp Pounces vast Destruction makes.
Some fall struck dead, some wounded slowly fly,
While Snowy Clouds of Feathers fill the Sky:
Those that the fierce Invader's Strokes survive,
With all the speed, Fear to their Wings can give;
To their belov'd *Cayster*'s Banks return,
And in their reedy Seats, their Wounds and Losses mourn.

So

So far'd the *Saxons*, and their shatter'd Fleet,
Octa forthwith Commands his Lords to meet
In Council, where they in long order sate,
T' advise, what best might save their threaten'd State.

Cissa first spoke, an able Counsellour,
Let us assemble all our present power,
And straight advance the *Britons* to Attack,
Who to our Arms can small Resistance make.
Sore with their Wounds, and weary with their Toil,
They tempt the *Saxons* to an easie Spoil.
Boldly fall on, before their Troops are eas'd,
With Food and Rest, and with Recruits increas'd.
Your Wisdom thus, and Courage will appear,
Who tho defeated, have not learn'd to fear.
The Foe surpriz'd must to your Mercy yield,
Or to their Ships Retreating, quit the Field.
He ceas'd, then *Osred*, who had always won
By his wise Counsel great Applause, begun:
Our late Defeat has too much Terrour strook,
Thro' all our Troops, too much our Empire shook,
And too much flush'd the Foe, to let me joyn
In this Advice, my Counsels more incline
To draw into the Field our utmost Power,
From all the *Saxon* States, and to secure
Our Empire, let us labour to perswade
The *Pict*, and *Scotish* King, to give us Aid.
The Cause and Interest is the same of all,
They and their Gods, if we are crush'd, must fall.
Our Arms united in a numerous Host,
We may before of certain Conquest boast.
The trembling Foe unable to withstand
Such mighty Armies, will forsake the Land.

Z 2 But

But if supported with vain hopes they stay,
They fall into our hands an easie Prey.

Pascentius next, a wise *Nestorian* head,
Whose Looks, and Words profound Attention bred :
Thus spoke-'tis true our Troops while thus dismay'd,
And of Prince *Arthur*'s Fame, and Arms afraid,
From present Action justly may disswade.
Seeking the Foe we too great Danger run,
Embolden'd by his Victory lately won.
And thus far *Osred*'s Thoughts and mine you see
Conspire, as in the rest they disagree.
If with our utmost Force we meet our Foes,
To too much hazard we our State expose :
Th' uncertain Game of War they little know,
That Stake an Empire on a single Throw.
While we delay to gather all our Force,
And to the *Picts* and *Scots*, shall have recourse ;
Prince *Arthur* will advance, and mightier grow,
Like rolling Balls, that gather up the Snow,
Or Rivers taking Streams in, as they flow.
The *Britons* led by ancient Prophecies,
Expect that near this time, a Prince shall rise
Heroick, Wise, a mighty Conqueror,
That all their lost Dominions shall restore,
And o'er the World, extend their Naval Power.
Something like this, our Augurs seem to fear,
From Prodigies, and Signs that oft appear.
Those hopes they all of *Arthur* now express,
Drawn by his Fame abroad, and late Success.
While this Belief, tho' false, the *Briton* warms,
He grows less fearful of the *Saxon* Arms :
He'll be more bold in Fight, while thus inspir'd,
And with such Zeal, and Expectation fir'd.

In-

Intoxicated thus Men Wonders do,
And by bold Deeds, make their vain Fancies true.
He therefore serves King *Octa*, that creates,
An Understanding first, between the States.
An Embassy may to the Prince be sent,
To treat how Blood and ruin to prevent,
They may propose the Kingdom to divide,
And offer *Octa*'s Daughter for his Bride,
Fair, *Ethelina*, whose perverted Mind,
To *Christian* Worship is too much inclin'd.
He ceas'd, and his Advice did chiefly please,
And of the Council most declar'd for Peace.

The Lords dispers'd, King *Octa* unresolv'd,
Long in his Mind his troubled Thoughts revolv'd;
With strong contending Tydes of Passion prest,
Now War he looks on, now on Peace, as best.
Long he appear'd on *Osred*'s Counsel bent,
And to the Neighb'ring *Saxon* Princes sent,
That all, the strong Necessity might know
Of joyning Arms, against the Common Foe.
At the same time an Embassy he sends,
To make the *Pict*, and *Scotish* King his Friends:
That of their powerful Aid he might not fail,
If *Arthur*, and his *Britons* should prevail.
But when he heard, that *Arthur* had as far
As *Glevum*'s Walls, advanc'd the threatning War,
Observing that the *Saxons* were dismaid,
And not yet strengthen'd by his Neighbours Aid,
He now declar'd, it was his setled Sense,
A Treaty with the *Briton* to Commence.

Then Orators he sent without delay,
Who to the *Britons* Camp direct their way.

Titullan

Titullan, Selred, and wife *Theocles*
For this Negotiation chiefly please:
Heldured of the Embassy was one,
Ofrick and *Thedred* noble *Ormar*'s Son.
Arriving at the Prince's Camp, they found
The *British* Youth in Crowds disperst around:
For then with various Sports, and manly Play,
The *Britons* solemniz'd, th' auspicious Day,
Of *Arthur*'s Birth, o'er all the Fields they spred,
To different Games, by different Passions led.
Here Chariots raising Clouds of Dust appear,
And run with smoaking Wheels their swift Career.
Here the robust *Danmonian* Nation swarms,
Hurling their massy Balls with vig'rous Arms.
Here the *Dobunians* to advance their Fame,
Toil at their Country's old laborious Game.
Long Ashen Staves across their Shoulders lie,
Then sway'd with both their Hands, strike thro the Sky
A mounting Orb of Thongs, or well sow'd Hide,
While at due distance rang'd, on th' other Side
The Foe inclining stands, to wait its Fall,
And with like Force, strike Back the bounding Ball.
Incircled Wrestlers here their Manhood try,
And with loud Shouts, that rend the lab'ring Sky,
The standing Ring proclaims the Victory,
Some to a Cudgel prize their Fellows dare,
Who strait spring out to meet the wooden War.
They brandish in the Air their threat'ning Staves,
Their Hands, a woven Guard of Osier saves,
In which they fix their Hazel Weapon's End,
Thus arm'd, the nimble Combatants contend
For Conquest, giving and receiving Blows,
And down their Heads a crimson River flows.

Here

Here flowry Garlands their proud Temples crown,
Whose airy Feet the Race had newly won.
Such were the *Britons* Sports, as thro' the Throng
The *Saxon* Orators pass'd slow along:
Who strait were to th' August Pavilion led,
Where *Arthur* sate, his Lords around him spread.

   To whom *Titullan* thus,
The *Saxon* King, whose ardent wishes are
To save *Britannia*, from Destructive War.
Who rather seeks t' enjoy the Fruits of Peace,
Then by his Arms his Empire to encrease:
Makes such Advances for these glorious Ends,
As may the *Britons* make his lasting Friends.
The *Saxons*, and the *Britons* shall command
Their equal Shares, of the divided Land:
Such Barrier shall be fixt, as shall secure
The *Britons*, jealous of the *Saxon* Power.
To give *Britannia* Peace, we condescend
To yield up what our Arms can well defend.
Such steps King *Octa* makes for Peace, beside
That both may yet with closer Bonds be ty'd.
Bright *Ethelina*, *Octa*'s chief Delight,
Shall be the Link, the Nations to unite.
This so much envy'd Favorite of Fame,
Whom all with Love, and Admiration name:
Octa consents shall be your beauteous Bride,
To you already, in her Faith Ally'd.
These Measures all Contentions may adjust,
Friendship confirm, and fix a mutual Trust.
But if rejected, *Octa* does declare
He's guiltless of the dire effects of War:
Upon the Christians Head, will rest the Guilt
Of all the Blood, that by the Sword is spilt.

                                       The

The Prince reply'd,
Affairs of such Importance to the State,
Require our thoughtful Care and calm Debate.
The two Proposals by King *Octa* made,
For lasting Friendship, shall be duly weigh'd.

Twice had the Sun broke from the Purple East,
Twice was he seen dilated in the West.
When *Arthur* seated on his Chair of State,
Thus spake, the *Saxons* with Attention wait:
An honourable Peace my Thoughts prefer,
To all the Triumphs of a Bloody War.
I, and my *Britons*, those just Terms approve,
King *Octa* makes t' establish Peace and Love,
To spare each Nation's Blood, and save the Isle
From Desolation, and destructive Spoil:
Indulgent Heav'n is to both Nations kind,
Which has your King to peaceful Thoughts inclin'd.
Ten Lords of *Saxon*, ten of *British* Blood,
May meet at *Spina* near *Cunetio*'s Flood,
T' adjust the Limits of each Nation's Power,
And Barriers fix, that may their Peace secure.
You for an Interview, the place will name,
Where I may see the beauteous *Saxon* Dame.
He ceas'd, and all the Audience pour'd around,
To this assented with a murmuring Sound:
A sudden Joy did in their Eyes appear,
While smiling Peace, triumph'd o'er vanquish'd War.

Mean time th' Infernal Monarch wings his Flight,
To the *White Hills*, whence his Angelick Sight
Might all the Fields, and subject plains survey,
Where in their Camp the hateful *Britons* lay.

While

While with malicious Eyes around he view'd,
The *Christian* Army fill'd with Joy, he stood
With Rage dilated, and with Envy blown,
Like glowing *Ætna*, on *Plinlimon* thrown.
Flashes of Fire from his red Eyeballs flow'd,
Like Lightning breaking from a lowring Cloud.
So when a Toad, squat on a Border spies,
The Gardner passing by, his bloodshot Eyes
With Spite, and Rage inflam'd, dart Fire around
The verdant Walks, and on the flowry Ground,
The bloated Vermin loathsome Poison spits,
And swoln and bursting with his Malice sits.
So the faln Angel sate, and thus begun,
Am I, and all th' infernal Powers outdone?
And must this *Briton* still pursue his Course,
And thus elude my Arts, and all my Force?
What Christian Towns, and States have I destroy'd,
Forc'd by my Power, or by my Arts decoy'd?
How few remaining Christian Regions are,
Where no deep Marks of my Revenge appear?
What glorious Ruin did my *Romans* spread
O'er *Asia*'s Christians; I the *Lombards* led,
And furious *Huns*, to rich *Ausonia*'s Soil,
And fill'd the Land with Blood, and Christian Spoil;
My *Maximins*, and *Neros*, mighty Names,
What Desolation, by devouring Flames,
What Slaughter by the Sword, these Heroes made,
With what Success did they the Saints invade?
And if the Fame be true that spreads in Hell,
In *Gaul* a Prince shall rise, that shall excel
All these, and more in Blood and Spoil delight,
And all Hell's Furies to his Aid invite.
Let that great Prince arise, and may his Birth,
Be honour'd with Convulsions of the Earth,

A a *Eclipses,*

Eclipses, Comets, Meteors, Lightnings, Storms,
Murders, and Monsters of tremendous Forms.
Nor are there Triumphs of my Power alone,
Much weaker Spirits, have great Conquests won.
Spirits of Lower Order, small renown,
In Hell of little Figure, scarcely known:
Inferiour, subaltern Divinities,
Could often their just Fury to appease,
To wreck their Rage, and honest Malice cloy,
Whole Armies of this hateful Sect destroy:
First tempt th' ungrateful Murmurers to Rebel,
And then with Plagues and Darts invisible,
With Fire, and Earthquakes lay all wast, disseize
Their God, and ruin all his Votaries.
And shall this *Briton* all my Force defy,
And introduce his banish'd Deity?
High States of Hell, ye mighty Gods below,
In your August Assemblies who will Bow,
Who Acclamations make when I appear,
Who dread my Power, my Greatness who revere?
If still this *Briton* shall resist my Power,
And all my Arts eluded, rest secure?
But if by irresistable Decree.
Pronounc'd by Fate, and unchang'd Destiny;
Arthur at last must mount the *British* Throne,
Beat down our Altars, and erect his own:
At least new hardships shall obstruct his Way,
And my Revenge his Triumphs shall delay.
That said he Flew, his Snakie Wings display'd,
Down to his Palace midst th' Infernal Shade.

From all their gloomy Regions to his Court,
At his Command, th' Infernal Lords resort.

To

To whom their Monarch from his glowing Throne,
Thus with a haughty, troubled Look begun:
Thus far in vain all our Attempts are made,
To crush the *Britons* that our State invade.
At Sea, they Triumph o'er King *Octa*'s Fleet,
At Land, Success above their Hopes, they meet.
Octa defeated, dreads Prince *Arthur*'s Arms,
And sues for Peace, by *Ethelina*'s Charms:
If this should once prevail, *Britannia*'s lost,
We, and our Priests, must fly this impious Coast.
Help'd by th' Almighty Enemy of Hell,
They yet our Arms escape, our Power repel:
Then Monarch's War with vast advantage wage,
When Heav'n its Power does on their part Engage.
This sure Expedient's left us to annoy
The *Britons*, and their tow'ring Hopes destroy:
Let us provoke them to some dire Offence,
Which may against their Armies, Heav'n incense,
Then the Seraphick Guards, that round them lie,
Or else patroling thro' the Region fly,
Scowring the Hills and Vales, with flaming Arms,
The Christians to protect from our Alarms;
These will displeas'd, withdraw their powerful Aid,
And we with Safety may their Camp invade.
What subtile Spirit of seducing Art,
And skill in tempting, will perform this part?

Then filthy *Asmodai*, who Men inspires
With wanton Passions, and unclean Desires,
Whose leud Adorers stand before his Shrine,
Transform'd to lustful Goats, and loathsome Swine,
Thus spake: This grateful Province I embrace,
I from their Minds will virtuous Passions chase.

My stronger Force shall all chast Thoughts expel,
And Heav'n's weak Flames, shall yield to those of Hell.
To solemn Groves, and lonesome Hermits Cells,
Where boasted Chastity in Triumph dwells,
To Cloyster'd Monks Admission I command,
And can a Camp my powerful Charms withstand?
On me such chosen Spirits shall attend,
Whose Skill and Power will most promote my End.
The Gods of *Riot*, *Luxury*, and *Wine*,
In this Attempt shall all their Forces joyn.
Doubt not great Prince, when we their Camp Assail,
Nature is on our side, we shall prevail.
Th' Infernal Diet with his Language mov'd,
With loud Applause the wise Design approv'd.

   Straight *Asmodai*, attended with a Train
Of soft Luxurious Spirits, to the Plain
Directs his Flight, where the glad *Britons* lay;
With lab'ring Wings he mounts the steepy Way,
And quickly reach'd the tender Verge of Day.
In Companies distinct the *Britons* sate,
Pleas'd with their wish'd Success, and prosp'rous Fate.
When to the Camp the Crew Infernal came,
Grasping in either hand *Tartarean* Flame.
About from Tent to Tent the *Demons* flew,
And midst the Troops their flaming Torches threw.
The wanton Fires about their Bosoms play,
And to their Hearts lascivious warmth convey:
The soft Contagion glides along their Veins,
And in their Breasts the pleasing Poison reigns.
Straight all in Riot and Debauches join,
Dissolve in Mirth, and sit inflam'd with Wine.
The Captains Snore on Scarlet spread beneath,
And with their lab'ring Breasts contend for Breath.
                                              Tables

Tables o'erturn'd and broken Swords betwixt,
And Dishes faln, with Armour intermixt,
Helmets and Harness, and bruis'd Goblets by,
A mad Confusion make of War, and Luxury.
Acted with lustful Fires, from Town to Town
Commanders, and their Men, promiscuous run:
With Outrages and ravish'd Virgins, Spoils
The vicious Army all the Land defiles.
Whoredoms in *Pagan* Cities they commit,
And at their Sacrifices feasting sit:
Heated with leud Religion, Lust, and Wine,
They in the Worship of their Idols join.
Then to the Camp the hot Adulterers lead
Their *Pagan* Women and avow the Deed.
Th' Angelick Guards th' enormous vices saw,
And in Displeasure from their Camp withdraw:
All Hell with Shouts of Triumph did resound,
That such Success had all their Wishes crown'd.

The Prince of Hell strait summons from beneath,
The chief supporter of the Throne of Death,
Vengeful *Megæra*, she without Delay,
From Hell's Abyss ascends, and in her Way
Gathers raw Damps and Steams from noisome Graves,
And putrid Reeks, from Subterranean Caves;
Where spotted Plagues first draw their poisonous Breath,
The Nurseries of Pain, and Magazines of Death.
These Seeds of Torment, and devouring Heats,
From whose Contagion vanquish'd Life retreats,
Megæra in compacted Hides dark Wombs,
For this infernal Purpose made, entombs:
In their distinct Repositories laid,
Sad choice of Death, she various Plagues convey'd.

Arm'd

Arm'd for Destruction thus the Fury came,
And brought from *Asmodai*'s, a different Flame.
Then Wolves were heard in neighb'ring Hills to howl,
Th' illboding Raven, and the screaching Owl
Sung o'er the Camp by Night, the Sun by Day,
Distain'd with Blood, shone with a dismal Ray.
The cruel Fury straight her Flight did take
To find her Prince, to whom th' Apostate spake:
Go, glut thy Rage, and let the *Britons* know,
Hell's Monarch is not yet a vanquish'd Foe:
Pass thro' their Camp with thy accustom'd Haste,
And on them all thy deadly Treasures waste.

 Straight did the vengeful Minister prepare,
T' infect the Camp, and poison all the Air.
Her Bottles turgid with imprison'd Death
She open'd, and releas'd the fatal Breath:
In livid Wheels the dire Contagion flies,
And putrid Exhalations taint the Skies.
The Region's choak'd with Pestilential Steams,
Malignant Reeks, raw Damps, and soultry Gleams.
Now with their Breath the hot Infection slides
Into their Breasts, and thro' their Vitals glides:
Their Lab'ring Hearts spout out the flowing Blood,
And fry the Limbs with an Ætnean Flood.
The raging Pest'lence, chases thro' the Veins
Retreating Life, and drest in purple Reigns.
While other Plagues run colder to the Heart,
And thro' their Breast strike like a poison'd Dart:
Rack'd with tormenting Pain some gasping lie,
Some only breath th' envenom'd Air, and die.
Their Hearts with chill, congealing Blood oppress't,
Throb a few moments in their panting Breast,
Then yield, and from their Vital Labour rest.

In vain for Help, in vain for Drugs they cry,
Friends and Phyſitians come, but with them dy.
Thro' all the Camp the fierce Deſtruction ſpread,
Deforming every Tent with Heaps of Dead.

   Mean time the pious *Arthur* proſtrate laid,
Thus in a Flood of Tears diſſolving pray'd:
Great King of Heav'n, thy Arm thou makeſt bare,
T' invade the *Britons* with reſiſtleſs War.
Thy glitt'ring Sword brandiſh'd with dreadful Sway,
Does thro our Camp with wide Deſtruction Slay.
Why did thy Aids the Shipwreckt *Britons* ſave,
From Rocks and Tempeſts, and th' inſulting Wave,
If we muſt only ſee our Native Soil,
And with our Dead th' encumber'd Land defile?
Th' inſulting Heathen will Blaſpheme thy Name,
And in their Songs advance their Idols Fame.
To their vain Gods loud Praiſes they'll return,
And Hecatombs upon their Altars burn.
Spare yet thy *Britons*, let ſome Reliques live,
That may due Honours to thy Temples give.
Let the Deſtroyer ceaſe at thy Command,
And Death at thy Rebuke arreſted, ſtand.
And may the Crimes which Heav'n provoke, be known,
That our deep Sorrows may its Wrath atone.

   The pious Prince's humble Cries ſucceed,
And glorious *Raphael*, with Angelick ſpeed
Deſcends, his Sword of Flame drawn in his Hand,
To chaſe the fierce Deſtroyer from the Land.
A Cryſtal Vial full of Od'rous Fumes,
Ambroſial Balm, and rich Etherial Gums;
His other hand pour'd out upon the Air,
To cure the Damps, and noxious Vapours there.

Megæra

Megæra flies the bright Archangel's Sword,
The Plague was ſtaid, and Health and Life reſtor'd.
Then to the room ſwift *Raphael* Wings his way,
Where *Arthur* ſtill devoutly proſtrate lay.

To whom the Seraph thus:
Heav'n by the *Britons* daring Crimes incens'd,
Almighty Wrath ſeverely has diſpenc'd
Your unprotected Camp it did expoſe,
To the dire Rage of your Infernal Foes:
Who by Divine Permiſſion ſoon o'erſpread
Your guilty Camp, with putrid Heaps of Dead.
Th' Angelick Guards return'd to Heaven, complain'd
That your flagitious Troops you n'er reſtrain'd.
Your Captains boldly Whoredoms, Riots, Rapes
Commit, and yet each Criminal eſcapes:
Thus you avow the Ills, by others done,
And their unpuniſh'd Guilt, becomes your own.
Had your Vindictive Arm been firſt employ'd,
Heav'n's had not thus your guilty Troops deſtroy'd.
But now th' Eternal yielding to your Prayer,
Has ſent me from his Throne, with ſpeedy Care
To ſtay the Plague, and make the Fiend retreat,
That ſpreads the Poiſon, to her *Stygian* Seat.
Heav'n's now appeas'd, may ne'er the *Britons* dare
By their Revolting, to renew the War.
The Seraph diſappear'd, and *Arthur* rais'd
Upon his Feet, th' Eternal Goodneſs prais'd.

Prince Arthur.

BOOK VII.

The Prince of Hell that on the Mountain ſtaid,
And with Infernal Joy, around ſurvey'd
The Camp, where Death did in ſad Triumph reign,
With wide Deſtruction, covering all the Plain;
Thus to himſelf: At laſt I have prevail'd
Againſt this Sect, tho other Arts have fail'd:
Their Troops half ruin'd with the Plague, afford
An eaſie Conqueſt, for King *Octa*'s Sword:
I'll break the Peace, although advanc'd ſo far,
And finiſh their Deſtruction by new War.
Arthur, prepare againſt the *Saxon* Arms,
'Tis time enough for *Ethelina*'s Charms.
Heroes delay'd, and diſappointed, prize
The Crown, which got too cheaply, they deſpiſe:
Pleaſures the farther off, the greater ſeem,
And Toil and Danger, beſt preſerve Eſteem;
That ſervice I will do, by taking care
To give freſh Fuel to th' expiring War.
That ſaid, he leaves the Cryſtal Plains of Light,
And to th' Infernal Regions takes his Flight.

There ſtands a Rock, daſh'd with the breaking Wave
Of troubled *Styx*, where in a gloomy Cave
Flowing with Gore, the fierce *Bellona* dwells,
And bound with Adamantine Fetters, Yells.

Around stand Heaps of mossy Sculls, and Bones,
Whence issue loud Laments, and dreadful Groans:
Torn Limbs, and mangled Bodies are her Food,
Her Drink whole Bowls of Wormwood, Gall, and Blood.
Long curling Snakes her Head with Horrour crown,
And on her squallid Back hang lolling down.
This gripes a bloody Dart, the other Hand
Grasps of Infernal Fire, a flaming Brand.
Treason, and Usurpation near ally'd,
Haughty Ambition, and elated Pride,
And Cruelty, with bloody Garlands crown'd,
Rapine, and Desolation stand around.
With these Injustice, Violence, Rage remain,
And ghastly Famine, with her meagre Train.
This Savage Rout to *Gallia* now resort,
Drawn by the Fame of proud *Versallia*'s Court:
There these Attendants on their Master wait,
And with their odious Forms, compose his horrid State.
To this wild Den now did th' Apostate fly,
Resolving all *Bellona*'s Aid to try:
At his Approach the Monsters cease their Din,
And bow at distance with a dreadful Grin.
The *Stygian* Prince, the Fury soon unchains,
Strait double Rage boils in her swelling Veins.

 Then thus he spoke, to *Octa*'s Palace fly,
Attended with perfidious Treachery,
And various Discord, let thy Arts perswade
That Prince, the ruin'd *Britons* to invade.
Go raise new Tumults, and dissolve the Peace,
For this high Task *Bellona* I release.

 Charg'd with these dire Commands, she flies away,
To the Superiour Regions, blest with Day.

Near

Near *Peak's* afpiring Mount, and fpacious Wood,
And the green Banks of *Dovus* Cryftal Flood:
A wide mouth'd Den, th' admiring Traveller fees
With thorny Shrubs o'er-fpread, and fhady Trees;
Which downward goes unfathomably deep,
Beneath the fubterranean Vaults, that keep
Imprifon'd Damps, and Winds tumultuous Store,
And the low Caves, where falling Waters roar.
It paffes thro' the Bowels of the Earth;
And the rich Beds, where Metals have their Birth,
Till it reveals the gloomy Mouth of Hell,
Bellona freed from her infernal Cell;
Thro' this dire Gulph afcends with hafty Flight,
And foon emerges in the Fields of Light.
The Air grew dark, the Rocks, and Mountains ftruck
With Horrour, at the *Fury's* Prefence fhook.
The Sphears diforder'd roll, the Starting Sun
Springs from the Heav'nly Courfe he us'd to run.
The Moon all drown'd in Blood, and blazing Stars,
Portended Tumults, and deftructive Wars.

Straight to King *Octa's* Court the Fury comes,
And *Acha Octa's* Mother's Shape affumes.
Then thus fhe fpoke:
From bleft *Elyfian* Gardens I defcend;
To teach thee how to gain a glorious End,
Of all thy Labours, and thy warlike Toil,
And fix thy Empire o'er the *Britifh* Ifle.
Heav'n has decreed that here thy Race fhall reign,
And therefore has the hateful *Britons* flain,
With a deftructive Plague, and poifon'd Darts
Shot from above, into their impious Hearts:
Not half their Troops furvive, make haft my Son
Their Ruine to compleat, by Heav'n begun.

Run then to Triumph, haft to certain Spoil,
And chafe the curfed Nation from the Ifle.
You fee how much your League the Gods offend,
Let not their Enemy, be *Octa*'s Friend.
They muft not be to us by Blood ally'd,
Nor *Ethelina* be a *Briton*'s Bride.
That faid, a fpotted Viper from her Head,
She to his Bofom fecretly convey'd.
The poifonous Vermin, with infernal Art
Glides thro' his Breaft, and twines about his Heart:
The fecret Poifon wanders thro' his Veins,
And warlike Fury o'er his Spirits reigns.
Hence ftraight-way to the *Picts* and *Scottifh* Court,
The Fury, and her hellifh Train refort:
Where they to bloody Wars found loud Alarms,
And make the barb'rous Nations fly to Arms.

Mean time, the *Saxon* Monarch raving flew
About the Court, and foon together drew
The chiefeft Lords, and thus himfelf expreft,
It was refolv'd to give the *Britons* Reft;
The Land between the Nations to divide,
And that the Princefs fhould be *Arthur*'s Bride:
But Heav'n againft this Treaty does declare,
And fingly with the *Britons* wages War.
In vain we offer what they can't enjoy,
We fpare the Men, Heav'n labours to deftroy.
Avenging Gods from their high Regions came,
Arm'd with bright Swords of keen, Etherial Flame,
And fatal Darts of pointed Lightnings made,
And with fure Death the *Britifh* Camp invade.
Their trembling Reliques fall our certain Prey,
Heav'n founds th' Alarm, and we muft Heav'n obey.

Tho'

Tho we by Sea their Power could not withstand,
Our Gods more potent are, then theirs by Land.
Th' unfinish'd Conquest we may soon compleat
Or from this Isle oblige them to retreat.
This fair occasion let our Arms improve
To fix our Power, and all our Fears remove.
He ceas'd, and all his Captains War desir'd,
And sprang into the Field with Martial Heat inspir'd.

   Straight Orders are dispatcht for all to Arm,
And thro' the Cities founds the loud Alarm.
The tremb'ling Husbandman his Toil forbears,
Fells his tall Ash, and shapes long Staves for Spears.
Some sighing o'er their Anvils forge the Blades,
Of Swords, instead of Hooks, and rural Spades.
Huge Gauntlets some, some hollow Helmets beat,
And some o'er brazen Backs, and Breastplates sweat.
Some shape their Darts, and some their Javelins Points,
Or fit their polish'd Armour's Manly Joints.
Sharp'ning their Arrows Heads, some stand inclin'd,
Some on revolving Stones their Axes grind.
Some serve on foot, some take the Horseman's Launce,
And to the Field their foaming Coursers praunce.
In haste, some from their high roof'd Halls, hung round
With all the horrid Pride of War, and crown'd
With dusty Trophies, take their massy Shield,
And flaming Sword, and fly into the Field.
Some clasp their Helmets on, some snatch their Spear,
And polish'd Buckler, and in Arms appear.
Ensigns display'd, and Trumpets voice delight
The *Saxon* Youth, and martial Minds excite.
The lighted Beacons from the Hills declare,
As blazing Comets do, approaching War.

The flaming Signals giv'n, the Regions round
With Hors'men, Arms, and warlike noise resound.
As when;
In some great Town a Fire breaks out by Night,
And fills with crackling Flames, and dismal Light,
With Sparks, and Pitchy Smoak th' astonish'd Sky;
Th' affrighted Guards, that first the Flame espy,
Straight give th' Alarm, and spread the dreadful Cry:
Th' amaz'd Inhabitants the Signal take;
And run in Crowds half cloath'd, and half awake,
To stop the spreading Ruin; and to tame
With spouting Engines the destructive Flame:
So when the frightful Cry of War begun,
Into the Fields in Troops the *Saxons* run.

Now *Muse* relate, and in their Order name
The People, which from different Regions came.
What fam'd Commanders did their Squadrons head,
And what great Lords their valiant Subjects led.
First the stout *Cantian* Saxon, from the Land
Which bravely once did *Cæsar*'s Arms withstand,
Where Joyful Nature, sits in Plenty crown'd,
Hesperian Woods, and Sylvan Scenes surround
Her shady Throne, that with rich Fruit abound.
Of these some on the flowry Banks reside,
Of fair *Medvaga*, that with wanton Pride,
Forms silver Mazes with her crooked Tide.
The *Durobrovian* Youth of war-like Fame,
And bold *Vagniacans*, together came,
With those about the fruitful Region bred,
Where *Durovernum*, reers her stately Head.
They march from *Thanatos*, and from her Towers
Her valiant Youth sublime *Rutupiæ* pours.

Rutupiæ

Rutupiæ, whose rich Gems, and Pearly Store
Inticed Victorious *Cæsar*, to her Shore.
Their chief Commanders were great *Amades*,
Valiant *Theodorick*, *Osred*, and with these
Hengist, a splendid Youth, the Blood, and Name
Of the first *Saxon*, of Illustrious Fame,
That from the *Belgick* Shore, to *Albion* came.
From the fat Glebe they come, and flowry Land
Which the stout *Trinobantes*, did Command.
Augusta sends her warlike Youth, a Town
Of ancient Fame, to Foreign Merchants known,
Ev'n then for Naval Power of great Renown.
But since her stately Head is rais'd so high,
Her glorious Towers surmount the wondring Sky.
Her Royal Fleets the watry World controll,
Where the vast Ocean can his Billows roll,
Far as the *Indies*, and from Pole to Pole.
Her Power by trembling, Neighbour States is fear'd,
By distant Empires, and new Worlds rever'd.
Her bellowing Oaks, with louder Thunder roar,
Then what annoy'd them, on their Hills before,
Shaking the *Gallick*, and the *Belgian* Shore.
Britannia's Head she reigns in Wealth and Ease,
Mart of the World, and Emp'ress of the Seas.
Edgar and *Cissa*, both Illustrious Names,
From the delightful Banks of famous Thames,
Into the Field, *Augusta*'s Squadrons bring,
None fought more bravely for the *Saxon* King.

They from the Forests come, whose Sports invite
Augusta's Youth, that in the Woods delight.
From the sweet Gardens of the fruitful East,
With smiling Flowers, and od'rous Saffron blest:

From

From *Camelodunum* pop'lous once, and proud
Of its fam'd Colony of *Roman* Blood.
From round *Canonium*, arm'd with Swords and Shields
The warlike People March, and from the Fields
Where *Idumanum* verdant Wealth bestows,
Whose wanton Tide in wreathing Volumes flows;
Still forming Reedy Islands, as it goes.
Brave *Sebert* led them, valiant *Oga*'s Son,
Whose Arms had great Renown in Battel won.
The chearful Youth from *Verolamium* came,
A Town of ancient, and illustrious Fame:
Where fortify'd with Trenches, Lakes and Wood,
The valiant *Casibellan*, once withstood
The *Roman* Arms, oblig'd at last to yield,
Where *Cæsar* fights, who can maintain the Field?
Since cherish'd by th' indulgent Conquerour,
The City was advanc'd in Wealth and Power:
Its Towers, gilt Fanes, and Palaces did rise,
Darting Terrestrial Glories thro' the Skies.
Now where the City stood, the Ploughman toils,
And as he works, turns up old *Roman* Spoils,
Medals and Coins, enrich th' admiring Clown,
Pavements and Urns, by ancient Figures known.

From the rich Seats they came, from whence their Sword
The *Coritanian* chas'd, the rightful Lord.
From all the Towns, around the spacious Wood
Near which sublime *Tripontium*'s Castles stood.
From *Bannavenna* well-arm'd Squadrons came,
And *Durobrevis*, on *Aufona*'s Stream.
Their chief Commanders were brave *Alopas*,
And valiant *Egbert*, both of *Horsa*'s Race.

They

They came, who dwelt along the Southern Coaſt,
On which the *German* Ocean's Waves are toſt:
The Soil the brave *Icenian Britons*, bleſt
With Peace, and envy'd Plenty, once poſſeſt.
Venta they left, where *Gariena*'s Tide,
Does to the Boſom of *Bardunus* glide;
An ancient, wealthy Town that did abound,
With warlike Youth, and rul'd the Soil around.
High *Branodunum* does her Squadrons ſend,
Where *Roman* Arms, did once the Coaſt defend.

They leave the Towns along fair *Theta*'s Flood,
And happy Soil, where *Gariononum* ſtood.
Thoſe from the Banks of winding *Stourus* came,
And the rich Town, that bore *Fauſtinus* name.
They come from *Oza*'s Banks, and from the Land
Which lofty *Combritonium* did Command.
This numerous *Saxon* Youth, that then obey'd
King *Ella*'s Laws, advance to *Octa*'s Aid.
Ella their Valiant Prince, was at their Head,
And to the Field, his warlike People led.

From *Camboritum*, and the Neighb'ring Hills,
The chearful Youth drawn out, the Region fills:
From *Camboritum*, then a warlike Town,
Since for the Muſes Seat, much better known.
Her learned Sons have gain'd Immortal Fame,
And high as Heav'n, have rais'd *Britannia*'s Name.
Redwal, whoſe Lands a vaſt Revenue yield,
Led them, compleatly arm'd into the Field.

They leave the reedy Lakes, and marſhy Soil,
Once happy by the *Britiſh* Farmer's Toil:

Now the vext Land a Foreign Master knows,
Which o'er the Country, like a Deluge flows,
That from the Sea, the Banks born down, is roll'd,
And o'er their Fields advances uncontroll'd.
The Valiant Youth from all the Region goes,
Which *Trent* and *Lindis*, confluent Streams, enclose.
High *Margadunum*, all her Squadrons lends,
And stately *Lindum*, which her Power extends
O'er the wide Province, her Battalions sends.
Mighty *Ebissa*, from the Fenny Land
Into the Field, did lead this warlike Band.
Orla, and *Imerick*, a Valiant Lord,
Fam'd for his Strength, and vast unweildy Sword,
Drew all their Squadrons, and Battalions forth,
From all their Towns, that lay the farthest North.

King *Cerdic* from the *West* his Army brought,
Who for the *Saxon* Empire bravely fought.
He all the *Saxon* Heroes far excell'd,
Whose conquering Arms, were never yet repell'd.
A great Commander, Brave and Fortunate,
That founded first the *Western Saxon* State.
Those seated on *Halenus* verdant Banks,
Draw out, and Muster their Victorious Ranks.
They March from *Trisantona*'s Crystal Flood,
From *Venta*'s Downs, and *Regnum*'s spacious Wood.
From rich *Clusentum*, and fair *Vecta*'s Isle,
From *Briga* and *Segontium*'s fertile Soil.
On *Sorbiodunum*'s Plains arm'd Youth appears,
With nodding Plumes, and moving Groves of Spears.
The famous Captain, who had chief Command,
That with his Prince came to invade the Land,
Was *Lothar*, born on *Belgick Mosa*'s Flood,
Whose noble Veins were fill'd with Royal Blood:

Him

Him did fair *Emme Cerdic*'s Sister bear,
And dying, left him to her Brother's Care.
With all this Strength King *Octa* takes the Field,
Nor doubts, but *Arthur* to his Arms must yield.

The *Britons* now a solemn Fast proclaim
To mourn their Guilt, and take th' attendant Shame:
To own the dreadful Plague, their Crimes desert,
And by their Grief, like Judgments to avert.
That Heav'n appeas'd, from its relenting Hand
May drop its Bolt, and spare the threaten'd Land.
Sorrow untaught on every Face appear'd,
And only Sighs and sad Laments were heard.
They weep aloud, and mourn their impious Fall,
And with united Prayers for Mercy call.
The prostrate Penitents for Pardon Cry,
And from Heav'n's Justice, to its Pity fly.
To Grief, and flowing Tears, no Bounds are giv'n;
Th' Artillery alone, that Conquers Heav'n.
Righteous Resolves fill every humble Mind,
And all in Vows of blest Obedience joyn'd.
The mournful Camp's a Scene of pious Woe,
Where thro' their Eyes, their Hearts dissolving flow.
Their loud and fervent Supplications, rise
Above the Clouds, and penetrate the Skies.
Contending thus with Heav'n they weep, and pray,
And strive to turn th' impending Storm away,
Which charg'd with Vengeance o'er their Camp appear'd,
More Plagues they had deserv'd, and therefore fear'd.

Prince *Arthur*, that in Piety was chief,
And now chief Mourner, thus exprest his Grief,
Th' attentive *Britons* hear, and hope Relief

Of Wrath Divine, what Vials have been pour'd,
And empty'd on our Heads, that have devour'd
The guilty *Britons*, and our Camp consum'd;
Where pil'd in Heaps, the Dead, the Dead entomb'd!
Th' Eternal's Sword around did widely waft,
And carried Death, and Ruin where it paft.
It reek'd in Blood, and fhone with Slaughter dy'd
Red, as the Crimfon Sins, which for its Vengeance cry'd
This day we deprecate the Curfe, and all
With wounded Souls, for Heav'n's Compaffion call.
To ftill the Storms of Wrath which on us beat,
And caufe the fiery Torrent to retreat.
The God we Worfhip Jealous is; and Pure,
His *Wrath* advances flow, but reaches fure;
His threat'ning Arm does long extended ftay,
But then defcends with the more fearful Sway.
Who then can his confuming Fire withftand,
Who bear the ftrokes of his Revenging Hand?
There's hope your Prayers have found Succefs above,
And Heav'n aton'd, will this fierce Plague remove.
May ne'er our impious Crimes, his Arm provoke
To end our Ruin, by a fecond ftroke.

    He ceas'd. His Men their facred Vows renew,
And for Devotion to their Tents withdrew:
Where while Celeftial Warmth their Breafts extend,
The Day in Prayers, and Hymns of Praife they end.
Heav'n the Returning Penitents embrac'd,
And far away th' Infernal Legions chas'd.
Their Guardian Angels once more take their Poft.
Drawn out in bright Array, around their Hoft.

    Twice had the Sun, with dawning Glories bleft
The World, and call'd the Lab'rer from his reft,

As

As oft the Night her Sable Vesture, set
With pearly Dew, ascends her Throne of Jet:
When certain Tydings *Arthur*'s Camp alarm'd,
That *Octa*'s Men against the *Britons* arm'd;
Believing that the *Britons* thus distrest,
By *Saxon* Arms, might be with Ease opprest.
With *Octa* Leagues, and Overtures of Peace,
When War shall offer more advantage, cease.
The Tydings soon thro' all the Army ran,
Whence in their Minds tormenting Fears began.
They thought their weaken'd Troops, could not oppose
The fierce Attack, of their insulting Foes.
The trouble spreads, all, their sad State bewail,
That those the *Plague* had spar'd, the *Sword* should now assail.

The pious Prince with heavy Grief opprest,
To Heav'n thus vents the trouble of his Breast:
Thou that from dark *Egyptian* Prisons freed,
As Shepherds do their Flocks, did'st *Israel* lead.
Who from between the Cherubs, did'st display
Thy Heav'nly Glories, to direct their Way.
Whose mighty Arm extended, did secure
Their trembling Host, pursu'd by *Pharoah*'s Power:
Shine forth, and with thy Beams dispel this Night,
Whose horrid Shades, my lab'ring Soul affright.
Stir up thy Strength, thy Foes, and ours invade,
And bring thy shining Myriads to our Aid.
Thou God of Light. reveal thy glorious Face,
Thy Rays will from the Sky, this Tempest chase.
Thee, all the unnumber'd Hosts of Heav'n obey,
Drawn in embattl'd Lines, and bright Array
Along th' Etherial Plains, and here below
Monarchs to thee, precarious Empires owe.

Prest

Prest by our Enemies, to thee we fly,
How long wilt thou neglect thy People's Cry?
Bath'd in our Tears, and pleas'd with Grief, we moan
Our solitary State, for God is gone.
Our Foes around, despise our Mournful State,
And on those Loads that press us, heap more Weight.
Our Enemies enrag'd, no Mounds between,
On us, like rising Waves, come roaring in.
Against the Reliques thy fierce Wrath has spar'd,
The Foe's Inexorable Sword's prepar'd.
On me with Scorn th' insulting Scoffers look,
As one, whom Heav'n displeas'd has now forsook:
The *Pagans* make my Woes their sportful Theam,
Reproach thy Vot'ries, and thy Name blaspheme.
Stir up thy Power, thy glitt'ring Arms assume,
Bowing the Heav'ns, to our Deliverance come.
As from th' aspiring Mountains, rais'd around
Jerusalem, while it stood, Protection found:
So let a Guard, from thy bright Host detach'd,
T' encamp about our Army be dispatch'd.
Thou God of Truth arise, let th' Heathen see,
Thy Wrath pursues perfidious Treachery.

   While thus Prince *Arthur* Heav'ns Protection sought,
The God-like *Raphael*, this kind Message brought:
Thy Prayer prevails, O Prince, be not dismay'd,
Th' *Almighty*'s Arm is stretcht out for your Aid.
Highly your Crimes Heav'n's Majesty displeas'd,
But your Repentance hath his Wrath appeas'd.
His People's Faults do but his Rod enploy,
But his fierce Vengeance shall his Foes destroy.
Let not the *Saxon*'s Numbers be their Pride,
You're stronger far, for God is on your Side,
Abundantly your Loss is thus Supply'd.

                                       Arise,

Arise, and let the *Britons* Courage take,
Their Arms shall drive th' advancing *Saxon* back.

The Prince with *Raphael*'s heav'nly Message cheer'd,
Octa's unequal Force, no longer fear'd.
His chearful Looks the drooping *Britons* saw,
And thence reviving Warmth, and Courage draw.
His God-like Language calms their troubled Minds,
And with its Charms reluctant Passions binds.
He to their frozen Veins new Life procures,
Dispels their Doubts, and fainting Hopes assures.
The *Britons*, that before did scarcely dare
T' expect it, now resolve to meet the War.
They now no more the Fears of Danger own,
While Heav'n assists, and *Arthur* leads them on.

Mean time ill-boding Prodigies, affright
King *Octa*, and disswade his Men from Fight:
The Birds of Heav'n the gazing *Augurs* scare,
Crossing with inauspicious Flights the Air!
The Fowl as sacred kept, projected Meat
Coldly regard, and sullenly retreat.
From hollow Oaks, obscene Night Ravens sung,
And clustring Bees upon their Ensigns hung.
Bullocks with Garlands crown'd reluctant come,
Break from the Altar, and run lowing home.
Near silver *Thamisis* sweet Banks, there stood,
Awful for solemn Shade, a lofty Wood:
Where they ador'd their God *Irmanful* nam'd,
A war-like Idol, thro' *Germania* fam'd.
His Right Hand did a flowry Garland bear,
His Left held up a Balance in the Air:
His Breast a grisly Bear's fierce Figure bore,
And in his Shield a Lyon seem'd to roar.

Fresh

Fresh gather'd Flowers difpers'd in Heaps around,
Gay Superftition, paint their facred Ground.
Hither the *Saxons*, and their Priefts repair,
T' atone their God, with *Victims* and with Prayer.
His Aid againft the *Britons* to invoke,
While the tall Oaks with Clouds of Incenfe fmoak:
The Priefts the Wood to burn the Victim lay,
And a crown'd Bullock at the Altar flay.
Their reeking Hands, ranfack in vain the Breaft,
To find the Heart of the prodigious Beaft:
The Priefts grow pale, and from their Altar ftart,
Finding a *Victim* flain without a Heart.

But that which moft the gazing *Saxons* fcare,
Are Armies feen engaging in the Air.
The higheft ground of all the heavenly Way,
The Sun had gain'd, darting a downright Ray:
When two black Clouds appear'd, one from the Eaft
Threat'ning arofe; the other from the Weft.
They ftretcht their lowring Fronts acrofs the Sky,
And frowning, feem'd each other to defy.
Between, a Glade of free and open Air,
Did, as betwixt two fpacious Woods, appear.
Then iffuing from the Womb of either Cloud
Two Armies met, and drawn in Battel ftood.
The fick'ning Sun fhone with a gloomy Ray,
Scar'd with the bloody Bufinefs of the Day.
Between them ftraight began a furious Fight,
And glitt'ring Arms fupply'd the want of Light.
Eager of Glory from Heroick Deeds,
The Airy Knights fpur on their foaming Steeds:
They rufh to Battel with a full Career,
And Tilting break their Lances in the Air.

Swords

Swords clashing Swords, and Shields rencountring Shields,
Fill with the Din of War th'Etherial Fields.
Vaulting the Air, thick Showers of Arrows fly,
And warlike Labour troubles all the Sky.
A bloody Field was fought, and Heaps of Slain
Seem'd to o'erspread the wide Etherial Plain.
Chariots o'erturn'd, and scatter'd Harness by;
Steeds, and dismounted Riders, mingl'd ly.
Erom gaping Wounds, a Crimson Sea of Blood,
Along the Heav'nly Pavement reeking flow'd.
At last the Squadrons, in the Eastern Sky
Fell in Disorder, and began to fly.
The Conquerors hung upon their Backs, and chas'd
Their Troops, with mighty Rout thro' all the Waft:
Into the Clouds and Heav'nly Wilds they fled,
And left upon the Bloody Field their Dead.
Next off the Theatre the Victors go,
And into shapeless Air dissolving flow.
The lab'ring Scene, and Actors disappear'd,
And of the War the Airy Stage was clear'd.

Octa that view'd th' important Prodigy,
Trembled to see the Eastern Army fly.
He wisely hid his Fears within his Breast,
And to his Captains thus himself exprest.
Let not vain *Prodigies* the *Saxons* scare,
Form'd by the wanton Demons of the Air:
Wrapt in dark Clouds, the Will of Heav'n's conceal'd,
To Mortals only by th'Event reveal'd.
Think not fantastick *Portents*, can declare
The Fate of Kingdoms, and Results of War.
These only weak, and vulgar Minds affright,
Like Phantoms, borrowing Horrour from the Night.

Which, as capricious Nature's Play, the wife,
From timerous Superstition free, despise.
The valiant on their Arms make Fortune wait,
And carve out to themselves propitious Fate.
Neglect these Dreams, the Gods are ever kind
To the best Troops, and to th' undaunted Mind.
Great *Cæsar* thus condemn'd his Augurs Tales,
Fights, and o'er Foes, and Portents too, prevails.
Thus *Octa* strove their Passion to appease,
And give them what himself enjoy'd not, Ease.

At a small Village, now unknown by Name,
There dwelt a Sorcerer of wondrous Fame.
The Pagan *Briton Merlin*, that of late
For his dire Art, driv'n from the *British* State;
Did with the Pagan *Saxons* safely dwell,
And kept his Correspondence up with Hell.
With potent Juices, and Infernal Charms,
The black Magician, Plagues, and Mortal Harms,
And various Kinds of Mischiefs, did inflict
On those, whom Heav'n was pleas'd he should afflict.
He in the silent Night while Mortals sleep,
By Hedg-rows, Lakes, or o'er the Hills would creep;
To gather baleful Herbs, with which he drew
Familiar Fiends; which round, like Ravens, flew.
Mounting his Magick Wand, he thro' the Air
To rich Nocturnal Feasts would oft repair,
Spread on green Hills, or near some shady Wood,
Or Grassy Banks of some sweet River's Flood:
Where when th' infernal Company are met,
Rich Meats, and Wines, on stately Tables set,
They seem to taste, and by the Moon's pale Light,
Spend in Fantastick Luxury, the Night.

But

But from th'imaginary Banquet come,
At the grey Dawning, lank and meagre, home.

King *Offa*'s Servants at their Lord's Command,
With their unrighteous Wages in their Hand,
To *Merlin* come, and soon prevail'd to bring
The fam'd Magician to their anxious King.
Whom *Offa* thus bespoke,
The Miracles, your sacred Art has shown,
Make you thro' all the wondring Island known
Let your prodigious Power my Army guard,
Honour and Riches shall be your Reward.
The Foe we'll now engage, but let him first
Be here by you, and your Enchantments curst:
Curse then this impious Enemy; your Breath
Will blast their Strength, and fatal prove as Death.
Your Curse and that of Fate, is deem'd the same,
And whom you bless the World does blest proclaim.
Assault their Camp with all your Magick Powers,
You'll curse your Mortal Foes, as well as ours.
Revenge your Wrongs, and by your potent Charms,
Draw off the Guardian Gods, that help their Arms.
Come with me then, I will a Mountain shew,
From whose high Top you may their Army view:
There we'll atone the Gods with Prayer, and thence
You shall your Curses on the Foe dispense.

Then *Offa* to a Mount the Sorc'rer led,
Whence thro' the Vale he saw the *Britons* spred.
Seven Altars they erect, and in the Flames,
Seven Bullocks sacrifice, and seven Rams.
Here *Offa* and his Lords their Gods ador'd,
And kneeling round the Flames, their Aid implor'd.

At laſt, the Night advancing to her Noon,
Merlin conducted by the ſilver Moon,
From *Octa*, to a neighb'ring Hill withdraws,
T' obſerve infernal Rites, and magick Laws.
He ſeeks out noxious Plants, whoſe powerful Juice,
Magicians for their ſtrong Enchantments uſe.
Green Henbane, Wormwood, Hemlock, Savine Tops,
In whoſe preſt Juice he dipt his magick Sops;
With Plants that to the Moon their Vertue owe,
And Toadſtools, which from Storms of Thunder grow.
Which mixt with humane Fat, red Hair, and Blood,
He offers up caſt on the Burning Wood.
Then with his potent Wand, he walks around,
And with dire Circles, marks th' enchanted ground.
Then did he with a mutt'ring Voice rehearſe
Wondrous, myſterious Words, and potent Verſe.
Th' infernal Charms all Nature did affright,
The waning Moon ſtraight ſickned at the Sight:
The Hill with Horror trembled, and around
With howling Wolves the neighb'ring Woods reſound.
Then Storms of Rain enſue, ſwift Lightnings fly,
And dreadful Thunderclaps torment the Sky.
Spectres, and Ghoſts break from their hollow Tomb,
And glaring round the Necromancer come.
All Hell was mov'd, the Powers drawn from their Seats
Ariſe, while *Merlin* his dire words repeats:
Whom with his Charms, he labours to engage
Againſt the *Britons*, and excites their Rage.
His powerful Arts incline them to employ
United force, their Army to deſtroy.
But Hell and all its Friends, vain Rage expreſs,
And Curſe in vain, when Heav'n deſigns to Bleſs.

Merlin

Book VII.   *Prince* Arthur.   105

Merlin, his impious Ceremonies done,
Returns to *Octa* with the rising Sun.
Before the *Saxon* Lords he stood, prepar'd
To Curse their Foes, and merit his Reward.
When the Magician's Breast an unknown Fire
Laps'd from above did suddenly inspire:
A Warmth Divine his Spirits did invade,
And once a Sorcerer a Prophet made.
The Heav'nly Fury *Merlin* did constrain
To Bless, whom he to Curse design'd in vain.

How beautiful the *Britons* Tents appear!
What goodly Heads his Tabernacles rear!
As the rich Vales they spread their verdant Pride,
Or flowry Gardens by the River's side.
As shady Aloes in th' *Arabian* Woods,
Or lofty Cedars planted by the Floods.
Indulgent Heav'n upon the *Briton*, pours
Prolifick Dews, and sweet refreshing Showers.
His Seed shall flourish midst surrounding Streams,
Blest with mild Air, and pure reviving Beams.
His Prince's Glory, shall his People's Love,
And Neighbour Monarchs Fear, and Envy, move.
He, like a fearless Unicorn shall stand,
Sure of his Strength, and all the Fields command.
Those hostile Nations who oppose his Power,
He with resistless Fury shall devour.
He'll break their crashing Bones, his Bow he'll bend,
And thro' their Flesh, his piercing Arrows send.
He couches like a Lyon on the Sand,
Like a vast Lyon in a Desart Land:
Stretching his fearful Limbs at Ease he lies,
What Creature dares provoke him to arise?

Bless

Bless him, and be of happy Men the first,
Curse him, and thou thy self shalt be accurst.

He ceas'd. King *Offa*, tho' incens'd, suppreſt
His Trouble and Diſpleaſure in his Breaſt,
And to the Sorcerer, thus himſelf addreſt:
By ſolemn Execrations, to devote
The *Britons* to Deſtruction, you were ſought;
But, you this impious Nation chuſe to Bleſs,
And all your Words preſage their Arms Succeſs.
Withdraw a ſecond time, perhaps you'll find
The Gods, by your Enchantments, more inclin'd:
Perhaps ſome Errour might at firſt diſpleaſe;
A ſecond Eſſay will the Powers appeaſe.

The Sorcerer a ſecond time retreats,
And all his potent Charms with Care repeats:
He added ev'ry poiſonous Juice, and Spell,
He knew had force to ſhake the Realms of Hell.
Merlin, his impious Rites perform'd, returns,
And acted by Satanick Fury, burns.
All Hell within ſhook the Magician's Breaſt,
But by a Power Divine ſtraight diſpoſſeſt,
Th'affrighted Demons fled, and in their ſtead
A pure Celeſtial Spirit did ſucceed.
Tranſports Divine his lab'ring Soul engage,
And thus he ſpake, mov'd with Prophetick Rage:
In vain with Divination, we aſſail
The *Chriſtian* Arms, where all Enchantments fail.
Our Curſes by the powerful Breath of Heav'n,
Back on our Heads, with fatal Force are driv'n.
Thoſe God has bleſt, no Guards nor Bulwarks need,
Nor can their Arms, whom he has curſt, ſucceed.

Unchangeably he's on his Purpose bent,
Nor does he, like unstable Man, repent.
The Christian Army will prevail; that said,
Observing *Octa*'s Fury rise, he fled.

The King incens'd, cry'd, curst Magician, fly;
Spite of thy Charms, and thee, shall Victory
And Triumph, on the *Saxon* Arms attend,
Against such Troops what Signs can ill portend?
Thy impious Tongue Propitious Heav'n belies;
And for the *Britons* forges Prophecies.
Thy self of *British* Blood, the *British* Cause
Stronger than Wrongs, or ev'n Religion, draws.
So oft poor Slaves, who to a neighb'ring State
Fly for Protection from a Tyrants Hate,
If he does War against those Neighbours wage,
And with his Arms, upon their Frontiers rage:
Joy at th' Oppressor's Conquests and Success,
Against their own Protector's, they express.

Octa at this Defeat with Fury burn'd,
And to his Army with his Lords return'd.
Amidst his Troops he rode, and thus he spoke,
His Voice high rais'd, their Courage to provoke:
Saxons, you now to certain Conquest go,
To glean the Reliques of a ruin'd Foe.
The Gods do loudly for your Cause declare,
And call you, but to finish their own War.
Think on the Deeds by your great Nation done,
The Towns they took, their glorious Battles won,
And the rich Countries by their Arms o'er-run.
From this fair *Island* shall the *Britons* chase,
From these sweet Fields, great *Odin*'s warlike Race?

From

From these sweet Fields, for which our Leaders fought,
Which with the noblest *Saxon* Blood were bought.
Shall we with ignominious Flight retreat,
O'er the rough Main, to seek some milder Seat?
Or shall we back to our cold Region go,
To hide in Caves, and dwell Hills of Snow?
Can my victorious Friends the *Britons* dread,
Who from your conq'ring Arms so oft have fled,
A vanquish'd Nation by an Exile led?
Appear like *Saxons*, add this Conquest more,
To all th' immortal Lawrels won before.
Thus you'll the Grounds of lasting Empire lay,
And still the *Briton* shall your Laws obey.
Vain with Success at Sea, they draw their Swords,
And for Dominion strive with us, their Lords:
Let now your Arms chastise their wanton Pride,
And then in unmolested Peace abide.
He said, and brandishing his threatning Launce,
And springing forward, bids his Men advance.

Now from the Hills th'embattel'd *Saxon* swarms,
And covers all the Plain with hostile Arms.
As when the great Commanders, Orders give
To quit the straight Dominions of their Hive,
The *Bees* pour out a numerous Colony;
From their sweet Cells, the busie Youth on high
Wheel in the Air, and darken all the Sky.
While brazen Pans charm and compose their Heat,
In some tall neighb'ring Tree they fix their Seat:
Thither th' unnumber'd Vulgar streight resort,
And clustring Crowds surround their Monarch's Court.
So thick the *Saxons* on the Field appear,
Following their Leader with an endless Rear.

The

The gloomy Throngs look terrible from far,
Difclofing flow, the horrid Face of War.
The thick Battalions move in dreadful Form,
As lowring Clouds advance before a Storm.
So when the Sea grown black, the hazy Sky,
And rifing Winds, foretel a Tempeft nigh:
Th' experienc'd Mariners, with hafty care
Furl their fpread Sails, and for a Storm prepare.
Straight in the black *Horizon*, to the Skies
The dusky Billows threat'ning Heads arife:
Th' unnumber'd Troops upon each others throng,
And with a gloomy Afpect march along.
Advancing, they their boundlefs Front extend
O'er all the Main, and fearful Wreck portend.
The *Saxon* Hoft thus in its March appears,
And where it came, thick Groves of briftling Spears,
Broad Iron Backs, and Breaft-plates, brazen Shields,
Mail-Coats, and burnifh'd Helms o'erfpread the Fields.
Chariots of War in Clouds of Duft advance,
And tofling up their Foam, the thundring Courfers Prance.
Their Army's Wings ftretcht out, they to the Foes
A long extended Ridge of War oppofe.
The *Britifh* Squadrons tho' outnumber'd far,
Run boldly on the horrid Edge of War.
To make their Front, the thin Battalions ran,
But ftretcht not equal to the *Saxon Van*.
Both Armies thus, rang'd in Battalia ftood,
And Death prepar'd her thirfty Jaws for Blood.

   From the Celeftial Hoft, a glorious Band
Of Seraphs was detach'd by high Command:
Hither the fhining Warriours did repair,
And drawn in long Array, ftood in the Air.

Their Blades divinely temper'd flam'd on high;
And blazing Shields inlighten all the Sky;
Impenetrable Shields, drawn from the Towers
Of Heav'n's high Ars'nal, fill'd with warlike Stores.
Th' Angelick Cuirassiers, in Armour shone
Of *Adamant*, from Rocks Empyreal hewn.
High milk-white Plumes, like Snowy Clouds arise,
From their bright Crests, and Nod against the Skies.
Rich Helmets, of Immortal beaten Gold
Adorn their Heads, Brass of Etherial mould
Refin'd above, their joynted Gauntlets made;
Brass, that the Teeth of Time can ne'er invade.
Broad silver Belts richly embroider'd o'er,
Rare Seraph's work, their shining Shoulders bore,
And round them Sky-dy'd Purple Scarfs they wore.
Michael a Prince in Heav'n of first renown,
Who, like a Sun, high in his Chariot shone;
This bright Detachment did in Chief Command,
Charg'd to maintain strict Guard, and to withstand
Th' Attempts, that might by Hellish Fiends be made,
Sent by their Prince the Christian to invade.

While *Lucifer* on the white Mountain's Head,
His black, Infernal Crew about him spread;
With Malice, Rage, and Pride extended sate
High on his dusky Throne, resolv'd to wait,
And see, if this important Day's Event,
Would answer with success, his curst intent.

In glitt'ring Arms the dazling Prince, appears
Before his Troops, the *Saxon* sees, and fears.
His Helm of polish'd Steel brac'd round his Head,
Did o'er the Field, a glorious Terrour spread.

Bright

Bright Stones, and high rais'd Needle Work adorn
The shining Belt, across his Shoulders worn.
His fatal Sword, the Bane of *Gothick* Pride,
With fearful Grace hung by his warlike Side.
Odar the *Neustrian* of this famous Blade
Inur'd to Victory, a Present made
To *Arthur*, when from *Albion* first he came,
To *Odar*'s Camp, to win Heroick Fame:
Lodar did with this Gift King *Odar* grace,
A valiant Hero of the *Neustrian* Race.
His radiant Shield, of Brass its outmost Fold,
Th' inmost temper'd Steel, the midst of Gold,
Was the rare Work of *Lycon*'s skilful Toil,
From which unpeirc'd, the sharpest Darts recoil.
Bright, like a Sun, it did fierce Glory dart,
Where might be seen pourtray'd with wondrous Art;
Strong Towns besieg'd, and famous Battels won,
And great Exploits by ancient Hero's done;
Who to defend their Country, bravely fought,
By Men inspir'd, in sacred Volumes wrote.

Here th' *Israelites*, kind Heav'n's peculiar Care,
Their famous Gen'ral *Joshua* leads to War.
The Rocky Desart past with wondrous Toil,
With Marches worn, and heavy with the Spoil
Form vanquish'd *Baashan*, and King *Sihon* won,
Where their illustrious Triumphs first begun,
Advance their Ensigns, *Canaan* to invade,
Ripe by their full grown Sins for Conquest made.
To *Jordan*'s Streams they come, straight to his Head
His Waves roll'd back, obsequious *Jordan* fled.
The naked Channel shews his sandy Face,
And gives the Fav'rite Nation leave to pass.

Th' aftonish'd *Canaanites*, like *Jordan*, fly,
And weep to fee their Guardian River dry.

Here valiant *Gideon*, with his Troop by Night,
March'd out t' attack the haughty *Midianite*.
The Foe, like Locufts, numberlefs was pour'd
Around the Vale, and all its Fruits devour'd:
But dreading *Gideon*'s Arms, the Spoilers fly,
And by his Sword, and by their own, they die.
King *Zeba*, and *Zalmunna*, with a throng
Of Captive Princes, draw their Chains along.

Here in the plain, ftretcht like fome fpacious Wood,
In long Array, the throng'd *Philiftines* ftood.
Goliah iffuing from their opening Files;
Of Bulk ftupendous, hideous with the Spoils
Of yellow Lyons flain, and fhaggy Bears,
Towring before their fhouting Hoft, appears.
With haughty Air, the wondrous Figure ftrode,
His Sword his Truft, and his right Hand his God.
Beneath his Weight the Vally feem'd to fhake,
But his pale Foes did more than feem to quake.
Gnafhing his Teeth the grinning Monfter ftood,
Himfelf an Army, and his Spear a Wood.
Sufficient Stores whole Mines could fcarcely yield,
For his wide Cuirafs, and prodigious Shield:
Where Figures pourtray'd of fierce Monfters fhone,
But none fo fierce, and monftrous as his own.
High in the Clouds, his brazen Helm did fhow
Like fome vaft Temple's gilded *Cupilo*.
His mighty Legs, that brazen Boots embrac'd,
Tall Pillars feem'd, with *Corinth* Mettal cas'd.
Thus arm'd he ftood, and by his Mein did feem
To curfe aloud, to threaten and blafpheme.

His

His beck'ning Hand held proudly up, invites
To combate, all the trembling *Hebrew* Knights.
Tho vaſt of Bulk he bigger ſwells with Pride,
He curſt their Army, and their Gods defy'd.
Here, God-like *David*, in the flowry Bloom
Of Youth, and Beauty, brings the Monſter's Doom.
To kindle Love, or Pity fitter far,
Then the rough Paſſions, which attend on War:
And likelier by his Youth's engaging Charms,
To wound the *Anakite*, then with his Arms.
Yet bravely he 'embrac'd th' unequal War,
And ſcorn'd his Rage that curſt him from afar.
The fatal Stone by the young Hero flung,
Cut thro' the Air, and ſure of Triumph ſung:
It pierc'd the *Cyclops* Head, his Carcaſs fell
Swift to the Ground, his Soul, as ſwift to Hell.
Faln on his Face, he bites the trembling Ground;
And Brains, and Gore break thro the gaping Wound:
Wallowing he lay a vaſt extended Load,
Like a great Iſland, in a Sea of Blood.
His ghaſtly Eye-balls ſtrive with parting Light,
And ſwim, and roll into eternal Night.
Here *Saul* receiv'd the charming conquering Boy,
The Captains bluſh'd for Shame, and wept for Joy.
His Brothers griev'd to ſee the glorious Day,
Prompted with Pride, and Envy ſhrunk away.
Here *Judah*'s Daughters flowry Garlands bring,
They crown young *David*, and preſage him King:
In Songs and Dances they his Deeds proclaim,
And *Saul*'s is leſſen'd, to advance his Fame.

Here mighty *Sampſon*, hot with Martial Rage,
A numerous Army does alone engage.

His Sword high wav'd, reeking in Sweat and Blood,
O'er flaughter'd Heaps, th' invading Conqueror ftrode.
His fatal Arms, his Foes no longer bear,
But their whole Hoft flies from his fingle Spear.
Confus'dly o'er the Field lay fpread about,
Wide Ruin, Spoils, and ignominious Rout.

Here valiant *David*'s Troops victorious come,
From their *Affyrian* Expedition home.
Vaft were the Spoils, which from the glorious Day
Won on *Damafcus*'s Plains, they bore away:
King *Hadadezer*'s Arms in Triumph born,
And Purple Robes by their foft Princes worn,
And fparkling Gems, which did their Ears adorn.
Rich Collars, Chains, and blazing Shields of Gold,
Vaft Silver Bowls, that richer Metal hold.
High gilded Dishes, graven or embofs'd,
Treafure immenfe, that *Syria* had engrofs'd.
Purple Pavilions once in lofty Rows,
And Crimfon Beds, where Monarchs did repofe.
Unnumber'd Camels, laden and opprest,
With all th' Luxury of the wanton Eaft,
Beneath the Booty groan'd along the Road,
Themfelves a Prey, as was their precious Load.
Here ran gilt Chariots drawn by generous Steeds,
Such as the noble Soil of *Afia* breeds.
Here Royal Captives, and chain'd Lords appear,
And vulgar Slaves, preft with an endlefs Reer.

Here the great *Conftantine* of *Britifh* Race,
O'er *Tyber*'s Bridge, does fierce *Maxentius* chafe.
With *Roman* Blood the fwelling Rivers dy'd,
And Helms, and Shields fwim down the Crimfon Tyde.
Spears, broken Armour, Men, and Courfers flain,
The Streams encumber, and the Flood detain.

Great

Great *Constantine* in glitt'ring Armour shines,
And pressing on, breaks thro' the *Roman* Lines.
Maxentius Hopes are blasted in the Bloom,
He flies, and opens wide the Gates of *Rome*
To the Victorious Christian, and his God,
Where for a while, he made his blest abode.

Prince Arthur.

BOOK VIII.

THus in resplendant Arms Prince *Arthur* shines,
Darting bright Terrour thro' the *Saxon* Lines.
All at his fearful Presence were amaz'd,
And on the glorious Foe with Wonder gaz'd.
Confusion seiz'd them, and a chilling Damp
Went to their Hearts, thro' all the trembling Camp.
And now the vaulted Sky, rings with the Noise,
Of *Souldiers* Shoutings, and shrill *Trumpets* Voice.
The *British* Prince waving his flaming Blade,
The *Saxons* strong Battalions did invade.

First *Baldred* fell a bold and daring Knight,
That rushing forward did his Fate invite.
The Javelin thro' his Shield of treble Hide,
And Coat of Mail, pierc'd deep into his Side.
Eska the second Triumph did afford,
His Head struck off by *Arthur's* conquering Sword.
Next groveling on the Ground great *Ina* lies,
And the brave *Orla* of stupendous Size :
Whose Clubs like that *Alcides* us'd to weild,
Laid whole Brigades on Heaps upon the Field.
Neither their Arms, nor Stature, nor Descent,
From mighty *Osca* could their Fate prevent.
As *Pharo* boasted loud, and threatned Death,
The Javelin pierc'd his Throat, and stop'd his Breath

F f *Kinullar*

Kinullar next the conquering Prince withstood,
A valiant Captain, and of Noble Blood.
Resisted by his Shield, the *Saxon's* Spear
Flew off, and pass'd obliquely thro' the Air.
Here on the Prince *Cissa* exclaiming loud,
Rush'd in, and prest him with a numerous Crowd.
Thick showers of Javelins with a mighty Sound,
Like Storms of Hail, from his bright Shield rebound.
The Prince enrag'd caught up his Spear in hast,
Which he at *Cissa* with such Fury cast,
It pierc'd his famous Buckler's seventh Fold,
And his rich Coat dawb'd thick with pond'rous Gold:
Then deep between the Paps the Weapon went,
And its last Force in his warm Bosom spent.
Flat on his Face the Bleeding *Saxon* lies,
And ratling in his Throat stretcht out, and dies.
Mollo rush'd in and with his hand did wrest,
The bloody Weapon from his Brother's Breast,
And boldly to attack the Prince advanc'd,
But from his Shield th' unprosperous Weapon glanc'd.
The Prince's Spear thro' *Mollo's* Shield of Brass,
Thro' his Habergion, and his Breast did pass:
Mollo of Sence bereav'd fell to the Ground,
And spew'd black Blood, both from his Mouth and Wound.
Striving th' invading Hero to repel,
Alcinor, Peda, and *Darontes* fell,
Three Men of wondrous Strength and warlike Fame,
Who from the farthest Snows of *Scythia* came;
Descended all from *Otha's* noble Line,
Whose glorious Deeds in *Saxon* Records shine.
He was victorious *Odin's* constant Friend,
And all his Toils, and Conquests did attend.

Then

Then *Cerdic* with his Troops the Prince withstands,
Sustain'd by *Sebert*, and th' *East Saxon* Bands.
Now these, now those, the *British* Prince attack,
And press on every side, to force him back.
As when two adverse Hurricanes arise,
Must'ring their stormy Forces in the Skies:
Of equal Fury, and of equal Force,
Against each other bend their rapid Course.
The Clouds their Lines extend in black Array,
And Front to Front a fearful War display.
Exploded Flames against each other fly,
And fiery Arches Vault th' inlighten'd Sky.
Conflicting Billows, against Billows dash, (flash.
Thunder 'gainst Thunder roars, Lightnings 'gainst Lightnings
Nor Flames, nor Winds, nor Waves, nor Clouds will yield,
But equal strength maintains a doubtful Field.
Britons and *Saxons* thus in Battel strove,
And neither from their Ground the Foe remove.

Then Valiant *Cadwal* threat'ning from afar
High in his Chariot, plung'd into the War.
His strong, extended Arm his Javelin flung;
Cutting the Air, the hissing Weapon sung.
Falling on *Kingill's* Shield it pierc'd the Hide
Of treble Fold, and enter'd deep his Side;
Fainting and stagg'ring *Kingill* backwards reel'd,
Then fell with sounding Arms upon the Field:
Gasping he lay, and from his ghastly Wound,
His Crimson Life ebb'd out upon the Ground.
And next, his fatal Shaft at *Bertac* flew
With mighty Force, and pierc'd his Breastplate thro'.
The secret Springs of Life, the pointed Dart
Broke open, and transfixt his generous Heart.

His Wound from gaping Channels inward bled,
And on his Shoulder hung his lolling Head:
He fell, and shivering gasp'd his latest Breath,
And fainting, sunk into the Arms of Death.
A noble Youth worthy of milder Fate,
But Death's blind Stroaks distinguish not the great.
At last the *Saxon* Troops in Throngs surround,
The Valiant King, thus far with Conquest crown'd.
Thick Showers of Darts from every side invade,
And in his Shield a bristling Harvest staid.
Th' undaunted Hero long their Force sustain'd,
And held at Bay; th' unequal War maintain'd.
Like a chaf'd Boar that in a sheltring Wood,
The clam'rous Dogs surround King *Cadwall* stood:
A noble Rage did in his Breast arise,
And Streaks of Fire break from his burning Eyes.
So when by Night th' Islandian Ocean roars,
And rolls its angry Waters to the Shores.
Flashes of Light, and fiery Lustre glance
From raging Waves, that in bright Troops advance.
With his refulgent Sword the Warriour flew,
Upon the Crowd, and cut his passage thro'.
Soga and *Kenrick*, from the Hilly Land,
Where *Sorbiodunum*'s lofty Castles stand;
Two constant Friends, whom Fate could not divide,
Together by the *Britons* Weapon dy'd.
Then *Redburg*, *Alfry*, and *Theodrick* fell,
Striving in vain the Victor to repell.
Great Numbers more he slew, whose vulgar Name
To those, in after Ages never came.
As a high Rock, which the vast Ocean laves,
Expos'd to stormy Winds, and raging Waves,
On its fixt Base, unshaken does defy
Th' united Fury of the Seas, and Sky:

So

So 'midſt ſurrounding Foes, brave *Cadwall* ſtood,
About him flow'd a Sea of Hoſtile Blood.
He ſlew *Rovennar* with his mighty Sword,
And *Saradan*, a great *Weſt Saxon* Lord.
Valiant *Elmunor*, to his Country dear,
And *Oſith* dy'd, by his projected Spear.

Octa, enrag'd to ſee the numerous Spoils
Round *Cadwall* ſpread, ſprung thro' the thronging Files;
Ruſhing with Fury on, and threatning high
He thus aloud, did to the *Briton* cry:
Cadwall, on me let all your Force be ſpent,
Hither be all your pointed Javelins ſent.
Here ſee a Foe that will your Pride abate,
Or in the glorious Combate meet his Fate.
At this his maſſy Spear with Vigour ſent,
Thro' Valiant *Cadwalls* ſhining Buckler went:
Thro' all the Plates of Braſs, and all the Plies
Of thick Bull's Hyde, th' impetuous Weapon flies;
Which bruis'd his Thigh, and ſpringing from his Veins,
A Crimſon ſtream his poliſh'd Armour ſtains.
Cadwall incens'd, his Spear at *Octa* flung,
Which in his temper'd Shield arreſted hung.
A ſecond hiſſing weapon *Octa* caſt,
Which th' interpoſing Buckler never paſt,
But glancing on the Steel, away it flew,
And with an oblique Stroke, *Idwallo* ſlew.
Then *Cadwall* chaf'd, exerting all his Force,
His ſecond ſends, with unreſiſted Courſe:
Thro' *Octa*'s brazen Shield it Paſſage found,
Inflicting on his Side, a painful Wound.
Their miſſive Weapons ſpent with equal Chance,
To cloſer Fight the Combatants advance.

Equal

Equal in Strength, alike in Combate brave,
Their Swords on high, like circling Flames they wave.
Both traverſing the Ground for Fight prepare,
And with Heroic Ardor meet the War.
And *Octa* firſt diſcharg'd a noble Stroke
On *Cadwalls* Creſt, which thro' his Helmet broke:
Cadwall amaz'd; recoyl'd, and backwards reel'd,
And ſcarce his Spear his tott'ring Limbs upheld.
A loud Applauſe rang thro' the ſhouting Hoſt;
The *Britons* rag'd, and thought their Hero loſt:
But he recov'ring from th' amazing Blow,
Collects his Strength to meet the inſulting Foe.
His brandiſh'd Blade fell with prodigious Sway,
And thro' the yielding Cuiraſſe, forc'd its Way.
The gaping Wound pour'd out a Vital Tyde,
And Crimſon Streams his burniſh'd Armour dy'd.
Octa his wounded Body wreaths in Pain,
And viewing on his Limbs the Bloody Stain,
With angry Eyes calls back his Life again.
And then aſſaults the Foe with doubled Rage,
Who meets his Arms, as eager to engage.
Freſh Strokes, freſh Wounds, they give on either ſide,
While Vict'ry does for neither Sword decide.
Weak with their Wounds, and with bruiſ'd Armour pain'd,
An equal, noble Combate they maintain'd,
Feeble and Breathleſs ſtill they kept the Field,
Unable more their blunted Arms to wield.

And now the Throng ruſh'd in, the Combat done,
By neither Hero loſt, by neither won:
And rending with their Shouts the tortur'd Air,
Back to their Files, the Combatants they bear.
So when two Valiant Cocks in *Albion* bred,
That from th' inſulting Conquerour never fled:

A

A Match in Strength, in Courage, and in Age,
And with keen Weapons arm'd alike Engage;
Each other they affault with furious Beaks,
And their trim'd Plumes diftain with bloody Streaks.
Each nimble Warriour from the Pavement bounds,
And wing'd with Death, their Heels deal ghaftly Wounds.
By turns they take, by turns fierce Strokes they give,
And with like Hopes and Fears, for Conqueft ftrive.
Both obftinate maintain the Bloody Field,
Both can in Combat dye, but neither yield.
Till with their bleeding Wounds grown weak and faint,
And choak'd with flowing Gore they gafp, and pant:
Difabled on the Crimfon Floor they ly,
Both Honour win, but neither Victory.

Then *Morogan*, his Javelin in his Hand,
Charg'd the fierce Troops where *Ella* did Command.
Wigmunda, firft his deadly Weapon felt,
Who on the flowry Banks of *Oza* dwelt,
Faln on the ground, the *Saxon* groan'd aloud,
And dying, lay deform'd with Duft and Blood.
Next *Ethelbright* he flew, the Javelin paft,
Thro' the brave Leader's Hand, where fticking faft,
He from the Battel fled, and thro' the throng,
Complaining loud, trail'd the huge Spear along.
To fight the *Briton*, *Thedred* did advance,
And in his Buckler broke his pondrous Lance:
High in the Air the fcatter'd pieces flew,
When *Morogan*, his ample Fauchion drew;
He mift the mighty ftroke aim'd at his Creft,
But Cleft his Shoulder down into his Cheft:
Thro' the prodigious Wound, a Sea of Blood
Spouts from his Veins, and down his Armour flow'd,

Weltring

Weltring in Gore, upon the Ground he ſtretcht,
And his laſt Breath in thick Convulſions fetcht.
Next he his Spear at great *Merthellan* throws,
Thro' Breaſt, and Back the deadly Weapon goes.
Then warlike E*lla*, with exceſſive Rage
All fir'd, advanc'd the *Briton* to engage.
As two chaf'd Lyons on a *Lybian* Plain,
Contending which ſhall o'er the Deſart reign,
With raging Eyes, and fierce erected Hair,
Scowr o'er the Sands, to meet the horrid War;
So furious E*lla*, and great *Morogan*,
Eager of Conqueſt, to the Combat ran.
The *Saxon* firſt his maſſy Javelin flung,
With the vaſt Stroke, the *Briton*'s Target rung,
The temper'd Steel the Weapon did repel,
Which flew aſide, and at a Diſtance fell.
The *Briton* next, did his bright Javelin throw,
E*lla* his Head inclin'd, eludes the Blow.
E*lla* with all his Might his ſecond caſt,
Which miſt, but ſtroke the Plume off, as it paſt.
The *Briton* ſtoop'd, and lifted from the Field
A pond'rous Stone, which both his Hands did weild;
So vaſt, that two in our degenerate Days,
Tho Men of Strength, the like can ſcarcely raiſe;
With all his Strength he throws the craggy Stone,
Which thro' King *Ella's* Leg-piece, cruſh'd the Bone:
The wounded Warriour fell upon the Plain;
Adda advanc'd the Conqueror to ſuſtain;
While *Gomel* with his Men did E*lla* bear
From the hot Place of Action, to the Rear,
Where Charioteer, and Steeds, and Chariot ſtay,
Waiting his coming from the Bloody Day.
Mean Time great *Morogan*, had *Adda* ſlain,
The Spear had thro' his Forehead pierc'd his Brain.

Biting

Biting the Ground, th' expiring *Saxon* lies,
And Death's unwelcome shade o'erspreads his Eyes.
And with like Courage, and with like Succefs,
The brave Prince *Conan*, did the *Saxons* prefs
Which *Ofred* led; great Numbers he deftroy'd,
Whofe putrid Blood, the flipp'ry Field annoy'd.
Sefred, Carantes, Molinoc he flew,
And *Ethelfrid*, in Arms furpafs'd by few.
Ofwy, and *Baffa*, all of warlike Fame,
And many more, of unrecorded Name.
Thus Valiant *Conan*, triumph'd in the Field,
And all he met, did to his Courage yield.
Until a fculking, unknown hand, at laft
Did unperceiv'd, a pointed Javelin caft.
Deep in his Arm, th' inglorious Weapon goes,
His Wound the Blood upon his Armour fhows,
He drew the Steel out, from his bleeding Veins,
And from the Field, retir'd in tort'ring Pains.

 Mean time, out-number'd in another part,
Macor's *Danmonian* Troops began to ftart.
Macor to ftop their ignominious Flight,
And give them Spirit to renew the Fight ;
Now fharp Reproaches us'd, and bitter Threats,
And now with Prayers he earneftly intreats.
Enrag'd, afhamed, and fearing open Rout,
Exclaiming loud, he wildly flew about.
He ftays them with his Hands, and Voice, and Eyes,
And to confirm their finking Courage, cries,
Whither will my *Danmonians* madly run,
And leave behind a Vict'ry almoft won ?
What pannick Fear does my brave Friends invade ?
Till now, you never knew to be afraid.

     G g   Think

Think on the Brav'ry you have always shown,
And Laurels you and your great Fathers won.
By their great Deeds, and yours, by *Cador*'s Name,
By all my Hopes and yours which are the same:
By the *Danmonian* Fame, I all conjure
Trust not to Flight, your Arms must you secure.
Who will maintain their Ground, if you recoil?
Thus do you mean to guard your Native Soil?
To what new Seats will you from *Albion* fly?
Or will you in the Rocks and Mountains ly?
Britons return from your inglorious Flight,
Rally your Forces, and renew the Fight.
To Safety, and to Fame the way I'll show,
See, here it lies, across the thickest Foe.

He said, and straight amidst the Troops he flew,
Osber the first he met, the first he slew.
He pierc'd his Belly thro' the yielding Shield,
And out his Bowels gush'd upon the Field.
To aid his Friend, constant *Eballan* flies,
But wounded by the *Briton*, with him dies.
Then while *Adulphas*, *Bertham*'s Offspring stands,
Poising a pondrous Stone in both his Hands,
The mighty Fragment of a craggy Rock,
And aim'd at *Macor*'s Head, a deadly Stroke:
Thro' his pierc'd Side the Javelin made its way,
And buried, in his bleeding Liver lay.
Then you brave Youths, *Egbert*, and *Alopus*,
Both noble Branches of great *Horsa*'s Race,
Their Age the same, the same their youthful Charms,
Fell in the *British* Fields by *Macor*'s Arms.
This 'twixt the Ribs receiv'd the fatal Dart,
Where transverse Bounds the Breast and Belly part;

Lopt

Lopt from the Shoulder with a fearful Wound,
T'other's Right Arm lay quivering on the Ground.

Now the *Danmonians* who began to run,
Seeing the Wonders by their Leader done,
With Shame and generous Indignation burn,
And to the War with doubled Rage return.
Then *Macor* let his Spear at *Redwall* fly,
In his bright Chariot, passing swiftly by.
It pass'd his Shield, and went into his Reins,
A Purple Flood, springs from his wounded Veins,
And mixt with Dust, the fervid Wheels detains.
Projected headlong on the Ground he lay,
Fetch'd a deep Groan, and gasp'd his Life away.
With like Success, his Men no more afraid,
Of *Saxon* Arms, their thickest Files invade.
So when dissolv'd by Summer Rays, the Snow
Do's down the Sides of *Alpine* Mountains flow,
Below the several Rills, and Currents joyn,
And different Streams in one great Flood combine:
Then do's the Deluge rear its foaming Head,
O'erflow the Banks, and o'er the Meadows spread.
No lofty Mounds arrest th' insulting Tide,
But o'er the flowry Vale, the Waves triumphant ride.
So the *Danmonian* scatter'd Troops unite,
And with associate Arms, revive the Fight.

Here to restrain *Macor*'s Victorious Course,
Bartha, oppos'd a fresh collected Force.
From his strong Arm his singing Javelin flew,
And passing thro' his Neck *Guitardan* flew.
He hurl'd his Ball of Iron at the Head
Of stout *Gomallador*, and struck him dead.

His Helm in Pieces flew, his Bones were craſh'd,
And from his Scull his Blood and Brains were daſh'd.
Macor incens'd, advances to the Fight,
And pray'd to Heav'n, to guide his Weapon right;
Nor did he pray in vain, th' unerring Dart
Transfixt his Breaſt, and ſunk into his Heart.
Strong *Bartha* fell, the Blood his Armour ſtains,
And ſhivering Death crept cold along his Veins.

But to revenge ſo great a Captain's Fall,
Lothar aloud does on his *Saxons* call.
Firſt *Lodoic* he ſlew, who ſtood the Shock,
Of War before unſhaken as a Rock.
Strong *Mandubrace*, of whom the *Britons* tell
Such mighty Deeds, by the brave *Saxon* fell.
Beauteous *Codunan* the *Silurians* Pride,
And warlike *Hanomer* together dy'd.
Their Leaders brave alike, alike enrag'd,
The *Britons*, and the *Saxons* cloſe engag'd,
An obſtinate, and bloody Fight maintain,
And heaps of Dead, ly thick upon the Plain.
Dark Clouds of Duſt thro' th' airy Region fly,
And warlike Noiſe bounds from the vaulted Sky.
Helms mix with Helms, and Arms with Arms unite
Their bright Reflexion, to oppreſs the Sight.
Now Man at Man, Squadrons at Squadrons ruſh,
And Files at Files with Spears protended puſh.
Swords claſh with Swords, Bucklers on Bucklers bray,
And thro' the Field a horrid Din convey.
Slaughter and Death in dreadful Pomp appear,
And Brains and Gore, the ſlippery Field beſmear.
So when two adverſe Tides their Waves advance,
With equal Fury, and with equal Chance;
The foaming Forces, doubtful Fight maintain,
Where both by Turns loſe, what by Turns they gain.

On

On this Side now retreats the vanquish'd Tide,
And on its back th' insulting Billows ride.
Rallying its roaring Troops with swift Career,
It soon returns, and reassumes the War.
The Conquerour before is forc'd to yield,
And rolling back its Waves deserts the Field.
Alternate Conquest, and alternate Flight,
Between the Foes prolong a doubtful Fight.
So thick the Troops, so fast and close were prest,
The wedg'd Battalions standing Breast to Breast,
They scarce have space their Hands or Arms to move
But like contending Waves each other shove.
Here *Macor* urges, presses, and invades,
Here *Lothar* stops him with his strong Brigades;
Equal in Arms, in Beauty, and in Age,
But not allow'd each other to engage.
On both the valiant Youths a different Fate,
From a far greater Foe does shortly wait.

King *Cerdick* then advanc'd, exclaiming loud,
And with his rapid Chariot cuts the Crowd.
And to the Troops that stopt his way, he cry'd
Open to right and left, your Ranks divide,
Macor, and I this Contest will decide.
Nor did the *Saxon* Troops his Will oppose,
But open, and an ample Space disclose.
Then leaping to the Ground his pondrous Oak,
Pointed with polish'd Steel, he threatning shook.
At such a Sight th' amaz'd *Danmonians* start,
And their chill Blood congeal'd about their Heart.
Macor undaunted, traverses the Ground,
And at the *Saxon* aims a fatal Wound.
Then thro' the Air his Spear projected flew,
And from its Sheath his flaming Sword he drew.

The

The Bucklers Brims the glancing Weapons raz'd
And flying off, on the right Shoulder graz'd.
Then *Cerdick*'s Javelin pois'd, and aim'd with Care,
Flew from his Arm, and hissing cut the Air:
Who cry'd out as it went, go swiftly fly,
And the hard Metal of his Armour try.
While *Cerdick* thus insults th' impetuous Oak,
Thro' Buckler, Coat of Mail and Cuirass broke,
And pierc'd his Breast where the deep Springs abide,
Whence Life leaps out upon its circ'ling Tide.
The Vital Streams thro' his bruis'd Armour spout,
While he in vain wrests the warm Weapon out.
After the parting Dart, together crowd
From the wide Wound, his Soul, and Life, and Blood.
He fell, his Arms upon his Armour rung,
And Death in cold Embraces round him clung.
Thus fell the brave *Danmonian* who had slain,
Such Numbers pil'd on Heaps upon the Plain.
His Friends with Sighs, and Tears upon a Shield,
Bear his Pale Corps off from the bloody Field.

Cerdic his Weapon warm with *Macor's* Blood,
Advanc'd with Fury not to be withstood.
With his drawn Sword he does the Foe invade,
And midst their Ranks prodigious Havock made.
The *Britons* all enrag'd at *Macor's* Fall,
With Showers of Darts the raging *Saxon* gaul.
On every Side the Monarch they assail,
With thick Brigades, but cannot yet prevail.
As when a mighty *Stag*, that long had stood,
The unmolested Monarch of the Wood,
Safe in its Coverts, and protecting Shade,
Against the Foe, that would his Peace invade:

If at an ancient Oak, he ſtands at laſt,
At Bay, by furious Dogs too cloſely chas'd ;
Fearleſs he looks, and to his clam'rous Foes,
Does his thick Grove of Native Arms oppoſe.
The Dogs with diſtant Cries infeſt his Ears,
And from afar the Huntſmen caſt their Spears.
None daring to approach the generous Beaſt,
Project aloof their Darts againſt his Breaſt ;
Thus *Cerdick* ſtood, nor dar'd the boldeſt Knight,
Advance to undertake a cloſer Fight.
They caſt their Darts at diſtance, and from far,
Shower on his brazen Shield a ratling War.
With their loud Cries the ambient Air they rend,
And raging, all their miſſive Weapons ſpend.

Mean time around, King *Cerdick's* Jav'lins flew,
And *Arthurs* Men, with vaſt Deſtruction flew.
Cadwan he kill'd, whoſe Arms great Fame had won,
And *Vortiger* great *Ganumara*'s Son.

Then *Vogan* fell, and *Ottocar*, who trace
Their high Deſcent from *Hoel's* ancient Race.
Great Numbers dy'd where the chaf'd *Saxon* flew,
And with his Sword cut his wide Paſſage thro'.
So when a generous Bull for Clowns Delight,
Stands with his Line reſtrain'd prepar'd for Fight.
Hearing the Youth's loud Clamours, and the Rage,
Of barking Maſtives eager to engage ;
He ſnuffs the Air, and paws the trembling Ground,
Views all the Ring, and proudly walks it round.
Defiance lowring on his brinded Brows,
A round diſdainful Looks, the griſly Warriour throws.
His haughty Head inclin'd with eaſie Scorn,
Th' invading Foe high in the Air is born,
Toſt from the Combatant's victorious Horn.

Rais'd

Rais'd to the Clouds, the sprawling Mastives fly,
And add new Monsters to th' affrighted Sky.
The clam'rous Youth, to aid each other call,
On their broad Backs to break their Fav'rites Fall.
Some stretcht out in the Field lie dead, and some
Dragging their Entrails on, run howling Home.
But if at last on all Sides he's engag'd,
By fresh and fiercer Foes, strait all enrag'd
He flies about, some with his Horns he gores,
Some strikes, and mov'd with Indignation roars.
With Disproportion'd Numbers prest at length,
He breaks his Chain collecting all his Strength.
Then Dogs and Masters scar'd promiscuous fly,
And fal'n in Heaps, the pale Spectators ly.
He walks in Triumph, nods his conquering Head,
And proudly views the Spoils about him spread.

Hyalca fell, a Lord of *Neustrian* Birth,
Struggling with Death he bites the hostile Earth.
Rivollan dies, the brave *Armorican*,
Who swifter than a driving Tempest ran.
Mador, not daring *Cerdick* to engage
Fled from his Post to scape the Conquerors Rage.
Cerdick pursu'd him close, exclaiming loud,
And to o'ertake him, breaks th' opposing Crowd.
As when a *Lion* on the Mountains spies,
A well grown *Stag*, his furious Bristles rise,
And yawning horribly, with Hunger prest,
Away he flies to tear the trembling Beast:
He leaps upon him with his dreadful Paws,
And buries in his Sides his fearful Jaws.
So raging *Cerdick* flew faln *Mador* dies,
And everlasting Night shuts up his Eyes.

Ludvallo

Ludvalla, from the high *Silurian* Hills
Eldubert flew, *Poel Edella* kills;
Chelrick Adarc, *Tudor* pierc'd *Alwy* thro',
Ofwoll Pricarden, *Oven Kenfey* flew.
Bladoc kills *Athelmar* in fingle Fight,
Of goodly Stature, and a Valiant Knight.
Edwin gave *Vortimer* his fatal Wound,
Who from his Steed, fell headlong to the Ground.
Lovellines Blood the great *Barnulfa* fpills;
Kentwin Rodollan, *Pricel Uffa* kills.
Now equal Ruin Rag'd on either Side,
And Vict'ry mutual Favours did divide,
Flowing, and Ebbing with an equal Tide.
With like Succefs, by turns the doubtful Field,
The Victors, and the vanquifh'd, win and yield.
Such was the bloody Labour of the Day,
And in fuch even Scales their Fortune lay.

Now certain Fame had reach'd Prince *Arthur*'s Ear,
That his lov'd *Macor* dy'd by *Cerdick*'s Spear.
No Tydings more his Fury could provoke,
Or ftrike into his Breaft a deeper Stroke.
His Looks reveal'd his Wound, and Grief, and Rage,
His conquering Arms in deep Revenge engage.
With his refulgent Sword he hew'd his way,
Like Grafs mown down the flaughter'd *Saxons* lay.
His Stroaks are all as fure, as thofe of Fate,
And Death and Vict'ry on his Progrefs wait.
His Arms the Field with vaft Deftruction clear;
Wide Lanes made by his Sword, and fpacious Voids appear.
Thro' their thick Ranks the raging Tempeft flies,
And fearful Ruin all around him lies.

In vain his fatal Javelin never flew,
Ebissa, Edgar, Ethelburg he slew ;
And *Ethelwoll*, who fled the Conquerors Sight,
But the swift Dart o'ertook him in his Flight.

His deadly Spear at *Kenfred* was design'd,
Who stooping down the hissing Death declin'd :
Then at the Conqu'ror's Feet he prostrate falls,
And in sad Accents for Compassion calls.
Spare, God-like *Briton*, and let *Kenfred* live,
Me to my Father and my Children give :
Treasures immense of Silver and of Gold,
My Iron Chests, and buried Coffers hold ;
These Riches from the Sun, so long conceal'd,
Shall to discharge my Ransome be reveal'd.
Mine's but a single Life, if that be spar'd,
It can't the Progress of your Arms retard ;
On this does not depend your Empire's Fate,
Nor can my Life or Death affect your State.

He said, to whom the *British* Prince reply'd,
The Silver and the Gold your Cellars hide,
You to your Sons and Daughters must bequeath,
Expect your self, the present stroke of Death.
That said, he took his Helmet by the Crest,
And drawing back his Head, into his Breast
Up to the Hilts, he plung'd his fatal Sword,
And from the Wound a Crimson River pour'd.
Colmar, hard by *Odin's* and *Frea's* Priest,
Distinguish'd by his Dress, from all the rest,
And by the Garland round his Temples known,
In glitt'ring Arms, and splendid Garments shone :
Up flew his Heels while from the Field he fled,
Nazaleod set his Foot, upon his Head,

And

And struck into the Ground, quite thro' his Breast
His pointed Spear, and his rich Spoils possest.
Then *Arthur* with his Spear, pierc'd *Rufa* thro';
Then *Osmar*, *Seward*, *Ethellar* he slew,
Osa, *Beorno*, *Kendred*, *Edifwall*;
Penda, *Kenelmar*, *Osbert*, *Ethelbal*.
Pale *Oswald* fled, the Conqu'rour to prevent,
But thro' his Back the swifter Javelin went.
His flaming Sword did ne'er in vain descend,
But sure Destruction did its Sway attend.
The reeking Conquerour in Triumph reign'd,
Glutted with Slaughter, and with Blood distain'd.
Th' unnumber'd Dead, that round the *Briton* lay,
More than their living Troops, obstruct his way.
To reach their Men, that from his Fury fled,
He climbs their slaughter'd Piles, and scales the Dead.
Sometimes the *Saxons* with new Fury burn,
And rallying Squadrons to the War return:
They pour around the Prince their numerous Swarms,
And strive to crush him with unequal Arms.
As when Tempestuous Storms o'erspread the Skies,
In whose dark Bowels inborn Thunder lies;
The watry Vapours numberless, conspire
To smother, and oppress th' imprison'd Fire:
Which thus collected, gathers greater Force,
Breaks out in Flames, and with impetuous Course,
From the Cloud's gaping Womb, in Light'ning flies,
Flashing in ruddy Streaks, along the Skies.
So *Arthur's* flaming Sword, cuts thro' the Cloud
Around him spread, and rends th' opposing Crowd.
With daz'ling Arms, he flies upon the Foe,
Flashes amidst the throngs, and terribly Thunders thro'.

Autbum

Authum and *Alfrid*, with fresh Troops sustain,
Their stagg'ring Squadrons, and the War maintain:
To these Prince *Arthur* wing'd with Fury flew,
And first stout *Alfrid* with his Spear he slew:
Thro' the left Groin, the Weapon made its Way,
And stretcht along the Ground, the bleeding *Saxon* lay.
At *Authum's* Crest he dealt a furious Stroke,
The *Saxon* totter'd at th' amazing Shock,
And fell upon his Knee, and while he pray'd,
And for his Life, would many Things have said;
His sever'd Head off, from his Shoulders flies,
And bounded on the Field, his Body lies
At a great Distance, quivering on the Ground,
And Streams of Blood spring from his ghastly Wound.
As when the Summer's soultry Heats, draw forth
Th' exhaling Moisture, from the thirsty Earth;
When scorching Rays the gaping Plains have fry'd,
And from their Banks contracted Streams subside:
If then a Fire invades a spacious Wood,
Where ancient Oaks have long securely stood,
The conquering Flames advance with lawless Power,
And with contagious Heat the Trees devour.
The spreading Burning lays the Forrest waste,
And sooty Spoils lie smoaking where it past.
So *Arthur* with resistless Rage, around
Destroys, and loads with slaughter'd Heaps the Ground.
Next did the Prince at bold *Edburga* aim,
Who from the fertile Banks of *Abum* came,
Prince *Unna's* Son to vast Possessions born,
Broad Flowers of Gold his shining Coat adorn;
The piercing Steel deep in his Bosom sunk,
And Life's pure Stream at the warm Fountain drunk.

His

His Arms did next valiant *Titullan* meet,
Who fell and quiver'd at the Conquerour's Feet.
Ofrick, and beauteous *Hengift* next appear,
The firſt his Fauchion flew, the laſt his Spear.
Next ſtout *Eldanor* did his Fate provoke,
And off his Head flew, at a ſingle Stroke.
And next he threw at *Labert*, as he fled,
The Weapon ſtruck him, as he turn'd his Head;
In Gore and Brains the glitt'ring Javelin reeks,
And from his Veins a Purple Torrent breaks.

Mean time King *Cerdic* did around deſtroy,
And with thick Deaths his maſſy Fauchion cloy.
Him from afar the *Britiſh* Hero ſpies,
And wing'd with Fury to aſſault him flies,
Cerdick mean time undaunted did appear,
And forward ſtep't, ſhaking his dreadful Spear.
Like one of *Anak*'s mighty Sons he ſtalk'd,
Or ſome tall Oak, that after *Orpheus* walk'd.
Fixt like a vaſt *Coloſſus* by his Weight,
He ſtood, expecting his approaching Fate.
Lowring, like riſing Tempeſts from afar,
He rages, and invites th' advancing War.
Now the *Britannic* Hero did appear,
Within the Reach of his prodigious Spear:
King *Cerdic* curſt, and by his Gods defy'd
The *Briton*, and aloud to *Odin* cry'd;
The glitt'ring Arms by this gay Robber worn,
Great *Odin* ſoon thy Temple ſhall adorn:
Aſſiſt great Founder of our State the Dart
I caſt, and guide it to his impious Heart.
Then from his vig'rous Arm his maſſy Spear
Projected ſung, and hiſs'd along the Air:

Off

Off from the temper'd Shield the Weapon flew,
Wounded *Glendoran*, and *Alantor* flew.
Then his long Spear the pious *Briton* caſt,
Th' impetuous Steel, thro' all the Thickneſs paſt
Of Brazen Plates, rowl'd Linnen, tough Bulls Hide,
And entring deep, did in his Groin abide.
The fainting *Saxon* fell upon his Knees,
Pain'd with his ghaſtly Wound, and trembling ſees
The Conquering Prince advancing to aſſwage,
By ſtriking off his Head, his veng'ful Rage.
Here the brave *Lothar*, that had Wonders done,
And by his Arms immortal Praiſes won,
For thro' the Hoſt, the loud Applauſes rung
Of mighty Deeds, atchiev'd by one ſo young;
Tranſported with his pious Care, to bring
Aſſiſtance to his Uncle, and his King;
Spur'd his hot Courſer on, and forwards preſt
Off'ring to *Arthur's* Arms, his valiant Breaſt.
He bravely undertook th' unequal Foe,
To ward from *Cerdic's* Head the fatal Blow.
Then his long Spear he threw, with Manly Force,
But *Arthur's* Buckler ſtop'd th' impetuous Courſe:
Th' applauding *Saxons* gave a Shout to ſee
The Noble Youth's exceſſive Bravery.
But to his Prince's Aid in vain he flies,
Who by his former Wound expiring lies,
And everlaſting Sleep ſhuts up his Eyes.

But then the *Britiſh* Hero's Javelin fled
At *Lothar*, but it pierc'd his Courſer's Head:
Rais'd in the Air upright, the gen'rous Beaſt,
Gather'd his ſhiv'ring Feet up to his Breaſt,
Then ſpringing ſtrook them out, and ſtagg'ring round
Fell head-long with his Rider to the Ground.

A mighty Groan the dying Courser fetcht,
And on the Ground a Breathless Carcass stretcht.
And here Immortal *Elda*, shall my Verse,
Thy unexampled Deed of Love reherse:
Love which will universal Wonder raise,
And scarcely find Belief in future Days.
For whilst the *British* Hero step'd with Speed,
To take off, with his Fauchion, *Lothar*'s Head,
Who with his Steed opprest, and wounded lies,
Fair *Elda* rush'd between, and thus she cries:
Before your fatal Sword takes *Lothar*'s Life,
Victorious Prince, hear his unhappy Wife.
Faln on her Knees she did her Helm unlace,
And shew'd the charming Beauties of her Face:
The blooming Looks of Spring, and lovely Red
Of opening Roses on her Cheeks were spread.
Her Eyes that sparkled like the Stars above,
Appear'd both th' Armory, and Throne of Love:
Where thousands of alluring Graces wait,
And mingling Charms form Love's triumphal State.
Bright *Ethelina* her, and all excell'd,
She the next Place in Beauty's Empire held.
Nor did her Looks, less Admiration move,
While wild Confusion, Sorrow, Fear and Love,
With beauteous Conflict, for the Vict'ry strove.
A Shower of Tears flow'd down her lovely Face,
Which from her Grief, receiv'd yet sweeter Grace.

At the great Conq'rour's Feet she threw her Charms,
And lifting up to Heav'n, her snowy Arms,
Aloud she spoke, a wretched Woman's Prayer
Great *Briton* hear, and my dear *Lothar* spare.

Since first his Bride, within his Arms I lay,
Scarce two full Golden Months are ftoln away,
Which in Love's Calendar fcarce make a Day.
With Prayers, and Tears, and tender Words I ftrove,
And all th' ingaging Arts of mournful Love;
To keep him from the Dangers of the Field,
And when th' obdurate Man refus'd to yield,
About him my defpairing Arms I flung,
And on his Neck, o'erwhelm'd with Grief I hung.
I then conjur'd him, to avoid with Care,
Your fatal Arms, fo much renown'd in War.
Away he goes, and as he faid, adieu,
He touch'd my Life, and my ftretcht Heart-ftrings drew:
For ftill I fear'd that the Heroick Fire,
And thirft of Fame, that did his Soul infpire,
Would make him think no Dangers were too great,
Till rufhing on your Arms, he urg'd his Fate.
My confcious Fears, this fad Event prefag'd,
If e'er with you, in Combat he engag'd.
Therefore in Arms I did my Limbs difguife,
And undertook this dangerous Enterprize,
That if he rafhly fought fo great a Foe,
I might between him, and your fatal Blow,
My Bofom interpofe, and in my Heart
To fave his dearer Life, receive the Dart:
Or if Occafion were, to intercede,
As now I do, and for his Safety plead.

  I pray by all that is to Mortals dear,
By all the Gods that you, and we revere;
Let this fad Object your Compaffion move,
Regard his Valour, and regard my Love.
Oh! Let his haplefs Fate your Soul incline,
Pity his blooming Youth, or pity mine.

Oh,

Oh, melt beneath divine Compassion's Charms,
Let not your Breast be harder than your Arms.
Save his dear Life, he of his Noble Line
The only Branch remains, as I, of mine.
Christians profess Compassion, Mercy, Love,
Sure such Distress should those kind Passions move.
Sheath in my Breast the Sword, and take my Breath,
But Oh, preserve this wondrous Youth from Death.
My self will to my Veins the Sword apply,
And to prolong his Life will gladly dy.
Hear pious Prince, his aged Father hear,
Who thus entreats, or would if he were here:
Oh, spare the spring of all my Hopes and Fears,
The only Prop of my declining Years:
Your fatal Sword deep in my Bowels sheath,
And for the Son's, accepts the Father's Death.
If great Possessions, or if Gold would buy,
His far more precious Life, he shall not dy,
His Father will a mighty Ransome give,
And mine as much, say but the Youth shall live.
Let us your Prisoners be in Chains confin'd,
The Chains of Love will make those softer bind:
There his dear presence I may still enjoy,
And for his Ease my thoughtful Cares employ.
Free from the Noise of War, and anxious Fears,
I'll kiss his Wounds, and wash them with my Tears;
I'll watch his midnight Slumbers, and by Day,
My Love shall Solace to his Grief convey.
Let him be banish'd from the *British* Isle,
I'll go, and share the lovely Wand'rer's Toil.
I'll follow thro' the swarthy, burning Zone,
No Flames can scorch me, fiercer than my own.
Our tender Words the savage Kind will move,
They'll stand, and gaze, and wonder at our Love.

Th' inhofpitable Defart will appear,
A flowry Paradife, when he is there.
O'er Snows with him and Hills of Ice I'll ftray,
I know not how, but Love will find the way.
If his fharp Keel fhall cut the Foaming Tide,
In the fame Bark I'll on the Billows ride.
No ftormy Winds my ftable Soul fhall move,
Or fhake the ftrong Foundations of my Love.
But hurried with diftracting Fears away,
And wild with Grief, I know not where to ftay,
And in a Maze of Thought I lofe my Way.
Oh! let your generous Pity calm the ftrife
In my toft Soul, and fave his precious Life.
Thus you'll not only Triumph o'er your Foe,
But o'er your felf, and your own Vict'ry too.

  Thus *Elda* pray'd, nor did fhe pray in vain,
Her tender Accents did Admiffion gain,
To the relenting Prince's generous Breaft,
Who thus the beauteous Supplicant addreft.

  This unexampled Effort of your Love,
Does equal Wonder and Compaffion move.
True Chriftian Captains are both brave and good,
Vict'ry purfue, but not with Thirft of Blood.
Revenge and Cruelty we difavow,
And only juft and generous Arms allow.
Go, to your Tears your *Lothar*'s Life I give,
Pleas'd with each others Love together live.

  Then *Cerdick* flain on whom they trufted moft,
A fhivering Fear ran thro' the *Saxon* Hoft.
The *Britons* now believ'd the Battel won,
And fure of Conqueft on their Squadrons run.

Prince *Arthur* at their Head breaks thro' their Files,
And covers all the Plain with Hostile Spoils.
The *Saxon* Troops dismay'd, began to yield,
And to the raging Conquerour leave the Field.

   Mean time the Prince of Hell, who anxious stood,
And from his Hill the bloody Labour view'd.
Seeing the *Saxon* Troops at last give way,
Resolves the *Britons* Progress to delay.
That thro' the *Angelick Guards* he might escape,
His Form he chang'd to a fair *Seraph's* Shape.
A mild *Celestial* Youth he did appear,
Drest in pure Robes of white Empyreal Air.
What once he was, the Fiend seem'd charming bright,
Conceal'd in Beauty, and disguis'd in Light.
Assuming meek and Heav'nly Looks he strove,
To imitate the loveliest Face above.
Then taking from the Mountain's Top his Flight,
Did straightway at th' *Angelick* Camp alight:
And thus transform'd thro' the bright Camp he went,
As an Express from Heav'n to *Michael* sent.
Along he march'd, and slily looking round,
While unobserv'd, a fair Occasion found
Of passing thro' their Lines, without Delay,
Swift as a Ray of Light, he shot away:
He mingles with the fighting Armies, where
He moulds to various Shapes, the thickn'd Air.
In *Sebert*'s warlike Form he did appear,
With *Arthur*'s gasping Head upon his Spear;
Which newly sever'd from his Body seems,
So fresh the Wound, so red the bloody Streams.
Britons he cry'd, learn hence your wretched State,
See your Destruction in your Leader's Fate.

The towring Hopes you vainly once conceiv'd,
Are sunk, nor can your Ruin be retriev'd.
Whose Arms can guard your State now *Arthur*'s dead?
His Life, and with it, all your Strength is fled.
Fly *Britons* hence, and to your Hills repair,
Fly to your Woods, and in your Caves despair:
Protected in your Fastnesses remain,
Stay not t' encrease the Number of the Slain.
Cold to their Hearts this Sight and Language went,
And thro' their Veins a shivering Horrour sent.
Confusion and Despair their Souls oppreft,
And their sad Looks their inward Wound confeft.
Urg'd with their Fear, their Troops began to fly,
And leave behind th' unfinish'd Victory.

Prince *Arthur*'s Breast with Indignation burn'd,
Who from the fierce Pursuit, reluctant turn'd
To stop his Army's Flight, stay, *Britons*, stay,
He cry'd, and blemish not this glorious Day.
Whence this Distraction, whence th' ungrounded Fear
And wild Despair, that in your Looks appear.
The Battel's won, the *Saxons* quit the Field,
And to your Arms a perfect Conquest yield.
Let not the vanquish'd Foe escape Pursuit,
The Vict'ry's yours, stay but to reap the Fruit.

While thus he spoke, the *Britons* stood amaz'd,
And on their Prince with Joy and Wonder gaz'd.
Their Grief dispell'd, their dying Hopes revive,
And joyful Shouts proclaim the Prince alive.
Mean time the Sun declines, and dusky Night
Covers the *Saxons*, and protects their Flight.

Prince Arthur.

BOOK IX.

NOw did the beauteous *Morn* begin to rife,
   Streaking with Rofy Light the fmiling Skies.
Prince *Arthur* rofe, and folemn Thanks addreft
To Heav'n, that had his Arms with Conqueft bleft.
Then rode amidft his Troops, and one by one,
Their Brav'ry prais'd, and Conduct lately fhown:
Difpenfing great Rewards thro' all the Hoft,
To thofe whofe Courage was diftinguifh'd moft.
The *Britons* in their turn exprefs their Zeal,
And to the Prince the higheft Love reveal.
The Heav'n's around with Acclamations rung,
And loud Applaufes of the fhouting Throng.
Then to the facred Temples they repair,
In joyful Crowds to offer Praife and Prayer:
In low proftration, they the Soveraign Lord
Of Hofts Exalt, and future Aid implor'd.
Soon as their Hymns of Heav'nly Praife were fung,
High in the Temples they their Trophies hung;
Bruis'd Armour, broken Shields, and Standards torn
From the fierce Foe, the gilded Roofs adorn.
This Honour to th' Almighty *Saviour* done,
Prince *Arthur* to his *Britons* thus begun.

   Thus far *Succefs* and *Triumph* on us wait,
And to our Arms, prefage a profperous Fate.

Pro-

Propitious Heav'n is to your Part inclin'd,
And still more glorious *Vict'ries* crowd behind.
The vanquish'd Foe can't long maintain the Field,
But must your ravish'd Lands and Cities yield.
Chase anxious Thoughts far from your valiant Breast,
And on your Cause, and *Heav'n's* Protection rest.
A perfect Conquest shall your Labours Crown,
And your Victorious Arms, regain your own.
Fear not the Relicks of a conquer'd Foe,
Their tott'ring State, falls with another Blow.
Now let no *Funeral* Honours be deny'd,
To these brave Men, that for their Country dy'd:
Let us with Sighs and Tears lament their Fate,
Who fell, while striving to support our State.
Ages to come shall their great Virtue praise,
Viewing the Tombs that on their Graves you raise.

And first the Prince to the Pavilion went,
Whither brave *Macor's* breathless Corps was sent.
He lay extended on a Purple Bed,
With high rais'd Pillows; plac'd beneath his Head.
His Servants standing round their Grief exprest,
With old *Pendarvan* sad above the Rest.
Cador to him as to his faithful Friend,
For wise Instructions, did his Son commend;
His Counsels form'd his Youth, and did prepare
His Mind for all concerns of Peace, and War.
Now in his Face the deepest Grief appears,
He beats his Breast, and baths it with his Tears:
He wrings his Hands, and in his mournful Rage,
Tears off the hoary Honours of his Age.
Immoderate Grief in lamentable Sounds,
As *Arthur* enter'd, thro' the Room rebounds.

The

Book IX. *Prince* Arthur.

The pious Prince with heavy Sorrow preft,
Burft out in Tears, and thus his Grief expreft.

  Inexorable Death, at every Heart
Without diftinction, shoots her fatal Dart.
Could Beauty, Courage, Virtue, Youthful Age
Move her Compaffion, or divert her Rage;
Brave Youth, thou had'ft efcap'd, and liv'd to fee
Our Triumphs, for a Vict'ry due to thee:
But all thy Charms by ftronger Fate o'ercome,
Could not reverfe th' irrevocable Doom.
Oh! thy fad Sire, what fwelling Grief will roll
Its ftormy Tide o'er his afflicted Soul?
Can he the News of *Macor's* Death furvive,
Or me, with whom he trufted him, forgive?
T' allay the fmart may the *Danmonians* tell,
How bravely *Macor* fought, how Great he fell.
And how my own with *Cador's* Grief contends,
He mourns the beft of Sons, and I the beft of Friends.
Our Hopes are gone, may the *Danmonians* Cry,
And what *Britannia* can thy Lofs fupply?

  Then to embalm the Prince he gave Command,
That he might fend him to his Native Land.
Straight with hot Steams, they wafh his Body o'er,
And purge his Skin from Duft and putrid Gore.
Then in *Arabian* Spices, fragrant Gums,
Rare Aromatick Oyls, and rich Perfumes,
They lay his Snowy Body, which they fold
In Bands of Linnen, round him often roll'd.
Then from his Troops a Thoufand Youths he chofe,
Which might a folemn Equipage compofe
Which might accompany the Funeral State,
To the unhappy Father's Palace Gate.

Small

Small Comfort for so great a loss, yet due
To the sad Sire, and all the Prince could shew.
Forthwith the *Britons*, weave with bending Sprigs
Of Willow Trees, and tender Oaken twigs,
An easie Bier, and with soft Rushes spread,
Sweet Flowers, and fragrant Herbs, the lofty Bed.
The Roof on high fresh spreading Branches shade,
And here sublime the hapless Youth was laid.
Such on the Ground the fading Rose we see,
By some rude Blast, torn from the Parent Tree.
The *Daffodil* so leans his languid Head,
Newly mown down, upon his grassy Bed.
Tho from the Earth no more supplies they gain,
Their splendid Form in part, and lovely Hue remain.
Then a rich Garment, glorious to behold,
Pond'rous with Orient Pearl, and stiff with Gold:
A noble Present from King *Odar's* Hand,
Receiv'd when *Arthur* left the *Neustrian* Land;
Upon the Bier his Royal Bounty threw,
The last Respect, which a sad Friend could shew.
A noble Portion of the wealthy Prey,
And Spoils gain'd from the Foe, on Cars they lay;
With Arms, and Standards, which himself had won,
The Trophies of the Wonders he had done.

Now the magnificent, and pompous Woe,
Does from the Camp, in sad Procession go.
The lab'ring Axle mourns along the Road,
And groans beneath th' uncomfortable Load.
The Horses slowly March, and mournful look,
As they their share of Publick Sorrow took.
Pendarvin follows stooping with his years,
But more with Grief, and delug'd in his Tears.

Then

Then *Macor*'s *Chariot* rolls, diſtain'd with Blood,
On which ſublime amidſt the War he rode.
His *War-horſe Rapa*, with black Trappings ſpread,
And he too ſeem'd to weep, is after led.
His *Arms* and poliſh'd *Armour* others bear,
His Golden *Spurs*, his *Helmet*, *Shield*, and *Spear*.
Then in long Order the *Danmonians* mourn'd,
Their *Spears* trail'd backward, and their *Bucklers* turn'd.

Then *Arthur* ſtood, and with ſad Accent ſpoke,
Thus far I mourn the Fate I can't revoke.
Back I am call'd where Arms and bloody Strife,
With more ſad Objects, muſt renew my Grief.
Farewel brave *Youth*, farewel, till we above,
Meet in the peaceful Realms, of *Light*, and *Love*.
He ſaid no more, but turn'd, and took his way
Back to the Camp, which lofty Works ſurvey.

Mean time ten *Orators* from *Offa* ſent,
Arriv'd, and waited at the Prince's Tent.
Their Embaſſy a Truce was to obtain,
To clear the Field, and to inter the ſlain.
They urg'd that all Hoſtilities ſhould ceaſe,
Againſt the Dead, who ought to reſt in Peace.
That all Heroick Conquerors ever gave,
To thoſe, from whom they took their Lives, a Grave.
The *Saxons* Prayer ſeem'd juſt, and ten days Truce,
Prince *Arthur* granted for this pious Uſe.

To *Cador's* Court the heavy Tydings came,
Born ſwiftly thither on the Wings of Fame.
Loud Lamentation thro' the Palace went,
And bitter Cries, gave their ſtrong Paſſion vent.

K k   Officious

Officious Fame the difmal News relates,
And univerfal Sorrow propagates.
Pale Faces, croffing Arms, dejected Eyes,
O'erflowing Tears, and deep, defpairing Sighs,
Compofe a finifh'd Scene of Blackeft Woe,
The Tragick place does all fad Figures fhow.
The *Men* like pallid Ghofts pafs filent by,
Women outrageous in their Sorrow cry
Macor is dead; our Hopes too with him dy.
Thro' all the Streets prodigious Numbers flow,
And pour'd out from the Gates, promifcuous go,
To meet their Hero's *Herfe*, with flaming Brands,
And Pitchy Torches lighted in their Hands:
Which in long Order fhone along the way,
Difclos'd the Fields, and call'd back banifh'd Day.
Soon as they fpied the lofty *Herfe* from far,
Attended with the Pomp of mournful War;
A lamentable Cry the Valley fills,
Eccho repeats it louder in the Hills.
Wild with their Grief, diftracted with Defpair,
They ftrike their throbing Breafts, tear off their Hair,
And with their piercing Screams difturb the Air.
Both Troops unite, Rivals in Love and Grief,
And the fad Conqueft feek with equal Strife.

  As *Cador*'s Love, no Bounds his Sorrow knew,
Who from their Arms and Prayers diftracted flew.
Clofe in his Arms he did the *Corps* embrace,
Kifs'd his cold Lips, and bath'd with Tears his Face.
A Scene fo tender, fuch a moving Sight,
Melts all their Hearts, and does frefh Grief invite;
Touch'd with Compaffion to th' afflicted King,
From their exhaufted Eyes frefh Torrents fpring.

                When

When the fierce Tempeſt had its Fury broke,
With a deep Sigh th' unhappy *Monarch* ſpoke.
Oh, my dear Son! how mild had been my Doom,
Hadſt thou eſcap'd, I ſuffer'd in thy Room.
This Sight kills worſe than *Death,* Oh that the Dart
Had miſs'd thy Breaſt, and pierc'd thy *Father's* Heart!
Oh, that to ſee this fatal Hour I live!
And thee, and all that's dear in Life ſurvive!
How much I wiſh Life's tedious Journey done,
The empty Name remains, the thing is gone!
But ſure I ſhall not long thy Abſence mourn,
I'll haſt to thee, thou'lt not to me return.
My hoary Head with Sorrow to the Grave,
Makes haſt, the beſt Repoſe my Troubles crave.
Thrice happy *Wife* remov'd from us below,
You have no ſhare in this ſad Scene of Woe.
My ill preſaging Fears are now fulfill'd,
I ſtarted in my Sleep, and cry'd, my *Son* is kill'd.
I knew too well warm Blood and youthful Age,
Eager of Fame, and fir'd with Martial Rage,
His Arms in greateſt Danger would engage.
I pray'd, and oft conjur'd him to beware,
Not raſhly to provoke unequal War.
He promis'd me while on his Neck I wept,
But oh, how ill has he his Promiſe kept?
I can't reproach the pious *Arthur's* Name,
Nor on his Friendſhip ſworn reflect the Blame.
If by divine, unchangeable Decree,
Untimely Fate, *Macor,* attended thee;
'Tis beſt that thou art fal'n with ſuch Applauſe,
Aſſerting *Albion's* and the Chriſtian Cauſe.
But why do my Complaints thus endleſs grow,
And why thus tedious my loquacious Woe?

Why from new *Laurels*, should I thus detain
These valiant Troops, to hear my Sighs in vain?
Go, *Britons*, to your Prince, at your Return,
Tell him I live, but only live to mourn.
I groan beneath the heaviest Load of Grief,
And spend in Tears my sad Remains of Life.
May Heav'n his Arms with greater Triumph bless,
Great as his *Vertues*, let him meet Success.
Mean time must we this last kind Office pay,
And *Macor*'s Body to the *Dome* convey;
Where his illustrious *Fathers* lie interr'd,
Who reign'd by Subjects lov'd, by Neighbours fear'd.

Soon as the *Sun* had with his early Ray
Depos'd the Shades, and re-enthron'd the Day;
The pious *Britons* their slain Friends inter,
And on their Graves due Honours they confer.
Some with their Spades, and with sharp Axes wound
The groaning Earth, and casting up the Ground,
They form deep Vaults, and subterranean Caves,
Then fill up with their Dead, the gaping Graves.
Some cast up hilly Heaps, and Mounts of Sand,
Which for their Tombs, and Monuments might stand:
And to th' admiring *Britons* might declare,
In future Ages what their Fathers were.
Some Stones erect of a prodigious Size,
That bear the Hero's Glory to the Skies.

Mean time the *Saxons* bear away their Dead,
Whose putrid Heaps, the bloody Field o'erspread.
Innumerable Piles they raise on high,
Which kindled, fill with Smoak and Flames the Sky.
With uncouth Cries, around the Fires they mourn,
Where vulgar *Dead*, in Heaps promiscuous Burn.

The

Book IX. *Prince* Arthur.

The Lords, and Officers of high Command,
They send attended with a warlike Band,
Each to his City, there to be interr'd,
Where greater Funeral Pomp might be conferr'd.
But fair *Augusta* chiefly flow'd with Tears,
Where Grief in all her mournful Looks appears.
Distracted with ungovernable Woe,
Into the Streets in Crowds the *Matrons* flow.
Confusion in their Looks, and wild Despair,
They wring their Hands, and tear their flowing Hair.
Parents on *Children*, *Wives* on *Husbands* call,
Sons mourn their Fathers, Maids their Lovers fall.
For their dear Brothers, Sisters, Tears are spent,
Servants their Masters, Friends their Friends lament.
All mingle Tears, their Cries together flow,
And form a hideous Harmony of Woe.
Pale *Consternation* sate on every Face,
They fear'd the Prince would soon invest the Place.
They oft reproach'd their Monarchs Breach of word,
That had expos'd them to the Conquerour's Sword.
They wish'd that this Destructive War might cease,
And *Ethelina* be the Bond of Peace.
Octa's Affairs in this ill State appear,
Such was their publick Grief, and such their Fear.

Mean Time the *Briton* joyful Sports ordain'd,
For the great Vict'ry by their Arms obtain'd.
For Horsemanship the *Britons* always fam'd,
To run a Course his generous Gifts inflam'd.
Desire both of the Prize, and loud Applause,
The *British* Youth to mount their Coursers draws.
A neighbouring Hill ascending high, but slow,
Survey'd the Valleys, with his lofty Brow.

Upon the flowry Top a spacious Down,
Extended lay, which shady Woods did crown.
The grassy Plains, and rising Groves appear,
Like a rich furnish'd, native Theater:
Where *Sylvan* Scenes, their verdant Pomp display,
And charming Prospects to the Eye convey.
Soon as the Sun, had with his Rosie Light,
From the cold Air, dispell'd the dewy Night;
The *British* Hero with a numerous Train,
Directs his Steps, to this delightful Plain:
Where high amidst his Friends he takes his Place,
Who swarm'd around to view the noble Race.

Britons, *Armoricans*, and *Neustrians* stood
Mingled below, the foremost of the Crowd,
Stood E*ddelin*, in all his Youthful Pride,
His Purple Boots were of *Iberian* Hide,
Which fast with Golden Buttons held, and grac'd
With Silver Spurs, his comely Legs embrac'd,
A flaming Ruban of *Sydonian* Dy,
In a Close Knot, his curling Locks did ty,
Which playing on his Shoulders flew behind,
Danc'd in the Air, and sported with the Wind.
Close to his well shap'd Vast, he wore his Coat,
Of Silk and Silver, by his Mother wrought.
A Cap of Crimson did his Head equip,
And as he walk'd, he flash'd his breaded Whip.
His swarthy Groom his generous Courser leads,
That scarcely marks the Ground, so light he treads.
Swift as a Dove pursu'd, or Mountain Hind,
His nimbler Feet could overtake the Wind,
Leave flying Darts, and Swifter storms behind.
Illustrious Blood, he boasts with equal Pride,
Transmitted to his Veins on either side.

The

The Mother Mare was of *Eborac* Race,
The Sire *Augusta*'s Merchants, brought from *Thrace*.
His inward Fire thro' his wide Nostrils flies,
And noble Ardor sparkles in his Eyes.
His well turn'd Limbs did Admiration move,
Where Strength, and Beauty for the Conquest strove.
His Matchless Speed the Prize did ever gain,
From all the Rival Coursers of the Plain.

Next *Blanadoc* upon the Plain advanc'd,
And led behind, his fiery Courser pranc'd.
Lightly equip'd, and ready for the Race,
He marches to the *Base* with Manly Grace.
The gazing Crowd admire his comely Steed,
Nobly descended from the famous Breed,
That on the *Mauritanian* Mountains feed.
Fam'd for his Swiftness in the dusty Course,
Of wondrous Beauty, and of wondrous Force.
And next to him the gay *Lanvallo* came,
Eager to win the Prize, and raise his Name.
His dapled Courser to the *Base* advanc'd,
And neighing wantonly along the Champain danc'd,
His high Descent he did from *Draco* trace,
The swiftest Courser of th' *Iberian* Race.
A Race so famous for their speedy Feet,
Eurus himself, was not esteem'd more fleet:
So swift they run, that vulgar Fame declares,
The Western Winds, impregnated the Mares.

Next the fierce *Tudor* comes into the Field,
That did to none for Art or Courage yield.
A Velvet Bonnet on his Head, and drest,
For Lightness, in a thin embroider'd Vest.

Thirsty of Honour to the *Base* he flies,
And with his greedy Wishers grasps the Prize.
His well-train'd Courser was admir'd for Speed,
Sprung from *Calabrian*, mixt with *British* Breed.
Lightning flew from his Eyes, and Clouds of Smoak;
Darkning the Air, from his large Nostrils broke.
None of the Rival Steeds arriv'd before,
More Wonder rais'd, or promis'd Conquest more.

Next *Trebor* came upon a noble Horse,
And oft victorious in the rapid Course.
He gently stroak'd his Mane, and bid him shew
On this great Day, the Feet he us'd to do.
With many more, whose long forgotten Name,
Was ne'er inroll'd in the Records of Fame.
While round the *Base* the wanton Coursers play,
Th' ambitious Riders in just Scales they weigh:
And those that by their Rules were found too light,
Quilt Lead into their Belts, to give them weight.
All things adjusted, and the Laws agree'd,
Each eager Rival mounts his generous Steed.

To whom th' indulgent Prince himself addrest,
And to inflame their Zeal these Words exprest:
Let no brave Youth despair of his Reward,
Due Gifts, and Honours are for all prepar'd.
Whoe'er are Rivals of the rapid Race,
Two costly Spears shall win, their plated Base
Glitters in Silver Sockets, finely wrought
By rare Engravers, from *Germania* brought:
Their Points are gilt, illustrious to behold,
Whence a deep Fring depends of Silk and Gold.
Besides a Back-sword whose well temper'd Blade,
Is of the fam'd *Iberian* Metal made.

The

The happy Youth that smear'd with Sweat, and Dust,
Shall reach the Goal, midst loud Applauses first,
This Golden Goblet, his Reward shall boast,
By *Damon* wrought, with Figures high emboss.
The second Conqu'ror shall in Triumph wear,
In a rich Belt, this *Persian* Scimiter.
The Haft's a costly Stone, that Nature stains
With various Figures, and with bloody Veins:
The chiefest Workmen of the curious East,
Have in the inlaid Blade, their Art exprest.
The third shall win a noble polish'd Shield,
Three Coursers rarely pourtray'd on the Field.

The Signal given by the shrill Trumpet's Sound,
The Coursers start, and scowr along the Ground.
So *Boreas* starting from his Northern Goal,
Sweeps o'er the Mountains to the adverse Pole:
His furious Wings the flying Clouds remove,
From the Blue Plains, and spacious Wilds above.
Insulting o'er the Seas he loudly roars,
And shoves the tumbling Billows to the Shores.
While for the Palm the straining Steeds contend,
Beneath their Hoofs the Grass does scarcely bend.
So long and smooth their Strokes, so swift they pass,
That the Spectators of the noble Race,
Can scarce distinguish by their doubtful Eye,
If on the Ground they run, or in the Air they fly.
So when the Earth smiles with a Summers Ray,
And wanton Swallows o'er the Valleys play:
In Sport each other they so swiftly chase,
Sweeping with easie Wings, the Meadow's Face,
They seem upon the Ground to fly a Race.
O'er Hills and Dales, the speedy Coursers fly,
And with thick Clouds of Dust obscure the Sky.

With clashing Whips, the furious Riders tear
Their Coursers sides, and wound th' afflicted Air.
Never *Epirean* or *Arabian* Steed,
Flew o'er the *Olympic* Plains, with greater speed:
On their thick Manes the stooping Riders ly,
Press forwards, and would fain their Steeds outfly.
By Turns they are behind, by Turns before,
Their Flanks and Sides, all bath'd in Sweat, and Gore.
Such speed the Steeds, such Zeal the Riders shew;
To reach bright Fame, that swift before them flew.
Upon the last with spurning Heels, the first
Cast storms of Sand, and smothering Clouds of Dust:
The hindmost strain their Nerves, and snore, and blow,
And their white Foam upon the Foremost throw.
Eager of Fame, and of the promis'd Prize,
The Riders seize the Mark with greedy Eyes.
Now Hopes dilate, now Fears contract their Breast,
Alternately with Joy, and Grief possest:
Thus far with equal Fate the Riders pass,
Uncertain, who should Conquer in the Race.
But now the Goal appearing, does excite
New warmth, and calls out all their youthful Might:
They lash their Courser's Flanks with Crimson dy'd,
And stick their goring Spurs into their side.
Their Native Courage, and the Riders stroke,
T' exert their Force, the generous Kind provoke:
Each springs out to the Goal with loosen'd Reins,
Works all his Nerves, and staring Eye-balls strains.
In this fierce strife, *Tudor's* the best for wind,
Shot forth, and left the panting Steeds behind.
Eddelin the other Rivals overpast,
Trebor came next, *Lanvallo* was the last:
Draco, his Steed, had once unrival'd Fame,
When in the Pride, and Pomp of Youth he came;

Cur-

Curvetting o'er the Plain, to win the Courfe,
All yielded to his Swiftnefs, and his Force;
Stiff Limbs now fhew his Age, with drudging Pace
He fweats behind, and labours thro' the Race.
Now *Tudor* whips, and fpurs his Courfer on,
And near the Goal believ'd the Goblet won:
When running o'er a naked, chauky Place,
Slipp'ry with nightly Dew, and bare of Grafs,
Up flew the Courfer's Heels, and to the Ground
He, and the Rider, fell with mighty Sound.
The fudden Danger could not be declin'd
By *Eddelin*, that follow'd clofe behind;
For ftumbling on young *Tudor*'s haplefs Horfe,
His Floundring fell, and loft the hopeful Courfe.

The mean time *Trebor* fpur'd, and forwards fprung,
While all the Field with Acclamations rung:
Firft to the Goal his reeking Courfer came,
Next *Blanadoc*, *Lanvallo* third in Fame.
The Victors by the Goal triumphant ftood,
Surrounded by the thick applauding Crowd:
When *Tudor* rufhing in, cries out of wrong,
And challenging the Prize, broke thro' the Throng.
The Judges over-rul'd the Youth's Demand,
Urging the firft eftablifh'd Rules fhould ftand.
The Prince confirm'd their Sentence, and declar'd
Who firft arriv'd, fhould have the firft Reward.
But on the two, that by ill Fortune croft,
The Vict'ry almoft in Poffeffion, loft,
Rich Marks of Royal Bounty he conferr'd,
And with his Smiles, their drooping Spirits cheer'd.
A famous Quiver wrought by *Didon's* Hand,
With *Thracian* Arrows ftor'd, at his Command

Was first on *Tudor*, as a Gift conferr'd;
And cross his Shoulders hung the bright Reward.
Eddelin that never hop'd so mild a Doom,
Receives a silver Helm, and milk white Plume.
This Kindness to th' unfortunate exprest,
He gives the promis'd Prizes to the rest.

Arthur rose up, and all their Footsteps bend
Back to their Camp, which lofty Works defend.
And now the *Britons* all their Hands employ,
To fetch Materials in, for Fires of Joy.
All to the Mountains, and the Woods repair,
And with their Labour fill the ecchoing Air:
They raise their Axes, and with toilsome Strokes,
Fell the tall Elms, and lop the spreading Oaks.
They bear the nodding Trees to every Town,
And from the Mountains draw the Forrests down:
In every City with the shady Spoils,
The joyful Youth erected lofty Piles:
Nearer the Skies they raise th' aspiring Wood,
Than when before, upon the Hills it stood.
Soon as the Sun his Beamy Light withdrew,
And the brown Air grew moist with Ev'ning Dew:
The shouting *Britons*, set the Piles on Fire,
The tow'ring Flames to Heav'n's high Roof aspire:
Up the steep Air the ruddy Columns play,
And to the Stars their Rival Light convey.
Around the burning Piles the Crowds rejoyce,
And mingle Shouts, with the shrill Trumpets Voice.
Heav'n's starry Arch with Acclamations ring,
While the glad Throng, *Arthur's* loud Praises sing:
Let *Arthur* live, the Towns and Fields resound,
Let *Arthur* live, the ecchoing Hills rebound.

The

The Evening thus in Mirth and Triumph paſt,
The *Britons* to their Reſt retir'd at laſt.

Mean Time four Lords arriv'd from *Tollo*, crave
Audience of *Octa*; which the *Saxon* gave.
To hear their Embaſſy, in regal State
High on his Throne, the *Saxon* Monarch ſate.
Duncan the chief broke Silence thus, we bring
This Meſſage from the great *Albanian* King;
He is advanc'd, to give that powerful Aid,
Which by his Orator's King *Octa* pray'd.
A valiant Hoſt obeying his Command,
Whoſe conquering Swords, no force could yet withſtand,
Who laid the *Caledonian* Forreſt waſt,
And from their Forts the fierce *Meatian* chas'd;
Halts on a Plain, three Leagues remov'd from hence,
Ready t' engage their Arms in your Defence.
But our great Leader prays, that when you come,
The *Britons* all ſubdu'd, in Triumph home,
Fair *Ethelina* may be then his own,
The bright Reward that ſhall his Labours crown.
If to theſe happy Nuptials you incline,
He'll ſtraight with yours, his valiant Forces joyn.
Let not the *Saxons* doubt, great *Tollo's* Arms,
Will free your Kingdom from the Foes Alarms,

He ſaid, forthwith *Octa* in counſel ſate;
A Matter ſo important to debate.
When *Oſred* thus began:
Great Exigencies of our State perſwade,
That we comply with this Propoſal made:
We are compell'd by hard Affairs to court
Th' *Albanian* Arms, our Kingdom to ſupport.

You know too well, how much the *Saxons* Hoft,
Is weaken'd by the Numbers we have loft,
When Valiant *Arthur* did our Troops invade,
What Havock his victorious Progrefs made.
What wide Deftruction in our Army rag'd,
Where'er his fatal Weapons were engag'd:
Our frighted Troops, when he advances, fly
Swift as the Clouds, the Winds chafe thro' the Sky.
But warlike *Tollo*, rivals *Arthur*'s Fame,
Equal their Courage, and their Strength the fame:
Againft the *Briton* he'll the Field mantain,
And on his Buckler his vaft Stroaks fuftain.
No ftronger Champion travers'd yet the Field,
To him, or none the *Britifh* Prince muft yield.
Kind Heav'n has fent a Man fo great, and Brave,
From *Arthur*'s Arms, our threatn'd State to fave.
I would not then his juft Defire withftand,
But let him know, you grant him his Demand:
This Grant to fuch a Prince we muft allow,
Was always fit, but neceffary now.

He ceas'd, and next *Pafcentius* filence broke,
And wifely thus th' attentive Peers befpoke:
I once advis'd that to preferve the State,
We fhould ftrict Friendfhip with Prince *Arthur* make,
That we *Britannia* fhould between us fhare,
And with the Princefs Nuptials end the War.
The Terms propos'd the *Britifh* Hero pleafe,
And all things feem'd to promife lafting Peace:
But when we were inform'd the *Britifh* Hoft,
Had half their Force, by raging Sicknefs loft,
Thinking we might with Eafe, the Foe defeat,
We from the Terms our felves propos'd, retreat.

I wish that Rupture may not Heav'n provoke,
To bring our Necks beneath the *British* Yoke.
With all our Force the *Britons* we assail,
But *Arthur's* unresisted Arms prevail:
How great a Loss the *Saxons* undergo,
Our bleeding Wounds and endless Funerals show.
What Hero can be found to guard our State,
Against Prince *Arthur's* Arms, and prosp'rous Fate.
True, *Tollo's* Deeds give him a warlike Name,
But much inferiour to the *Briton's* Fame:
If we confiding in th' *Albanians* Sword,
Fresh Triumphs to the *Briton* should afford:
Who after, shall controuling Bounds oppose,
To the victorious Progress of our Foes?
Who then against the Torrent can contend,
And from th' o'erflowing Flood, our Towns defend?
We shall in vain our former Conquest boast,
The *Saxon* sinks and all *Britannia's* lost.
All things well weigh'd, Prince *Arthur* looks to me,
As one supported by divine Decree,
To Empire rais'd by unchang'd Destiny:
If so in vain all our Attempts are made,
In vain we build our Hopes on *Tollo's* Aid.
We shall oppose inevitable Fate,
And in our Ruin learn our Fault, too late.
I would Prince *Arthur's* Temper sound, and strive
Once more the former Treaty to revive.
This way we may controul the Conqueror's Arms,
And *Arthur* bind by *Ethelina's* Charms:
This way perhaps you'l stem the rapid Tyde,
And gain a Conquest to your Arms deny'd.

Pascentius ceas'd, *Crida* with Choler burn'd,
And with an Air disturb'd these Words return'd;

We all well know *Pascentius* Tongue, was made
Smooth, soft, and fluent fitted to perswade.
For courtly Arts, and fine Intreagues of State,
No *Saxon* Genius can *Pascentius* mate:
All to his Eloquence at home must yield,
As he to all, for Courage in the Field.
Men of the Cabinet take no Delight.
In bloody War, they are too wise to fight.
The *Briton*'s Strength, and *Arthur*'s Arms I find,
Strike fiercely on a prudent timerous Mind:
A brave Heroick Spirit can't despair,
Who minds the Turns and doubtful chance of War.
Joyn'd by the *Picti* and *Albanian* Horse,
We're much superior to the *British* Force:
Tollo and *Mordred*, both for Arms are fam'd,
Whose Deeds with greater wonder are proclaim'd?
We too have Heros left, that dare engage
The *Briton*'s Arms, and can sustain his Rage:
My self will meet him in the Field, and stand
Unmov'd against the Fury of his Hand.
Shall we at last a Conquer'd Nation fear,
And long inur'd to Victory despair.
Let not our vile Submission stain our Name,
And lessen thro' the World the *Saxon* Fame:
No, let the King, with *Tollo's* Prayer comply,
Our Forces joyn'd must make the *Britons* fly.
He ceas'd, the Council murmur'd their Applause,
And pleas'd with this Advice King *Octa* rose.

 He straight dispatch'd th' *Albanian* Orators,
By whom the Valiant *Tollo* he assures,
That he the *Britons* by his Aid subdu'd,
Shall *Ethelina* wed for whom he sued.

Withall he added, that Affairs requir'd
Their Troops should join, before the Truce expir'd.

 His Oratours return'd to *Tollo* bring,
The pleasing Answer, of the *Saxon* King:
Tollo transported with excessive Joy,
Believes no Rival could his Hopes destroy.
As if the Battel were already won,
He thinks the beauteous Princess is his own.
Glitt'ring in Arms, like a refulgent Star,
He leads his *Scotish* Nation to the War:
A Nation fierce and haughty by Success,
Which *Albions* Northern Soil did then possess.
For a rude, cruel People, bred to Spoil,
To Blood, and Rapine, from th' *Hibernian* Isle,
Did in this Age, infest th' *Albanian* Coast,
And landed there at last their barb'rous Host:
Scots they were call'd, from their wild Islands Name,
For *Scotia*, and *Hibernia* were the same:
Here their new Seats the prosp'rous Pyrates, fix,
And their course Blood, with the old *Britons* mix.
These their *Albanian* Seats, new *Scotia* stile,
Leaving *Hibernia*, to their Native Isle:
The *Calidonian Britons* dispossest,
And by a hard Tyrannick Yoke opprest;
Did these *Hibernian*, *Scotish* Lords Obey,
And felt the Curses of a forraign Sway.
This Nation then obey'd King *Tollo's* Laws,
And now in Arms asserts the *Saxon* Cause.

 The mighty *Donald*, of the *Northern Isles*,
Of Visage fierce, and dreadful with the Spoils
Of grisly Bears, and of the foaming Boar,
Which hideous Pride he o'er his Shoulders wore;

Marches his vig'rous Troops into the Field,
Whose thundring Swords, themselves could only weild.
By their rough Captains led, they left the Land,
Where once the old *Meatians* did Command:
And where the Walls from Sea to Sea extend,
By *Romans* built, their Province to defend;
Stupendous Bulwarks, whose unnumber'd Towers,
Repel'd th' Incursions of the Northern Powers.
But when proud *Rome* was weak and feeble grown,
Th' insulting Foe broke the high Fences down:
Now Ruins show where the chief Fabrick stood,
Between wide *Tinna's* and *Itunna's* Flood.
The Youth from all the Towns that did obey,
In ancient times, the mild *Novantian* Sway.
Such as possest the *Elgovian* Seats, and those
Who till'd the Land, where silver *Devia* flows:
Who on the wild and bleaky Shore reside,
Insulted by the rough *Hibernian* Tide;
To aid the *Saxon* from their Country came,
By *Dongal* led, a Lord of Martial Fame.
Those where *Kanduara* rears her lofty Towers,
And *Glotta's* Tide into the Ocean pours:
And where th' *Orestian* Princes heretofore,
And *Attacottian* Lords the Scepter bore.
Those where the *Otadenian* Cities stood,
Between *Alanus*, and fair *Vedra's* Flood.
They march from *Castralata* and the Shore,
Where wide *Boderia's* noisy Billows roar.
Then those from *Vindolana* and the Land
Where *Ælians* Bridge and high *Cilurnum* stand.

Mackbeth a great Commander of the North,
And rocky Highlands, draws his Nation forth.

Loose

Loose Mantles o'er their brawny Shoulders flung,
With careless Pride beneath their midleg hung:
Cerulean Bonnets on their Heads they wore,
And for their Arms, broad Swords and Targets bore.
The Youth pour'd out from fair *Victoria's* Gates,
From *Orrea* and the old *Gadenian* Seats:
And from the spacious *Caledonian* Wood,
And where fair *Celnius* rolls his rapid Flood.
These Troops were by the fierce *Congellar* led,
Of *Malcol*'s Royal Stock the famous Head:
Who first from wild *Jerne* wafted o'er,
His barb'rous Engines to th' *Albanian* Shore.
Those from the *Vicomagians* Cities came,
From high *Banatia*, and from ancient *Tame*:
And they who dwelt on either verdant Bank
Of *Longo*'s Stream, and those that *Itys* drank.
With those that stretcht along the *Western* Coast;
To whom the old *Creonian* Towns were lost,
Where high *Epidium* midst th' *Hibernian* Waves,
Protrudes his Head, and all their Monsters braves.
Those from the Towns along the flowry Side,
Of Northern *Tinna*, and fair *Tava*'s Tide;
Where once the happy *Venicontes* dwelt,
Before the forraign Conquerour's Yoke was felt.

There was a Northern Nation fierce and bold,
On whose dy'd Bodies, fearful to behold,
Wild Beasts inscrib'd, and ravenous Birds were born;
Which their vast Limbs did dreadfully adorn:
So fierce they seem'd, as ready to devour,
The naked Limbs, which the wild Monsters bore.
Their Hieroglyphick Armies, stain'd and smear'd
With various Colours, and strange Forms appear'd,

In Pageant Armour, and in painted State,
Like Troops of Heralds, who on Triumphs wait.
This Nation *Picts* were call'd, who wafted o'er
From *Scandinavia*, and the bleaky Shore
Of Southern *Scythia*, did these Seas infest,
And with their Fleets, the *British* Coast molest.
Their Pyracies by Sea, and Thefts by Land,
Th' exhausted *Britons* did in vain withstand:
No more of *Rome's* declining Power afraid,
They did the weak, defenceless Isle invade.
Th' affrighted *Briton* from the Shore retreats,
And leaves the Conquerour his abandon'd Seats.
Their King at Pleasure, this fierce Nation made,
And *Mordred* now th' Imperial Scepter sway'd:
He to King *Tollo* by his Queen Ally'd,
And now by closer Bonds of Interest ty'd,
Commands his Men, to take their Shield and Launce,
And with the *Scotish* Army to advance.

    They march'd, who then possest the Hilly Land,
Which th' ancient *Carnonatian* did Command.
From *Ricine*, and the frozen *Hebudes*,
Lav'd by the loud *Deucaledonian* Seas.
From all the Towns whence their victorious Sword,
Forc'd the *Carenian* Prince, the rightful Lord,
Where the wild *Hiperborean* Ocean raves,
And on the Rocks breaks his Tempestuous Waves.
They came who then the *Mertian* Cities fill'd,
And held the Lands that once the *Logian* till'd.
They left the Soil where swift *Tuesis* flows,
Where *Grampius* stands in everlasting Snows,
Which like the fam'd *Riphean* Hills appears,
And with his Head divides the neighb'ring Spheres.

From

From all the Land where *Loxa*'s Current flows,
Which *Uara*'s and *Tuefis* Streams inclose :
Where once the bold *Decantians* did reside,
And from their Hills the Power of *Rome* defy'd.
These with the *Saxon* Troops their Arms unite,
Who so well reinforc'd prepare for Fight;
While wounded in his Tent King *Octa* staid,
King *Tollo*, as their Leader, all obey'd.

Prince Arthur.

BOOK X.

Aurora's Beams now on the Mountains smil'd,
And adverse Clouds with Purple Edgings gild.
Boyling with Martial Rage King *Tollo* stands,
And his high Chariot, and his Steeds demands:
Steeds, whiter than the purest *Alpine* Snows,
And fleeter than the Gales that *Boreas* blows.
He triumph'd when his noble Breed appear'd,
Their Harness thick with Gold and Silver smear'd:
When he their thundring Neighings heard, and saw
Their wanton Hoofs the trembling Valley paw,
The Grooms and Charioteers about him stand,
Reining the snorting Coursers in their Hand:
Stroking their Backs, they their hot Spirits sooth'd,
And their high Manes with Combs, and Spunges smooth'd.

Tollo mean time, puts on his mighty Arms,
And all the Field resounds with loud Alarms:
Each Army does for Bloody Toil prepare,
And draw their Troops out, to renew the War.
The thund'ring Coursers shake the trampled Ground,
And warlike Clamours from the Hills rebound.
Across the Plain the rapid Chariots fly,
And with thick Clouds of Dust annoy the Sky.
An Iron Harvest on the Field appears,
Of Launces, burnish'd Shields, and bristling Spears.

Throng'd

Throng'd Heads in long embattl'd Ranks dispos'd,
The lowring Front of Horrid War disclos'd.
First furious *Tollo* springs out from the Lines,
And on the Plain in radiant Armour shines:
His polish'd *Helm* oppreſt the dazled Sight,
And shone on high, like a huge Globe of Light.
The Golden *Shield* his mighty Arm did bear,
Hung like a blazen Meteor, in the Air.
His Coat of Mail was on his Shoulders caſt,
And Golden Pieces his vaſt Thighs encas'd:
The Pieces round his Legs, Gold Buttons ty'd,
And his broad *Sword* hung dreadful by his Side:
Which when drawn out, like a destructive Flame
Of Light'ning, from the ample Scabbard came.
In such illuſtrious Arms King *Tollo* shone,
And Thought no Strength superior to his own.
Then shaking in his Hand his maſſy *Spear*,
He cry'd aloud, that all his Threats might hear,
This *Spear* ne'er yet deceiv'd its Maſter's Hand,
Nor could the braveſt Knight it's Force withſtand:
Witneſs *Alboadian*, and great *Locrine*, ſlain
In ſingle Combates, on th' *Albanian* Plain.
Witneſs ye *Caledonian* Princes, you,
Whom with vaſt ſpoil on *Tava's* Banks I ſlew.
Now, by this faithful ſpear shall *Arthur* dy,
If his juſt Fears perſwade him not to fly:
T' *Augusta's* Gates I'll bring his sever'd Head,
And in his Spoils, fair *Ethelina* wed.

Thus *Tollo* boaſts, thus did his Fury riſe,
And ſtreaks of Fire flaſh'd from his raging Eyes.
So when a tawny Lyon, from the ſide
Of ſome high *Lybian* Mountain, has deſcry'd,

A spotted Leopard, or a foaming Boar,
To rouze his Courage he begins to Roar;
He shakes his Hideous Sides, his Bristles rise,
And fiercely round he rowls his fiery Eyes.
Again he Roars, his Paws the Mountains tear,
A fearful Preface to th' ensuing War.
High in his Chariot *Tollo* then advanc'd,
And from his Arms amazing Lustre glanc'd:
A Martial Ardour sparkled in his Eyes,
And hot with Choler he the Foe defies.
So when the Spring's warm Breath, and chearing Ray
Calls from his Cave th' awaken'd *Snake*, that lay
Folded to Rest, while Winter Snows conceal'd
The Mountains Heads, and Frosts the Lakes congeal'd.
The sloughy Spoils from his sleek Back depos'd,
And the gay Pride of his new Skin disclos'd;
He views himself with Youthful Beauties crown'd,
Elated casts his haughty Eyes around,
And rolls his speckled spires along the Ground.
Fresh Colours dy his Sides, and thro' his Veins
Turgid with Life, reviving Vigour reigns.
The sprightly Beast, unfolds upon the Plain
The glossy Honours of his Summer Train.
His Crest erected high, and forky Tongue
Shot out, he hisses, bounds, and leaps along.
Such Life and Vigour valiant *Tollo* shows,
Marching with eager Haste to meet his Foes.

And now the *British* Host advanc'd in sight,
With chearful Looks, and eager of the Fight:
Prince *Arthur* in refulgent Arms appear'd,
High in the midst, the *Saxons* saw, and fear'd.
As when a Merchant richly laden spies,
A lowring Storm far in th' Horizon rise,

A deadly Fear o'er all his Vitals reigns,
And his chill Blood hangs curdled in his Veins:
He furls his Sails, and fits his Ship to bear
The dreadful Hurricane, ascending thro' the Air.
Now both th' embattled Hosts advancing near,
King *Tollo* shakes his long, outrageous Spear:
And crying out, and threatning from afar,
In his swift Chariot flew amidst the War.
His rapid Wheels cut thro' the thickest Files,
With fearful Ruine, and prodigious Spoils.
Hapless *Vodinar*, first his Arm did feel,
And in his Breast receiv'd the pointed Steel.
Next *Byron* on the Sand expiring lies,
Orpes flies to his Aid, and with him dies.
Kentwin, *Morosten*, *Caradoc* he slew,
And with his Javelin pierc'd stout *Mervin* thro'.
Then you brave Youths, *Risan*, and *Tudor* fell,
Who did in Strength, and Martial Skill excel.
His fatal Spear transfixt bold *Arnon*'s sides,
And from his Neck, his Sword the Head divides.
As *Udas* fled, the hissing Dart he sent
Enter'd his Back, and thro' his Navel went;
He fell, and on the Dust, sad to behold,
His Bowels issuing from his Belly roll'd.
Runo's right Knee his Javelin did invade,
And in the Bone the glitt'ring Weapon staid.
Strong *Runo* fell, and as he wildly star'd,
And many moving Words, in haste prepar'd
To beg his Life, th' insulting Conquerour flew,
And with his Spear pierc'd his pale Body thro':
Groaning he lay, and fetcht long double Sighs,
While in thick Mists Death swims upon his Eyes.

Next

Next *Leoline*, King *Cadwall*'s Son he kill'd,
A beauteous Youth, and not in War unskill'd:
His Head the Fauchion to the Shoulders Cleft,
And on the Duft his groveling Body left.
Ouenar felt within a fudden Dread,
And turning round his Chariot, would have fled;
When his long Spear the fierce *Albanian* threw,
Which crafht the Bones, and thro' the Temples flew:
Headlong *Ouenar* fell, and on the Ground
Lay weltring in his Blood, pour'd from his Wound.
His fatal Weapons vaft Deftruction made,
And where he pafs'd, the flain in Heaps were laid.
So when a Flood from th' *Hyperborean* Hills,
Comes thund'ring down, and all the Valley fills,
Where the high Snows diffolv'd by Summer Beams,
In one vaft Deluge joyn their various Streams:
The roaring Tide with its impetuous Courfe,
O'erflows the Banks, and with refiftlefs Force
Sweeps Houfes, Harveft, Herds, and Flocks away,
Nor can the loftieft Mounds its Progrefs ftay.
With equal Rage, with fuch impetuous Haft,
Great *Tollo* thro' the thick Battalions paft:
The rapid Wheels of his fwift Chariot burn,
And in their Courfe the throng'd Brigades o'erturn.
O'er fcatter'd Arms, bright Helms, broad Shields of Brafs,
And broken Spears, his raging Axles pafs:
O'er Heaps of Dead the furious Warrior flies,
And fills with Duft, and ratling Noife, the Skies.
The fquallid Field, a Crimfon Torrent choaks,
And mingled Duft, and Blood opprefs his Chariot's fpoakes.
The trembling Ground th' outrageous Courfers tear,
And fnoring, blow their Foam into the Air:

Their fervid Noſtrils breath out Clouds of Smoke,
And Flames of Fire from their hot Eye-balls broke.
With furious Hoofs o'er ſlaughter'd Heaps they fly,
And daſh up bloody Rain amidſt the Sky:
Reeking in Sweat, and ſmear'd with Duſt and Gore
They ſpurn the Sand, and thro' the Battel roar.

Then Valiant *Malgo* with a freſh Brigade,
Advanc'd, the mighty Warrior to invade;
While from another Part his warlike Band,
Bothan led up, and made a noble Stand.
Now Showers of Darts, and feather'd Arrows fly
At *Tollo*'s Breaſt, that darken all the Sky:
When Valiant *Marodan* approaching near,
With all his ſtrength, caſts his impetuous Spear;
It paſs'd the Buckler's Plates, and folded Hide,
And thro' his Armour, ſlightly raz'd his Side:
Tollo incens'd, collecting all his Might,
Broke thro' their Ranks, and put the Foe to Flight.
Now dire Deſtruction reigns amidſt their Files,
And all the Field was ſpread with warlike Spoils.
So when *Battavian* Harpooniers aſſail,
With their ſharp Launces, ſome prodigious *Whale*,
That like a floating Mountain, lies at Eaſe,
Vaſtly extended on the Frozen Seas:
When the *Leviathan* begins to feel,
Within his wounded ſide, the bearded ſteel;
And looking round, ſees all the ambient Flood,
Deeply diſtain'd with its old Monarch's Blood;
Straight all enrag'd, he throws himſelf about,
And thro' the Air does Crimſon Rivers ſpout:
Swift, as a Storm, he does the Foe aſſail,
With his expanded Fins, and hideous Tail.

Some

Some Barks are crush'd, as with a falling Rock,
And some o'erturn'd, sink with the dreadful Shock:
The rest ply all their Oars, and frighted Row,
Thro' Fields of Ice, to shun th' unequal Foe.

   Canvallo then brought up a stronger Force,
Whom *Galbut* joyn'd, to stop th' *Albanian*'s Course:
The fainting *Britons* these fresh Troops protect,
And with their Arms great *Tollo*'s Triumphs checkt.
And now their thick Brigades were close engag'd,
And thro' the bloody Field Destruction rag'd:
Now Man to Man stood close, and Spear to Spear,
Helms mixt with Helms, and Shields with Shields appear.
Arrows aloft in feather'd Tempests fly,
Darts hiss at Darts, encountring in the Sky.
A dreadful Noise distracting all the Air,
Came from the hoarce *Cerberean* Throat of War:
While Arms on Arms, Bucklers on Bucklers ring,
Swords clash with Swords, and flying Javelins sing.
Some threaten loud, while some for Quarter cry,
And some insult, while some in Torment dy:
As when a Torrent down some Mountain's side,
To the low Valleys rolls its rapid Tide,
Where mighty Stones and rocky Fragments, high
Within the rude, unfashion'd Channels ly:
O'er abrupt Tracks its Course the Deluge bends,
And roaring down with mighty Falls, descends.
Prodigious Noise th' Aerial Region fills,
The Shepherds hear, and tremble on their Hills.
Or as;
When high *Vesuvius* stow'd with wealthy Stores,
Preluding to some dire Irruption, roars;
While horrible Convulsions shake its Womb,
And lab'ring Sides, which hidden War entomb:

Th' imprifon'd Thunder bellows under Ground,
And the loud Noife fill all the Heav'ns around.
Auguft *Parthenope*'s gilt Turrets fhake,
And fair *Campania*'s wealthy Farmers quake.
Such was the loud diftracting Noife of War,
Such horrid Clamours tore th' afflicted Air,
While the fierce Foes againft each other rag'd,
And for *Britannia*'s Empire were engag'd:
The neighing Steeds, and wounded Warriors Cries,
And rifing Clouds of Duft confound the Skies.

Mordred mean time the mighty *Pictan* King,
Does to the Charge, his threatning Squadrons bring:
Sticking his Golden Rowels in the Sides
Of his huge Steed, amidft the Ranks he Rides.
The *Britifh* Horfe unfhaken as a Rock,
Bravely fuftain'd th' Invader's thundring Shock:
King *Meridoc*, who did the Horfe Command,
Confirm'd his Men, to make fo brave a ftand.
Yet many Valiant *Britons Mordred* flew,
Firft with his Spear he pierc'd brave *Jafper* thro':
The Valiant *Giffith* by unhappy Chance,
Came in his Way, and felt his fatal Launce;
Beneath his Ear, the Weapon pierc'd his Head,
He fell, and in a Moment ftretcht out Dead.
His furious Arm noble *Lodanar* felt,
On whofe high Creft fo fierce a ftroke he dealt,
The *Briton* ftunn'd with the prodigious Blow,
Drops the loos'd Reins, and lets his Weapons go:
The frighted Courfer thro' the Battel Flies,
Lodanor in the Duft difmounted lies;
The Horfes Hoofs in pieces crufh his Head,
And deep into the Mire his Bowels tread.

Then,

Book X.   *Prince* Arthur.   279

Then with great Fury he at *Adel* flew,
And grip'd him with his furious Hand, and drew
The *Briton* from his Seat, his fiery Steed
Scours o'er the Field, from his loft Rider freed.
Wrigling and spurning in his Arms the Prey
'Midst loud Applauses *Mordred* bears away:
So when an Eagle from some Mountain's Top,
To truss a timerous Leveret makes a stoop,
And in his crooked Pounces takes him up.
Struggling he mounts, and squeaks amidst the Skies,
And faster than he ran before, he flies.

To fight the *Pict* straight *Guinan* did advance,
But in his Shield broke his projected Launce.
Then at the *Briton Mordred*'s Javelin flew,
It mist the Rider, but the Courser slew.
Extended on the Ground the groaning Beast,
Th' unhappy Rider with his Weight oppress'd:
Mordred dismounts, and with his glitt'ring Dart
Loudly insulting, stabs him to the Heart.
Guinan a Friend to *Meridoc* was dear;
Who at his Death enrag'd, caught up his Spear,
And shaking it from far, with mighty Rage,
Spurs thro' their Ranks King *Mordred* to engage.
The *Pictan* Monarch who elated stood,
Like some tall Oak, that overlooks the Wood,
Or some high Tower, which with its lofty Head
Surveys the Towns beneath, around it spread;
Lifts his Gigantick Spear, and cry'd aloud,
To *Meridoc* advancing thro' the Crowd,
Briton come on, and but a Moment stand,
A glorious Fate expect from *Mordred*'s Hand:
Let not thy Fears perswade thee hence to flie,
Heav'ns give thee Courage to come up, and die.

King

King *Meridoc* his Spear in Anfwer fent,
Which in the Shield's third Ply, its Fury fpent.
Then *Mordred* threw, aloft the Weapon hift,
Ludar it flew, but *Meridoc* it mift.
Brave *Ludar* was a Lord of *Neuftrian* Blood,
Who long in vain the fair *Marinda* woo'd;
To blefs him with her Smiles, and heal his Wound,
But from the fcornful Maid no Pity found.
Loft in Defpair, he left his Native Soil,
His Torments to beguile with Martial Toil:
Now wounded by an erring Spear, he lies,
Cry'd out *Marinda*, cruel Fate! and dies.

Then did the *Briton's* fecond Weapon fly,
Which thro' his Armour, pierc'd King *Mordred*'s Thigh,
Which from the Flefh he ftrove to draw in vain,
Then flew about wreckt with tormenting Pain.
Wildly he ftar'd, and turn'd his Courfer's Head,
Aloud he roar'd, and from the Combat fled.
So when a Sword-Fifh, urg'd with generous Rage,
Does a vaft Whale, in Northern Seas engage:
The Finny Warriors, with a furious Courfe
To Battel rufh, and meet with wondrous Force;
A Noble Fight enfues, and dreadful Strokes
Afflict the Main, and fhake the Neighb'ring Rocks.
As they advance, they drive high Seas before,
The Monfters bellow, and the Billows roar.
The boiling Sea, with greater Fury raves,
Then when incumbent Storms prefs on its Waves.
The Surges raging with inteftine War,
With high curl'd Heads, look terrible from far:
The Foam of breaking Waves, in pointed Sleet
Like driven Snow, does on the Ocean beat.

At every Shock the dashing Waters fly,
And Clouds of Liquid Dust obscure the Sky.
At last the Whale his shining Belly goar'd,
By his fierce Enemy's invading Sword;
Wild with his Rage and Pain, whole Seas does spout,
And like a floating Island, rolls about.
The wounded Monster does the Seas out-roar,
And tumbles thro' the Billows to the Shore,
Leaving behind broad Tracks of Purple Gore.

Thus strove the *Pictan* and the *British* Horse,
While pious *Arthur* with resistless Force,
In radiant Arms, bright as th' Autumnal Star,
Flies thro' the Foe, himself a fearful War:
With his victorious Sword, which wav'd on high,
Made flaming Bows, and Arches in the Sky.
The Body of their Battel he invades,
And thro' a Sea of Blood victorious wades.
Where'er the Conqu'ror did his progress bend,
Ruin and wide Destruction did attend.
Prodigious Numbers by his Weapons fall,
And on their Gods in vain the *Saxons* call:
He made his way, like an impetuous Flood,
Or furious Burning, raging thro' the Wood.
Where'er he pass'd, the Dead lay thick behind,
As sapless Leaves, spread by a boistrous Wind.

Ussina first, a Valiant Lord, did feel,
In his Left Side, the *Briton*'s piercing steel.
Next *Godred* fell from Valiant *Ingulf* sprung,
And as he fell, his Arms upon him rung.
Next fell the famous *Ethelbert*, betwixt
The Head and Shoulders with a Dart transfixt.

O o   Nothing

Nothing his Courage, or illustrious Blood,
That to his Veins from mighty *Odin's* flow'd;
Nothing his well-prov'd Armour, when assail'd
By *Arthur's* Hand, the noble Youth avail'd:
Struggling he lay, and wallow'd on the Ground
In the warm Streams that rush'd out from his Wound:
A gloomy Night o'erwhelms his dying Eyes,
And his disdainful Soul, from his pale Bosom flies.
Then *Imerick* he slew a valiant Chief,
And *Lodocan* that rush'd to his Relief:
One with his Fauchion, th' other with his Spear,
That cleft the Head, this pierc'd from Ear to Ear.
Next from his Arm a singing Javelin sent,
Thro' the left Groin of mighty *Crida* went:
The wounded Chief retires in tort'ring Pain,
And Tracks of Blood his halting Leg distain.
Then *Sigebert* a noble Youth he slew,
The fatal Weapon pierc'd his Temples thro'.
His furious Dart did next at *Ebald* fly,
Which thro' his Shield pierc'd deep into his Thigh:
Inflam'd with Rage, and roaring out with Pain,
He strove to pull the Weapon out in vain.
His Javelin next transfixt *Congellar's* Reins,
And out his Life gush'd from his open'd Veins.
Then *Edbert* fell;
Thro' the bright Helmet which his Head encas'd,
Thro' Bones, and Brains, the furious Javelin pass'd;
And his left Eye from out its Circle struck,
On the sharp Point, a ghastly Prospect stuck.
Then *Ethelrick* a stout *West Saxon* Lord,
And *Ida* fell, by his victorious Sword.
The first, his Head down to his Shoulders Cleft,
Fell to the Ground, of Breath and Sense bereft.

The

The heavy Blade falling with oblique Sway,
Half thro' the other's Neck, did make its way.
The Head half fever'd on his Shoulders hung,
And from the Wound a bloody Torrent sprung.
Rolling in Gore upon the Field he lay,
Wildly he star'd, and groan'd his life away.
As when a mighty Tempest from the East,
The Sea assail'd, and on the Billows prest
By Heav'n's Command, that *Jacob*'s Fav'rite Race,
Might *Pharaoh*'s Arms escape, and safely pass.
Th' astonish'd Ocean did its Force obey,
Open'd his watry Files, and clear'd the pathless way.
The Waves retreated, and erected stood,
As fear and wonder had benum'd the Flood.
Then Front to Front they kept their Line unmov'd,
And those that crowd behind, they backwards shov'd.
Like a long Ridge of Crystal Hills they rose,
And the low Wonders of the deep disclose.
So valiant *Arthur* prest upon the Foe,
And so their Troops retir'd, and let the Conqueror thro'.

Now he advanc'd to *Tollo's* foremost Band,
Where mighty *Fingal* and *Dolavian* stand;
Both which he slew, next valiant *Duncan* falls,
While he in vain for Help on *Tollo* calls.
And now on every side the *Saxon* Host
Began to fly, and yield the Battel lost.
Only King *Tollo* with enormous Rage
Breaks thro' the Troops, Prince *Arthur* to engage.

Mean time the Prince of Hell stood full of Care,
And fear'd th' Event of this unequal War.
To save the *Saxon* Squadrons which remain,
Whereof such Numbers lay already slain,

And to prevent *Tollo's* impending Fate,
Whose Arms the *British* Hero's could not mate.
The conquering *Britons* fierce pursuit to stay,
And once more *Arthur's* Triumphs to Delay,
By Heav'n's Permission, causes to arise
A dreadful Tempest in the troubled Skies.
The blustring Powers, and Demons of the Air,
Straight at his Summons to their Prince repair.

To whom thus *Lucifer* :
Aerial Powers, who my Commands obey,
And in these Regions own my soveraign Sway ;
Know, I intend to end this bloody Strife,
To part the Hosts, and guard King *Tollo's* Life.
Go hasten then, each to his known Employ,
And let your loudest Storms the Heav'ns annoy.
Swift, as your own projected Lightnings fly,
And in a Moment trouble all the Sky.
The dusky Fiends obedient fly away,
Some fetch up misty Stores to choak the Day.
Some Pitchy Clouds of *Stygian* Fleeces made,
And in their Bowels Trains of Brimstone laid.
Some ram in Seeds of unripe Thunder, some
With mighty Hailstones charge their hollow Womb.
Some fetch strong Winds, which on their Wings may bear
The heavy Tempest lab'ring thro' the Air.
O'erspreading mists th' extinguish'd sunbeams drown,
Dark Clouds o'er all the Black Horrizon frown,
And hang their deep Hydropick Bellies down.
Hoarse Thunder rolls, and Murm'ring try's its Voice,
Preluding to the Tempest's dreadful Noise.
Infernal Torches now the Fiends apply,
And light the fiery Seeds that hidden lie.

The Heav'n's wide Frame outrageous Thunder shocks,
Loud, as the mighty Crack of falling Rocks.
The Cloudy Machines burst amidst the Skies,
And from their yawning Wounds exploded Lightning flies.
Confusion fills the Air, Fire, Rain, and Hail
Now mingle Tempests, now by Turns prevail.
No more the *Britons*, and the *Saxons* strove;
For that below, yields to the War above.
The conquering *Britons*, to the Camp return,
Their Loss in theirs, the vanquish'd *Saxons* mourn.
So when a summer Cloud the Sky o'erspreads,
The Bees that wander o'er the flowry Meads,
Or to the Tops of lofty Mountains climb,
To fetch the yellow spoils of od'rous Thyme,
Forsake their Toil, and lab'ring thro' the Air,
To their known Hives, with hasty Flight repair.
All to their Cells returning from abroad,
Depose their luscious Dew, and strutting Thighs unload.
Perplext, and sad, the *Saxon* Troops appear,
And horribly they curst Prince *Arthur's* spear.
They saw no *Saxon* could his Arm withstand,
And doubt Deliverance from King *Tollo's* Hand.

When half of this uneasie Night was spent,
To all the great Commanders *Octa* sent,
To bring them quickly to his royal Tent.
And first the Summons they to *Tollo* bear,
Who to equip himself did straight prepare.
A Wolf grin'd horribly upon his Head,
And o'er his brawny Back a Leopard's Hide was spread.
He girds his mighty Fauchion to his side,
Which hung across his Thigh, with fearful Pride.
Frowning, and on the great Affair Intent,
He straight to *Octa's* high Pavilion went.

Next

Next *Mordred* halting with his Wound, and lame,
And by his maſſy ſpear ſupported, came.
A Beaver's Skin upon his Head he wore,
And a fierce *Tyger*'s his wide ſhoulders bore.
A ſilver Belt, illuſtrious to behold,
Held his broad ſword, adorn'd with ſtuds of Gold.

Then *Ella* roſe newly laid down to Reſt,
And button'd on his rich embroider'd Veſt.
O'er which a pompous ſcarlet Cloak he threw,
Faſten'd with Golden Claſps, and lin'd with coſtly Blue.
Then putting on his mighty ſword, in Haſt
Tho lame, he to the Counſel ſternly paſt.
Then valiant *Amades*, and *Chuline* went,
With wiſe *Paſcentius*, to their Monarch's Tent;
Follow'd by *Oſred*, *Sebert*, and the reſt
Of their chief Lords, who great Concern expreſt:
And now th' auguſt Aſſembly fill'd apace,
Where all the Leaders took their proper Place.

Then their Attention *Octa* did demand,
And leaning on his Scepter with his Hand,
He thus began, Princes, you ſee the Field,
To the victorious *Britons* ſtill we yield.
By Sea, and Land we've felt their fatal Arms,
And all our Realm trembles at their Alarms.
Our Heaps of Dead the Field with Horrour crown,
And Seas of *Saxon* Blood the Valley drown.
All *Albion*'s Iſle reſounds with dying Groans,
White with her Rocks, but whiter with our Bones.
Prince *Arthur*'s Sword the Field with Ruin ſpreads,
Like Storms, which from the Trees diſhonour'd Heads

Their

Their shady Leaves, and spreading Branches tear,
Cover the Ground, and leave the Forrest bare.
On us th' offended Gods severely frown,
But on the *British* Arms look smiling down.
While we oppose the rapid Tide of Fate,
We think to stop, what we precipitate,
And learn our Errour, at too dear a Rate.
He said, the *Saxon* Chiefs, who found their Host
Feeble, and sunk by frequent Battels lost:
Thinking their Arms unable to oppose,
The rapid Course of their victorious Foes:
Upon *Pascentius* straightway cast their Eyes,
As one above the rest accounted Wise,
And who the King to Peace did still advise.

Pascentius then began:
Octa, the Counsel which at first I gave,
From *Arthur's* Arms our threaten'd State to save;
What since has happen'd, shows was just and right:
For who can meet the *British* Prince in Fight?
Our sinking State, and hard Affairs demand
A Remedy of Force, and near at hand.
He that in such a Storm, would safely steer,
Must have a Head that's steady, cool, and clear.
The lab'ring Ship on all sides feels dire Shocks,
Charybdis shunn'd, she's dash'd on *Scylla's* Rocks.
'Tis hard to give a Monarch Counsel, where
On either Hand such frightful Shelves appear.
Statesmen, in such a Case as this, debate
How best to save themselves, and not the State.
But if my Judgment still I must declare,
I would at any Price compose the War.
And till a more effectual can be found,
This as a safe Expedient I propound.

Sore

Sore with their Wounds, and sunk with ill success,
The *Saxons* strong Desires for Peace express.
This to obtain, we must to *Arthur* sue,
And the first Treaty, which we broke, renew.
The Princess *Ethelina*'s Heav'nly Charms,
Are only stronger, than the *Briton*'s Arms.
She must be offer'd as the Prince's Bride;
This once prevail'd, and must again be try'd.
But then you break the Promise, that you made
To *Tollo*, who'll complain he is betray'd.
Since hence to Peace, our chief Obstructions spring,
I move that *Arthur*, and th' *Albanian* King,
May by their single Arms the strife decide,
And let the Princess be the Conqueror's Bride.
If o'er the *Britons* we th' Advantage gain,
And *Arthur* by th' *Albanian* King is slain;
The *Britons* shall repass *Sabrina*'s Tide,
And in their Rocks, and Hilly Lands abide:
But all the Cities, Castles, and the Land,
That lie on this side, *Octa* shall Command.
But if King *Tollo* slain by *Arthur*'s Sword,
New Triumphs to the *Briton* shall afford;
We'll meet no more their Armies in the Field,
But all our Towns, and conquer'd Places yield.
Those who shall ask it, shall be wafted o'er,
To our old seats along the *German* Shore:
The *Cantian* Kingdom still we will retain,
And in its Limits circumscrib'd remain.
This, as the best Expedient, I propose,
He said, the *Saxons* murmur'd their Applause.

Then *Tollo* answer'd with a haughty Air,
Pleas'd with my Fate, I undertake the War.

Book X.   *Prince* Arthur.   289

My Sword and *Arthur's*, shall the Strife decide,
And let the Princess be the Victor's Bride.
This conquering Arm the *Saxon* Realm shall guard,
Repell the Foe, and win the bright Reward:
For if the Foe does not my Sword decline,
The War is ended, with his Fall or mine.

Th' Assembly rose, and back the Captains went,
Praising King *Tollo* much, but fear'd th' Event.
At the first opening of the tender Day,
Six Orators, King *Octa* sent away
To *Arthur's* Camp, who introduc'd declare,
The Measures taken to compose the War:
The Challenge *Arthur* heard with great Delight,
And readily accepts the single Fight.

Straight to the sacred Temples all repair,
Heav'n to solicite with united Prayer,
That *Arthur* in the Combate might succeed,
And vanquish'd *Tollo*, by his Weapon bleed.
With warmer Zeal, and with more earnest Cries,
The *Britons* never importun'd the Skies:
A deep Concern at Heart they all exprest,
And mighty Passions struggled in their Breast;
For if the Prince fell in the Combat, all
Well knew their unsupported State must fall.

Soon as the Sun had streak'd the Skies with Light,
Prince *Arthur* rose, and Arm'd himself for Fight.
Pieces with silver Studs his Legs encas'd,
And Plates of Gold his warlike Thighs embrac'd:
And on his Head he lac'd his burnish'd Helm,
Whence flashing Brightness did the Sight o'erwhelm.

P p   Like

Like some Celestial Orb his blazing Shield,
Darted amazing Lustre thro' the Field:
And then he girded to his Martial Side,
His faithful Sword, so oft in Battel try'd.
Thus arm'd the Hero mounts his thundring Steed,
Nor *Thrace*, nor *Greece* can boast a nobler Breed.
With his strong Arm he grip'd his trembling Spear,
His very Friends, tho pleas'd, yet seem'd to fear:
And as he spurr'd his Courser, and advanc'd,
Unsufferable Splendour from his Armour glanc'd.
As glorious *Michael*, when the Foe alarms
The blisful Realms, clad in Celestial Arms
Bright as the Sun, leads forth th' Angelick Host,
To chase th' Invaders from the Heav'nly Coast:
In such illustrious Arms the Prince was seen,
His warlike Grace was such, and such his God-like Mien.

  Mean time King *Octa* from his Camp proceeds,
High in his Chariot, drawn by milk white Steeds:
And by his Side, *Tollo* appear'd in sight,
Compleatly Arm'd, and coveting the Fight.
His Coat of Mail was o'er his Shoulders flung,
And by his side his dreadful Fauchion hung.
Like a high Beacon lighted in the Air,
His Buckler flam'd, denouncing horrid War:
In his right Hand he shakes his pondrous Launce,
And on his Steed did to the Lists advance.
The Marshals of the Field, had markt out Ground
Fit for the Fight, and fixt high Pales around,
Which with arm'd Troops, on either side were lin'd,
Their Spears stuck in the Ground, their Shields reclin'd.
On either Side the Armies stood in sight,
Drawn up, as they too were design'd for Fight.

           Attended

Attended with his Heralds on the Place,
Prince *Arthur* firſt appear'd with Martial Grace.
When *Octa* and his Prieſts advancing near,
Raiſing his Voice that thoſe around might hear:
His Hand devoutly on his Breaſt, his Eyes
Fixt in a ſolemn manner on the Skies;
To ratifie the Treaty, thus he ſwore,
Th' Eternal Mind whom Chriſtians do adore;
The God of Truth I here to witneſs call,
That if this Day by *Tollo*'s Arms I fall;
We will no more Hoſtilities repeat,
But o'er *Sabrina*'s Waters will retreat:
We will no more the *Saxon* State moleſt,
But in our Hills and ſnowy Mountains reſt:
But if we find this an auſpicious Day,
And by Heaven's Aid, my Arms ſhall *Tollo* ſlay;
Then if the vanquiſh'd *Saxons*, ſhall reſtore
The Towns and Lands, which we poſſeſt before,
They in the *Cantian* Kingdom ſhall reſide,
And unmoleſted in thoſe Bounds abide.

    Then did King *Octa* by an Altar ſtand,
Rais'd with Green Turf, and on it laid his Hand;
And thus his Idols he invok'd.
Irmanſul God of Arms, and mighty *Jove*,
Tuiſco, *Odin*, all ye Powers above,
And you green Gods, and blew-ey'd Goddeſſes,
Who rule the ſpacious Empire of the Seas:
And you tremendous Powers, who all reſort,
At *Pluto*'s Summons, to th' Infernal Court:
Ye rural Gods, who rule the Hills and Woods,
Ye watry Powers, who dive beneath the Floods:

By gloomy *Styx* I swear, bear witness all,
That if King *Tollo* does in Combate fall,
The Treaty now agreed to, shall be kept,
The *Cantian* Kingdom only we except,
All other Lands, our once victorious Sword,
Won from the *British* Kings, shall be restor'd:
He who shall Conquerour in the Field remain,
Shall for his Bride fair *Ethelina* gain.

He said, and to confirm the Oath he swore,
He drew his Sword, that by his Side he wore;
And with its Point did his full Veins divide,
And let out from his Arm, the Crimson Tide:
A golden Bowl receiv'd the vital Flood,
Which *Octa* took, and drank the flowing Blood.

Arthur and *Tollo* now themselves prepare,
By a brave Combate to decide the War.
The Martials, Heralds, and the Fecial Priests
The Ceremonies finish'd, clear the Lists.
Then the loud Trumpet's Clangour did invite,
The mighty Warriours to begin the Fight.
Both in their Hands grasping their pointed Launce,
Spur their hot Steeds, and to the War advance.
And now the Combatants approach'd so near,
Their Voices rais'd, they might each other hear.

Then *Tollo* cry'd aloud:
Till now distress'd without a Friend or Home,
In forraign Lands, you did an Exile roam,
Here stop your Course, your Soul mean time shall go,
A wandring Exile to the Shades below.
I'll take off with this Sword your gasping Head,
And in your Spoils, fair *Ethelina* wed.

Were

Were you brave *Hector*, or his braver Foe,
Or Godlike *Hercules*, I'd stand your Blow:
Did you advance, with Thunder in your Hand,
Against your Bolts I would undaunted stand:
But such a mighty Foe I need not fear,
You bear not such a Shield, nor such a Spear.
Oh! that bright *Ethelina* now stood by,
To see her Lover, and my Rival dy.
Thus boastful *Tollo* did his Choler vent,
And thus in Air his empty Threats were spent.
The pious Prince enrag'd, without Reply,
Shakes his long Spear, and hastes to Victory:
As when a roaming Lyon from a far,
Sees a strong Bull stand threat'ning furious War,
Who flourishes his Horns, looks sowrly round,
And hoarcely bellowing, traverses the Ground.
For want of Foes, he does the Wood provoke,
Runs his curl'd Head against the next tall Oak,
Wishing a nobler Object of his Stroke.
The Lyon fir'd, regards him with Disdain,
And to insult him scowrs along the Plain:
So *Arthur* boyling with Heroic Rage,
Springs with a full Carier, King *Tollo* to engage.
Collected in himself th' *Albanian* stood,
Like some tall, shady Pine, it self a Wood,
Or a vast *Cyclops* wading thro' the Flood.

Then *Tollo* first, *Arthur* advancing near,
With all his Force casts his long Ashen Spear;
Which *Arthur* on his temper'd Buckler took,
While with the vast concern the *Britons* shook:
Thro' the first Plate of Brass the Weapon went,
But in the next its dying Force was spent.

Then

Then from his valiant Arm the *Briton* threw,
His Javelin, finging thro' the Air it flew;
The yielding Buckler did its Force obey,
And thro' the Plates, and Hide it made its Way;
Thro' the thin Joynts of Steel the Spear did fly,
And wounded, as it paſt, his mighty Thigh:
The Blood ſprung thro' his Armour, from the Wound,
And trickling down the Plate, diſtain'd the Ground.

Then did King *Tollo*'s ſecond Weapon fly,
Which broke within the Buckler's ſecond Ply.
The *Britiſh* Prince another Weapon threw,
Which, *Tollo* ſtooping, o'er his Shoulders flew;
And falling went ſo deep into the Ground,
No Arm, of Force to draw it out, was found.
Theſe Weapons ſpent, to end the noble Fight,
The furious Warriors from their Steeds alight:
And as they nimbly leapt upon the Ground,
The moſt undaunted Chiefs that ſtood around,
So fearful was the Chinck their Armour made,
Started, as Men ſurpriz'd, and look'd afraid.
Then furious Strokes on either Side they deal,
The ecchoing Air rings with the dreadful Peal:
Pale with the vaſt Concern both Armies look,
And for their Champion's Life with Terror ſhook.
So when two vig'rous Stags, each of his Herd
The haughty Lord, thro' all the Forreſt fear'd,
Reſolv'd to try which muſt in Combate yield,
In all their Might advance acroſs the Field;
They Nod their lofty Heads, and from afar
Flouriſh their Horns, preluding to the War.
The Combatants their threatning Heads incline,
And with their claſhing Horns in Battel joyn:

They

They rush to combate with amazing Strokes,
And their high Antlets meet with dreadful Shocks;
The mighty Sound runs ratling o'er the Hills,
And Eccho with the Fight the Valley fills:
Retiring oft, the Warriours cease to push,
But then with fiercer Rage to Battel rush.
The trembling Herds at Distance gaze, and stay
To know the Conquerour, whom they must obey:
No less concern'd *Saxons*, and *Britons* stand
To see the Victor, who must both command.

Now *Tollo* backwards shrinks, and panting stood
Faint with his Labour, and his Loss of Blood.
The *British* Prince enrag'd to see the Fight
So far prolong'd, collecting all his Might,
With double Fury on th' *Albanian* prest,
And his bright Sword high rais'd, upon his Crest
Descended with so horrible a Sway,
It stun'd the Foe, and took his Sense away;
He dropt his Arms, and giddy reel'd about,
The joyful *Britons* raise a mighty Shout.
Arthur on fire, lets not th' Advantage go,
But stepping forward with a back hand Blow,
Drawn with prodigious Strength, from side to side,
Did his wide Throat, and spouting Veins divide:
A crimson River gushing from the Wound,
Ran down his burnish'd Armour to the Ground.
Reeling and tott'ring for a While he stood,
And from his Stomack vomits clotted Blood;
Then down he fell, the Field beneath, and all
The *Saxon* Army tremble at his Fall:
Groveling in Death, and smear'd with Gore he lay,
And his dim Eyes scarcely admit the Day:

Rolling

Rolling in Duſt his wounded Body bled,
Away his Soul with Indignation fled:
Convuls'd and quivering, for a while he fetcht
A dreadful Groan, and breathleſs out he ſtretcht
As when a Whirlwind, with outrageous Force
O'erturns a lofty Oak, that ſtops its Courſe,
Its Roots torn up, the Tree's caught from the Ground,
And with the furious Eddy carried round:
Then falling from the Sky, his ſtately Head,
And ſhady Limbs, the groaning Hill o'erſpread:
So by Prince *Arthur*'s Arms, King *Tollo* ſlain,
Fell down, and lay extended on the Plain.

THE
INDEX,
EXPLAINING

The Names of *Countries, Cities,* and *Rivers,* &c. mentioned in this BOOK.

A.

ABum, *the River* Humber.
Agencourt, *or* Azencourt, *in the County of St.* Paul, *in France.*
Alanus, *River* Alne *in Northumberland.*
Alda, *a suppos'd Port in* Hampshire.
Allobroges, *Inhabitants of* Savoy *and* Piedmont.
Alpes-British, *Mountains in* Caernarvonshire.
Apulia, *a part of* Italy, *famous for Wool.*
Ariconium, Kenchester; Hereford *is suppos'd to have its original from Ariconium.*
Armorica, Little Bretaigne, *in France.*
Attrebatians, *Inhabitants of* Barkshire.
Attacotians; Ortelius *makes them to inhabit between the* Horestii *and* Otadenii, *in Scotland: But* Camden *places them more Northward, beyond the* Venicontes.
Ausona, *River* Nine *in* Northamptonshire.
Augusta, *the City of* London.
Ausonia, Italy.
Ælian's-bridge, *an old Town, so call'd by* Hadrians Wall.
Ætna, *a famous burning Mountain in the Island of* Sicily.

B.

BAnnavena, Wedon *in* Northamptonshire.
Banatia, Camden *supposes it to stand where* Bean-Castle *does, in* Murray, *in* Scotland.
Bardunus, *a River near* Norwich, *in* Norfolk.
Barry-Isle, *about three Miles from the River* Taf, *in* Glamorgan-shire.
Battavia, Holland.
Blackmoor-land, *that which was call'd* Whitehart-forrest, *in* Dorset-shire.
Boderia, *or* Boteria, Edenburg-frith, *in* Scotland.
Bolerium, *the utmost Promontory of* Cornwal, *or the* Lands-end.
Bosworth, *a Town in* Leicester-shire.
Bovium, Boverton *in* Brecknock-shire.
Brannodunum, Brancaster *in* Norfolk.
Brechinia, Brecknock-shire; *likewise* Breckncok-town.
Brigantes, *the Inhabitants of* York-shire, *Bishoprick of* Durham, Lancashire, Westmorland, *and* Cumberland.
Brigæ, *suppos'd to be* Broughton, *an old Town in* Hampshire.
Bulleum, *some suppose it to be* Bualhtcastle *in* Brecknock-shire. *The Additions to* Camden, *apprehends it to be* Caerphilli-castle, *in* Glamorgan-shire; *both under the* Silures.

C.

CAlabria, *the furthest part of* Italy.
Caledonian-forrest, *the great Forrest in* Scotland, *divided by Mount* Grampius, *or* Grantzbain.
Caledonians, *those that inhabited on both sides of Mount* Grampius, *in* Scotland.
Camboritum, *the City of* Cambridge; *near to which are* Gogmagog-hills.
Camelodunum, Malden *in* Essex.
Campania, *a part of* Italy, *in the Kingdom of* Naples.
Canonium, Chelmsford *in* Essex.
Cantians, *Inhabitants of* Kent.
Catenians, Camden *places them in* Cathness, *in* Scotland. Ortelius, *more Northward than the* Carnonacæ, *on the West-side of* Scotland.
Carnonations, *they inhabited beyond the River* Longas, *on the West-side of* Scotland.
Carphillis, *a famous Castle, suppos'd to be but by the* Romans, *in* Glamorganshire.
Cartinia, *a suppos'd Port in* Normandy.
Castralata, *City of* Edenburg, *in* Scotland.

* Cel-

The INDEX.

Celnius, *suppos'd to be the River* Keillan; *it rises below Mount* Grampius, *and falls into the German Ocean.*
Chaluz, *a Castle in France, belonging to the Viscount* Limoges.
Charybdis, *a dangerous place in the Sicilian Sea.*
Cilurnum, *it is suppos'd to stand where* Collerford *does, or else not far from it, at* Silchester in the Wall.
Clamorgania, Glamorgan-shire.
Clusentum, *where old* Hanton *stood, by* Southampton.
Combretonium, Bretenham *in* Suffolk.
Conda, *for* Condate, *a Town of* Bretaigne *in* France.
Conovius, *River* Conwy; *it divides* Caernarvon-shire *from* Denbigh-shire.
Coritanians, Darby-shire *was a part of the* Coritani.
———— Northampton-shire, *was part of the* Coritani.
Cornavians, *the Inhabitants of* Shropshire, Cheshire, *&c.*
Creonians, *or* Cerones, *the Inhabitants of* Assenshire *in* Scotland, *according to* Camden.
Croissy, *or* Cressy, *in* Ponthieu, *in* Lower-Picardy, *in* France.

D.

Danmonians, *Inhabitants of* Cornwall *and* Devonshire.
Danus, *River* Dan, *in* Cheshire.
Darventia, *River* Darwent, *in* Darbyshire.
Decantians, *or, as* Camden *calls them,* Cantæ; *he places them in* Ross *in* Scotland.
Dimetians, *those that inhabited* West-Wales, *viz.* Caermardhin-shire, Pembroke-shire, *and* Cardigan-shire.
Deucaledonian-Ocean, *that on the Westside of* Scotland.
Deva, *River* Dee *in* Cheshire.
Devana, *the City of* Chester.
Devia, *River* Dee *in* Scotland; *it falls into the Irish Sea.*
Dobunians, *Inhabitants of* Glocester-shire *and* Oxford-shire.
Dornavaria, Dorchester.
Dorus, *River* Dore *in* Hereford-shire; *it runs through the* golden Vale.
Dovo, *River* Dove *in* Darby-shire.
Druids, *the Pagan Priests among the* Britons *and* Gauls.
Durobrevians, *Inhabitants of* Rochester.
Durobrevis, *an old Town, call'd* Dormanchester, *on the River* Nyne, *in* Northampton-shire.
Durotriges, *Inhabitants of* Dorset-shire.
Durovernum, *the City of* Canterbury.

E.

EBorac Race, York-shire *Breed.*
Elgovians, *or* Selgovians, *Inhabitants of* Liddesdale, Eusdale, Eskdale *and* Annandale *in* Scotland.
Epidium, Cantyre *in* Scotland: *The Island that is near* Cantyre, *is likewise call'd* Epidium.
Epirus, *a Country of* Greece.

F.

FAustinus, Villa Fastina, *now St.* Edmundsbury *in* Suffolk.
Fial, *one of the chief Mountains in* Swedeland.
Froma, *River* Frome *in* Dorset-shire.

G.

GAdenians, *Inhabitants of* Teifdale, Twedale, Merch, *and* Lothian, *in* Scotland.
Gallens, Wallingford *in* Barkshire, *on the borders of* Oxford-shire.
Garienus, *River* Yare, *on which* Yarmouth *stands, in* Norfolk.
Gariononum, *suppos'd to be* Burgh-castle *in* Suffolk.
Gaul, France.
Gevini, *a River in* Wales, *that runs into the River* Usk.
Glevum, *the City of* Glocester.
Glotta, *River* Cluyd *in* Scotland: *Also an Island now call'd* Arran, *lying in the Bay of* Cluyd.
Gobanium, Abergaenna *in* Monmouth-shire.
Gobeum, *a Promontory of* Bretaigne *in* France.
Goths, *Inhabitants of the* Lower-Scythia, *in the Northern part of* Europe.

H.

HAga, *the* Hay, *or* Haseley, *in* Brecknock-shire.
Halenus, *River* Avon *in* Hampshire.
Hebudes, *or* Hebrides, *a Cluster of Isles that lye on the West-side of* Scotland, *in the* Deucaledonian-Ocean.
Hibernia, Ireland.
Hunns, *a People that came out of* Scythia *and dwelt in* Europe, *in* Hungary.
Hybernian-Ocean, *the Irish-Seas.*
Hydaspes, *a River in* India.
Hyperborean-Ocean, *that which washes the North part of* Scotland.

I.

IBeria, Spain.
Icenians, *Inhabitants of* Suffolk, Norfolk, Cambridge-shire, *&c.*
Idumanum, Black-water *in* Essex.

Ierne,

The INDEX.

Ierne, Ireland.
Imaus, *a Mountain which parts* India *from* Scythia, *and divides* Scythia *into two parts.*
Isca, *River* Usk *in* Monmouth-shire.
——— *an old Town on the River* Usk, *in* Monmouth-shire.
——— *River* Ex, *on which the City of* Exeter *stands.*
Isis, *a River in* Oxfordshire.
Ithaca, *an Island in the* Ionian *Sea.*
Itunna, *River* Eden, *or* Solway *Frith in* Scotland.

K

Kanduara, *or* Vindogara, *suppos'd to stand in* Kyle, *in* Scotland.

L

Lake, *in* Brecknockshire, *now call'd* Brecknock-mere.
Lapland, Lapponia, *it belongs partly to* Swedeland, Norway, *and* Moscovy.
Latium, *a part of* Italy, *now call'd* Campagna di Roma, *or* St. Peters *Patrimony.*
Liddenus, *River* Ledden *in* Herefordshire, *by* Malvern Hills.
Liger, *River* Loire *in* France.
Lindis, *River* Witham *in* Lincolnshire.
Lindum, *City of* Lincoln.
Loghor, *a River which is the Western limit of* Glamorganshire.
Logians, *they Inhabited from Mount* Grampius, *to the German Ocean, by the* Mertæ *in Scotland.*
Longo, *a River on the West side of* Scotland, *that falls into the Western Ocean, 'tis call'd* Logh Longas.
Loxa, *River* Losse *in* Scotland.
Lugas, *River* Lug, *it rises in* Radnorhills, *and falls into* Wye, *Three Miles from* Hereford.

M

Mantua, *a Town in* Italy *where* Virgil *was born.*
Margadunum, *an Old Town suppos'd to stand where* Bever Castle *does.*
Maridunum, Caermardhin, *in* Wales.
Mauritania, Barbary.
Meatians, *They Inhabited near the Picts Wall.*
Mediolanum, *an Old Town in* Montgomeryshire.
Medvaga, *River* Medway *in* Kent.
Mersel, *River* Mersey *in* Cheshire.
Mertians, *those that Inhabited the North part of* Scotland, *which lies towards the German Ocean.*
Mervinian-mountains, *those of* Meirionithshire.

Milford-haven *in* Wales.
Mona's-isle, *the Isle of* Anglesey.
Mosa, *the* Maes, *in* Gallia-Belgica, *it falls below* Dort, *into the German Ocean.*
Muno, *River* Munow, *it rises in* Hatterillhills, *and parts* Herefordshire *from* Monmouthshire.

N

Nannetum, *the City of* Nants, *in* Brittany, France.
Neustrian-coast, *that of* Normandy.
Nidus, *River* Neath, *on which stood a Town of the same Name, in* Glamorganshire.
Nile, *the Famous River of* Egypt.
Novantians, *they inhabited*, Galloway, Careck, Kyle, Cuningham, *and* Glotta, *the Promontory which here runs into the Sea, was call'd the* Novantian *Promontory.*

O

Octopitarum, *St.* David's *Land, in* Wales.
Olympic, *the Olympick Games were kept in the City* Olympia, *in* Peloponnesus.
Ordovicians, *Inhabitants of* North-Wales, *and* Powisland, *viz.* Montgomeryshire, Meirionithshire, Caernarvonshire, Denbighshire, Flintshire.
Orestians, *or* Horestians, *Inhabitants of* Argyle, *and* Perth, *according to* Camden, *in* Scotland.
Orrea, *a Town on the North of the River* Tay, *in* Scotland.
Ottadenians, *those that Inhabited next the* Brigantes.
Oza, *River* Ouse, *there is the great and little* Ouse, *the former divides* Norfolk *from* Cambridgshire.

P

Pactolus, *a River in* Lidia.
Parthenope, *the City of* Naples.
Peak, *in* Darbyshire.
Pictavian-fields, Poictou *a Province in* France, *its Capital City is* Poitiers, *within Two Leagues of which was fought the Famous battle between the* English *and* French.
Picts, *they Inhabited part of* Scotland, *some place them in the South, in* Lothian *and* Fife: *Also* Camden *places them in* Orkney, *and the Northern Isles.*
Plinlimon, *a high Mountain in* Wales, *whence* Severn, Wye *and* Rydol, *take their rise.*

R

Ratostibium, *River* Taf *in* Wales.
Regnums-wood, Ringwood *in* Hampshire.

Repan-

The INDEX.

Repandunum, Repton *in* Darbyſhire.
Rhemnius, *River* Remny *in* Glamorganſhire.
Rhine, *a River which parts* France *from* Germany, *after it has run* 300 *Miles, it falls into the River* Moſa, *and the* German Ocean.
Ricine, *the Firſt Iſland of the* Hebudes.
Riphæan-hills, *Mountains of* Scythia *ſo call'd.*
Roman-military-way, *call'd* Watlinſtreet.
Rutunium, Routon *in* Shropſhire.
Rutupiæ, *an Old Town* Richborrow, *near* Sandwich *in* Kent.
——— *The* Foreland *in* Kent.

S.

SAbrina, *River* Severn.
Salopia, Shropſhire.
Scandanavia, *or* Scandia, *the Country between the* Belt *and Northern Sea*, *containing* Norway, Swedeland, &c.
Scylla, *a dangerous place in the* Sicilian *Sea.*
Scythia, *otherwiſe call'd* Sarmatia; *now that part of* Tartary, *which lies in* Europe, *about the* Euxine Sea, *and the* Meotick *Lake.*
Segontium, Caernarvan *in* Wales.
——— Silcheſter, *in* Hampſhire.
Sein, *the River on which* Paris *ſtands.*
Seſtus, *a Caſtle of* Thrace, *by the* Helleſpont.
Severus-wall, *the* Picts *Wall.*
Silures, *Inhabitants of* South-wales, *viz.* Radnorſhire, Brecknockſhire, Glamorganſhire, Herefordſhire, *and* Monmouthſhire.
Sirius, *the* Dog-ſtar.
Spinæ, *an Old Town hard by* Newbery.
Stourus, *River* Stoure *in* Dorſetſhire.
——— *River* Stoure *in* Suffolk.
Stuccia, *River* Yeſtwith *in* Cardiganſhire.

T.

TAme, *a Town on the River* Celnius *in* Scotland.
Tava, *River* Tay *in* Scotland.
Tegæan-lake, Pimble-mere, *in* Wales.
Thamiſis, *River of* Thames.
Thanotos, *Iſle of* Thanet.
Thet, *the River on which* Thetford *ſtands.*
Thrace, *now* Romania.
Tinna, *River* Tine, Tinmouth *ſtands on it, there is likewiſe another* Tine *more Northward.*
Trenta, *River* Trent, *it divides* Lincolnſhire, *from* Yorkſhire *and* Nottinghamſhire.
Treſantona, *River* Teſt, *it runs into* Southampton-Bay.
Trinacrian-Iſle, *the Iſland of* Scicily.
Tripontium, *ſuppos'd to ſtand where* Towceſter *does, in* Northamptonſhire.
Trojans, Troy *was a City of* Phrygia, *in the leſſer* Aſia.
Tueſis, *a River in* Scotland, *that riſes below* Grampius, *and falls into the* German Ocean.
Turobius, *Rever* Tcivi *in* Wales.
Tyber, *the famous River of* Rome.

U.

URiconium, *an Old Town call'd* Wroxceſter, *near the place where* Severn *and* Tern *joyn*, Shrewsbury, *is ſuppos'd to have its riſe out of the Ruins of* Uriconium.
Uſocona, *ſuppos'd to be* Oxenyate *in* Shropſhire.

V.

VAga, *River* Wye, *it riſes in* Wales, *and runs thro'* Herefordſhire.
Vagniacans, *Inhabitants of* Maidſtone *in* Kent.
Vandals, *they Inhabited about* Meklenburg *in* Germany, *on the Coaſt of the* Baltick Sea.
Vara, *or Bay of* Vavaris *in* Scotland.
Vecta's-Iſle, *the* Iſle *of* Wight.
Vedra, *River* Ware, *in the Biſhoprick of* Durham.
Vindogladia, Winburn *in* Dorſetſhire.
Venicontes, *or* Vernicontes, *they Inhabited North of* Tay *in* Scotland, Camden *places them in* Mernis.
Venta, *an Old Town near* Chepſtow *in* Monmouthſhire.
——— *An Old Town call'd* Caſter, *near* Norwich, *out of whoſe ruins* Norwich *is ſuppos'd to have its Original.*
——— Wincheſter, *in* Hampſhire.
Verolamium, *an Old Town near St.* Albans, *out of whoſe Ruins it had its beginning.*
Veſuvius, *a Famous burning Mountain in* Italy.
Vicomagians, Camden *makes them to Inhabit* Murray, *but* Ortelius *places them between the* Creones *and* Carnonacæ, *in the Weſtern part of* Scotland.
Victoria, *ſuppos'd to be* Inch-Keith-Iſland, *broke off from the Land.*
Vindolana, *Old* Wincheſter *in* Northumberland.

FINIS.

www.ingramcontent.com/pod-product-compliance
Lightning Source LLC
Chambersburg PA
CBHW030757230426
43667CB00007B/996